Warlocks and Warpdrive

Contemporary Fantasy Entertainments with Interactive and Virtual Environments

KURT LANCASTER

Foreword by Brooks McNamara

McFarland & Company, Inc., Publishers
Jefferson, North Carolina, and London

Library of Congress Cataloguing-in-Publication Data

Lancaster, Kurt, 1967–
    Warlocks and warpdrive : contemporary fantasy enter-
tainments with interactive and virtual environments / by
Kurt Lancaster.
        p.   cm.
    Includes bibliographical references (p.) and index.   ∞
    ISBN 0-7864-0634-8 (library binding : 50# alkaline paper)
    1. Interactive multimedia.   2. Virtual reality.   I. Title.
QA76.76.I59 L36 1999
006.721—dc21   99-44740

British Library Cataloguing-in-Publication data are available

Manufactured in the United States of America

McFarland & Company, Inc., Publishers
  Box 611, Jefferson, North Carolina 28640
    www.mcfarlandpub.com

For Jen

Acknowledgments

I would like to thank all my professors who actually made a difference. Marshal Blonsky's passionate lectures on semiotics fascinated me. Barbara Kirshenblatt-Gimblett always has a critical eye, tempered with supportive encouragement. Brooks McNamara encouraged me to write about science fiction and fantasy and was kind enough to write the foreword. Tom Mikotowicz, a mentor and friend, got me hooked on performance studies and scholarly writing in the first place. Richard Morse made me love theater despite myself. Richard Schechner's books and lectures inspired me to love performance studies. Their insightful comments brought new angles to my work.

I would also like to thank my colleagues who encouraged me during my years at NYU, including Abdul, Sudipto (who provided support and guidance my whole time there); Patrick (who always gave me moral support and not just the trips to Wendy's); and especially Daniel (a good friend whose work on role-playing games is second to none).

Table of Contents

Foreword

In a way this book is about popular entertainment as a branch of performance. Behind much of *Warlocks and Warpdrive*, in fact, lies a revised view of the previously much-ignored areas of entertainment theory and history. Although it is plain — as it has always been — that a great many forms of popular entertainment are not of especially high literary quality, it is now equally clear that this is not really the issue at all. We are beginning to see that all sorts of amusements — with literary merit or without it — are unique forms of focused play that tell us quite clearly what is on the minds of a culture. Popular performances that previously have been looked at as essentially self-referential, with no particular cultural meaning — or have been ignored altogether by scholars as not really performances at all — are now being seen for the first time both as performances and as important cultural artifacts.

Perhaps this is partly the result of a new perspective — an acknowledgment of the ongoing "genealogy" of theater and other traditional forms of performance. Theater and the conventional varieties of live performance are now beginning to be seen not as *all* of entertainment but as *one part* of it. They have spawned, or helped to spawn, many other kinds of performance — including popular entertainment — both in the past and in our own time: Contemporary entertainment forms — media, environmentalism, and the many different kinds of fantasy games, for example — clearly owe their origins in part to traditional theater and related conventional forms of performance. Specifically, as this book points out, new insights into our end-of-the century culture may be gained through the study of entertainment, one of these "descendants." And the book also makes clear that our entertainment culture may be comfortably examined under an expanded definition of performance that includes popular entertainment.

Warlocks and Warpdrive does not take received academic wisdom as the starting place for the study of such contemporary entertainments as cyberspace, artificial environments, role-playing games, among others. Instead, Kurt Lancaster looks for new questions and suggests new answers, always keeping firmly in mind the cultural meanings of entertainment. His book will undoubtedly become one of the standard texts on the turn-of-the-twenty-first-century performance and will bring new meaning to the study of the other, previously neglected, topics in popular culture as well. The book is a valuable guide to entertainment as a descendant of theater and to a whole multitude of its forms.

What is most significant about *Warlocks and Warpdrive* is that it does not look for conventional answers; instead, it posits a comprehensive theory about the origin and meaning of overlooked but indisputably important forms of contemporary culture.

Brooks McNamara, Professor Emeritus
Department of Performance Studies
New York University

Introduction:
Virtual Fantasies
and the Cultural
Mise-en-Scène

"Virtual worlds offer experiences that are hard to come by in real life."

— Sherry Turkle (1995:192)

Cyborgs, Virtuality, and Simulacra

Cyborgs are living next door. They're walking down our streets. We see them at work, and we see them in grocery stores. Not only do we hear about people dressing up in medieval costumes and hacking at each other with mock weapons in the woods, but we also hear about their romantic cyberspace encounters with people they never see. Masked behind costumes and computers, millions of people are stepping into new kinds of interactive virtual environments. Alternative forms of entertainments, sites of performances unlike anything we have seen before, are pervading society's virtual landscapes. The "mask" of virtual performances allows us to perform in ways that we could not without this mediation. As social scientist Sherry Turkle says, "The notion 'you are who you pretend to be' has mythic resonance. The Pygmalion story endures because it speaks to a powerful fantasy: that we are not limited by our histories, that we can re-create ourselves" (1995:192).

One way we can recreate ourselves is by participating in such performance events as role-playing games, where we can virtually visit worlds in outer space or go back in time to a medieval world of knights and dragons in unfolding interactive oral stories. We can also visit chat rooms online and have a textual fantasy date. These kinds of virtual activities share some qualities of feminist scientist Donna Haraway's manifesto for cyborg culture: "The cyborg is a condensed image of both imagination and reality" (1991:150). Haraway uses the cyborg as a metaphor to explicate society's relationship to fantasy, reality, and technology — especially how people meld technology with their lives in an attempt to create not just new fictions but new lifestyles that circumvent how an industrial (or postindustrial) society tells them to live. For the cyborg, Haraway contends, "[n]o objects, spaces, or bodies are sacred in themselves; any component can be interfaced with any other if the proper standard, the proper code, can be constructed for processing signals in a common language" (163). The rule books for role-playing games provide the "code" for players to interactively share in the construction of virtual worlds and personalities, whether participants play around a table at home, in a transformed forest, or online. Behind the Web page, computer code gives the cyberspace visitor preconstructed worlds of virtual fantasies just waiting for a click of the mouse. The cyborg is a postmodern figure.

Those who construct these virtual fantasies are *imagineers*— the term given to Disney employees who engineer the environmental rides of the famous theme parks. They don't build these rides from actualities like bridges, cars, buildings, and airplanes but from their imagination, from fantasy. Imagineers, by combining "a unique blend of creative imagination and technical know-how" (Disney 1996), construct simulacra — a term used by the postmodern philosopher Jean Baudrillard to describe copies of objects lacking an actual original pattern. Simulacra get closer to my understanding of virtuality, which is different from that of the common definition: "a mode of simulated existence resulting from computation" as found in Benjamin Woolley's work, *Virtual Worlds* (1992:69). To limit virtuality to something computational is to limit what a virtual environment can be. It is not something that exists only in cyberspace — the perceived space evinced from a computer's performance of digital code. Ironically, it's closer to what Woolley says about the development of the first computers. Woolley believes that since the mathematician Alan Turing designed the first computer on paper in 1936, every computer is but a "shadow" of this model (60). In fact Woolley calls this computer a "virtual Turing machine" because it is an "abstract entity or process that has found physical expression, that has been 'realized.' It is a simulation, only not necessarily a simulation of anything actual" (68–69). According to this line of reasoning, a computer is a simulacrum.

I contend that simulacra, whether objects or environments, represent sites of virtuality: the objects that *are* appear "as if" they participate in a space that is *not*. Material objects and sites are the physicalization of, and interface to, imaginary fantasies. This process is virtuality. The virtual, like fantasy, is a simulation, an environment or object that has no "actual" existence but that of a simulacrum. In *Simulacra and Simulation* (1994) Baudrillard says that simulacra are "the generation by models of a real without origin or reality" (1), "signs that dissimulate that there is nothing" (6), and a state of being where "the models come first" (16). In essence this means that the model precedes the actual—flipping reality by inverting the process of natural cause and effect.

Simulacra are not "real" because they are not modeled from something real. Even art—which, according to Plato, is thrice removed from the originating idea—is still based on some model of reality: Artistic objects or events are a mimesis of the real, and the real is an attempted mimesis of an ideal (Plato 1945:327). In *Performance Theory* (1988) Richard Schechner agrees with the Platonic art process, contending that "[t]here is no way for raw food to 'come after' cooked food. So it is with art and life. Art is cooked and life is raw. Making art is the process of transforming raw experience into palatable forms. This transformation is a mimesis, a representation" (38). However, according to Baudrillard, in a simulacrum the cooked food would precede the raw—an improbable (if not impossible) state in normal life. But fantasy, like other simulacra, including the virtual worlds of cyberspace, makes alternate fantasies (if not realities) possible.

Whether we go online and talk to someone on the Babylon 5 space station at AOL (chapter 5), have an aural close encounter of the third kind through Michael Stearns's music (chapter 1), hack our way through the woods of a Boston park in an attempt to rescue Princess Arianne in a live-action role-playing adventure (chapter 2), or enter a symbolic world of myth and legend at the National Museum of the American Indian in New York City (chapter 4), we experience virtualities. These simulated environments are unlike anything else found on this planet before the latter half of the twentieth century. Through simulation people explore alternate realities. Marcel Duchamp attempted to do this by locating virtual sound in his experiment "Virtuality as fourth dimension" (Adcock 1992:121)—a locus where what can't be seen can still be perceived by its effect. I'm calling these kinds of sites *virtual fantasy* (as opposed to virtual reality). Environments and objects of virtual fantasy do not exist in the "real" or actual world. They may or may not be based on any predecessor except from those things that exist only as something not real. As Baudrillard theorizes, they constitute the hyperreal: "Simulation is no longer that of a territory, a referential being, or a substance. It is the generation by models of a real without origin or reality: a hyperreal" (1994:1). It would seem that virtual fantasy is beyond reality, more real than the real. For some, it replaces reality (for a period of time).

When visitors enter the starport at Disneyland's Star Tours ride, for example, they are standing in a site whose only model (or predecessor) is Lucasfilm's space fantasy movie *Star Wars* (1977). This hyperreal site has no existence outside that of a movie. Visitors can see droids and aliens peer at them from all around a starport dock environmentally filled with girders, cross beams, flashing lights, video monitors, and clanking machinery. This environment seeps into them so deep that if they did not know that just some distance away is a doorway opening to the sunny California weather, they may feel as if they really are on a space station—a meeting place of aliens, humans, and droids. According

to Baudrillard's logic, however, this site is not real because it has no predecessor in the real world — it is the creation of Disney Imagineers, and its predecessor (model) is the fantasy creation of George Lucas, not God: in an "era of
simulacra and simulation, ... there is no longer a God to recognize his own"
(1994:6). Baudrillard terms the natural world as the creation of God. Simulacra
of virtual fantasies exist as something other than the paradigm of linear modernism or classicism where meaning is scientifically logical and discoverable —
where identity is centered in the praxis of a natural order.

   However, if fantasy and virtuality seem like a contradiction to reality and
actuality to a modernist state of thought, we must remember that we do live in
a cyborg age, as Donna Haraway describes the postmodern social state that just
may "be about lived social and bodily realities in which people are not afraid of
their joint kinship with animals and machines, not afraid of permanently partial identities and contradictory standpoints" (1991:154). If that metaphorical
cyborg seems to be an abstract creature that enjoys simulations, imagination,
fantasy, nonlinearity, and "decentered" identities, it is because, according to
Turkle, "computers now offer an experience resonant with a postmodern aesthetic that increasingly claims the cultural privilege formerly assumed by modernism" (1995:45). Turkle believes that postmodernism — being, as she claims,
abstract — becomes concrete in current cyberspace culture. I disagree with this
assessment. As postmodern subjects, cyborgs are not just found in online communities or virtual reality experiments. They appear in such concrete sites as
those described in this book — where citizens are unafraid of aliens or technology (those other than themselves, whether based on race, gender, or humanity).
Cyborgs live among simulacra. They take on aspects of simulacra. And for them,
the hyperreality of virtual fantasies is no less important, no less real, no less
actual than what noncyborgs would call "everyday life."

   Whether we live in "a whole new postmodern space in emergence around
us," created by an aura of a "technological sublime," or whether this is but a
"distorted figuration of something even deeper, namely, the whole world system
of a present-day multinational capitalism," as that other postmodern philosopher, Fredric Jameson, would argue the notion of a cyborg culture (1991:37), we
do in fact live in a virtual age where humans and their technologies conflate into
a postmodern social state known as the cyborg. The cyborg can be found in sites
of simulation, where "identity can be fluid and multiple, [where] a signifier no
longer clearly points to a thing that is signified" (Turkle 1995:49). Ultimately,
the virtual is a state of mind that results from living in Baudrillard's semiosphere — a milieu permeated by images connoting symbolic fantasies that lack
natural denotative qualities. The nineteenth-century metaphysician Mary Baker
Eddy contends that both fantasy and reality — whether made up of a semiosphere or something from the actual world — come from the same source: "Mortal mind sees what it believes as certainly as it believes what it sees. It feels, hears,
and sees its own thoughts" (1906 [1875]:86). Cyborgs evolved out of minds
immersed in the late-twentieth-century semiosphere, and as citizens they devel-

oped their own kinds of performances, entertainments, cultural artifacts, and fantasies. They have made their imaginations concrete. The postmodern matrix of virtual fantasies is found in such places as cyberspace, in role-playing games, and at physical artificial environments like those found in Disneyland.

Describing the Cultural Mise-en-Scène

For the most part, the essays contained in this book do not praise or condemn virtual fantasies. They observe them — a description both analytical and theoretical. Some people may be upset that I have not taken a "dissident" or "resistant" reading of my subjects of study. After all, isn't fantasy dangerous? Aren't those who go to Disneyland being subverted by white middle-class values (as some scholars claim)? Don't those who play fantasy games lack the ability to cope with real life? And what about those adults who go to science fiction conventions in *Star Trek* uniforms — will they ever grow up? However, value judgments, like feelings, are tricky things: unpredictable, indefinable — what someone dislikes, others will like, and vice versa. With that in mind, if I do not criticize or condemn virtual fantasies, I do resist the dark play of fantasy — where people live a fantasy as if it were real, as the Heaven's Gate cult did (chapter 9), or utilize fantasy as a means to enact a technological foreign policy (chapter 10).

So, those who end up placing cultural events on some hierarchical cultural scale (this is High Art, this is Low Art/pop culture) are still living on the leftovers of modernism, not yet educated by a cyborg society, a culture where at least a multiplicity of values and meanings are more important than just an authoritative one — a view that grew out of the Enlightenment. Gregory Ulmer, reading Peter Sloterdijk, talks about the "invention of conceptual reason," which led to "the possibility of 'enlightened false consciousness,' which arose when the enlightened got into power," wherein "people stick to their positions for anything but 'rational' reasons" (1994:19). Because of this, a "combative stance" replaced a "friendly invitation to a conversation" (Sloterdijk 1987:15). Opposed to negative criticism (which is usually more combative than perceptive), I instead attempt to perceive the nuances of social, cultural, historical, and theoretical forces shaping these different sites — revealing to some extent what these fantasy events are, how they work, and why some find them so important. As a scholar I find this far more interesting and rewarding than mere self-inflated elitist-style culture bashing.

After reading this book, someone who has never been online and had a cyberspace date or visited the National Museum of the American Indian will have some idea what those experiences are like — not the whole of it, but perhaps some essence. However, if I merely placed a value judgment on the National Museum of the American Indian, for example, and claimed with scholarly authority that this is a "bad" museum because it fails to display artifacts by a conventional anthropological standard — such as with tribal classification — some people may be instantly turned off and not go, perhaps causing such a reaction as, "How do people expect to learn anything about Native Americans if different cultural objects and ideas are melded together? Who do those people think they are?" Rather than being a condemning cynical critic, I describe various cultural and theoretical forces influencing such sites. Only then can readers make an intelligent decision as to whether they want to go and experience the described event. They will at least learn something about the sites other than mere opinions, vacant analyses, and intellectually strapped value judgments promulgated by cynical critics and cynical scholars.

I do this by attempting to avoid a culturally logocentric reading of my subjects. Far too many movie critics, theater critics, and scholars describe their subjects of study from the basis of literature, summarizing their observations as if giving a plot synopsis of a literary text rather than actually analyzing a performance. Most movie and theater reviewers not only place unneeded value judgments on their subjects — this film is good, this one bad — but they also describe them as if they were reviewing a book. This twofold approach to criticism — labeling what's good/bad and describing the plot as if what they saw were a novel — is "Always predictable," Dubravka Vrgoc writes about conventional theater criticism, and "gives the spectator a 'sure' line of direction for the performance and establishes in advance a settled relation between the event on the stage and the audience.... [It] reduces the complexity of theater as well as the complexity of every spectator" (Vrgoc 1996). It seems strange to me that, in an age where literary texts are not the only purveyors of knowledge, so many critics (apparently trained in English literature) continue to analyze nonliterary cultural events as if they were "reading" something from the English canon.

To read culture as a "text" would be similar to how Woolley describes what happens when people read or analyze information as data: "Money, phone calls, an architectural model, the smell of rose petals, pi, 'Stairway to Heaven' by Led Zeppelin, DNA, and the light of a distant star are all information. What does that tell us about them? Lumping them together in this way tends to serve more to *hide than reveal important distinctions*" (Woolley 1992:70; emphasis added). According to performance scholar and theater director Richard Schechner, critics have a similar problem in hiding (rather than revealing) important distinctions when they describe theater from the basis of dramatic texts: "The accepted methods and vocabularies are inadequate for the analysis of both orthodox and new theater. The close textual readings of the New Critics, enlightening as they are, seem more related to literature than performance. [There is a] need to analyze the *action* of theater" (1988:27–28). The analysis of the *action* of theater is not just the analysis or description of a plot unfolding onstage (what can be described by reading the play itself) but the analysis of the entire performance event: the activity of performers, sets, lights, spectators, and so forth occurring on- and offstage — the physicality of the entire performance milieu. If, as Schechner maintains, "the theater 'in life' will permeate more and more activities, both ordinary and special" (115), then it is time to apply this approach to other cultural, social, and political occurrences. By looking at these events *performatively*, we begin to understand how they function in action, as opposed to stripping away their performance qualities and leaving behind a sterile plot synopsis.

To focus on a subject through the lens of performance does not mean that one is necessarily studying performances, however. Rather, performance is a way to study a large array of behaviors, some of which may not even be considered performance in the conventional sense. Be that as it may. Human beings are essentially performative creatures. Performance studies recognizes the fact that all the world's a stage and offers its unique way of looking at life in such a way as to explain, show, and describe certain patterns of behavior occurring in our society irrespective of its cultural status. To describe an event performatively is to describe not just its textual plot but its cultural mise-en-scène. The field of performance studies emerged as a scholarly complement to the experimental theater of the 1960s. As experimental theater opposed mainstream theater, performance studies rebutted conventional theater scholarship, which continued to focus (and still does) on the analysis of play texts and trade school–like training.

What Is Performance Studies?

One of the conventional myths in theater scholarship was that theater evolved out of ritual on an increasingly aesthetic evolutionary ladder. So, under this logic you have on the right hand the tragic "high art" theater of ancient Greece, which, on the left hand, evolved out of the "low" dithyramb rites. This theory has since been proved not only doubtful and inaccurate but also irrelevant — a leftover token of linear-based thinking that attempted to prove classical tragedy was a "higher" form of "art" than the ritual it purportedly came from. "If one argues that theater is 'later' or more 'sophisticated' or 'higher' on some evolutionary ladder and therefore must derive from one of the others," Schechner says in his seminal work *Performance Theory* (1988), "I reply that this makes sense if we take fifth century BCE Greek theater (and its counterparts in other cultures) as the only legitimate theater" (6). Contending that there are many different kinds of performance types and rituals, he adds: "there is no need to hunt for 'origins' or 'derivations.' There are only variations in form, the intermixing among genres, and these show no long-term evolution from 'primitive' to 'sophisticated' or 'modern'" (6). Schechner broke the artificial compartmentalization of performance made by conventional scholars. He was not the first to do so.

Johan Huizinga, some years before Schechner, says in *Homo Ludens* that "civilization arises and unfolds in and as play" (1955:i). In fact, he contends, "[p]lay is older than culture," and "human civilization has added no essential feature to the general idea of play" (1). When one plays one performs, and when one performs one is playing. Play encompasses all performance genres from ritual to theater to cyberspace chats, and it would be ridiculous to assign different genres of play to some kind of cultural hierarchy. During the same moment as Huizinga, J. L. Austin explained *How to Do Things with Words* (1955), positing that speech acts are *performative*. They do not rely on any kind of artistic forms or genres. One example of this occurs during a marriage ceremony, when the groom says to the bride: "I, with this ring, do thee wed." So, theorists see performance paradigms as intergeneric, located on what Schechner calls a "web": "Theater is only one node on a continuum that reaches from the ritualizations of animals (including humans) through performances in everyday life — greetings, displays of emotion, family scenes, professional roles, and so on — through to play, sports, theater, dance, ceremonies, rites, and performances of great magnitude" (1988:xiii).

The idea of an interconnected performance web lies at the root of such contemporary catchwords as *nonlinear, systemic,* and *pattern-based thinking,* so popular in many science trade books. From the study of quantum physics to weather pattern predictions it has become clear that the artificial designations scientists have placed on different phenomena — isolating and reducing them to their constituent parts — only revealed their own nonisolationist tendencies. Phenomena are interconnected. Where before objects of study were analyzed as independent things, placed in separate compartments, now many scholars recognize that even entire disciplines are just as interconnected. Interrelated scientific objects and cultural products are nodes having the potential to be contextualized across a web of disciplines. This shift from linear to nonlinear patterns emerged in the sciences with parallel processors and cellular automata — tools used to study economies, ant behavior, and weather research, among other subjects. A similar nonlinear process has also emerged in the humanities. The interdisciplinary and nonlinear field of performance studies is one such academic field that is quietly producing scholars equipped to study the patterns and forms of social and cultural behavior emerging in a nonlinear, postmodern world. Rather than inventing its own discipline, performance studies uses already existing methodologies in new ways. It applies theories from linguistics, semiotics, philosophy, anthropology, Marxism, feminism, among many others in order to further understand human behavior *as, in,* and *through* performance.

Theater scholar Gautam Dasgupta, for example, proposed an interdisciplinary model of study between theater and science. He offers "a re-working of dramatic and artistic thought as the locus of prevalent scientific ideas of the time" and attempts to "outline on a provisional basis modalities of thought that seem to recur in the exercises of the theatrical imagination and of the scientific temper" (1985:238). He then goes on to analyze Richard Foreman's theater as a process by which matter and energy shape — algebraically and geometrically — the mise-en-scène, unlike language and gesture as found in conventional theater. Robert Wilson's theater — at once expressing simultaneity of time and space, as well as a dream-like subjective quality — corresponds to the ideas of quantum mechanics and the theoretical possibilities of alternate dimensions that grew out of Einstein's early-twentieth-century relativity theories, Dasgupta posits.

I believe that the 1960s experimental theater scene not only paralleled anti-linear developments in the sciences but that because of the changes occurring in theater, a new way of explaining these shifts had to develop. Conventional theater scholarship was unable to explain these experiments in a satisfactory way. These scholars were still steeped too much in a classical model of drama and science, as Dasgupta contends: Aristotle's "emphasis on dramatic action as the first principle of dramaturgy may have reflected his own scientific studies in motion" (1985:238). It seems that not only has most conventional theater reflected Aristotle's concept of drama, but theater scholarship has expressed it as well. Theater studies had to change because the former conservative theater education — based mostly on the study of dramatic texts and trade school–like training — was ill-equipped to study these changes. Schechner explains: "Steadily over the past twenty-five years or more, theatre and dance departments, obsessed with professional training, have let the intellectual aspects of performance studies — historical, political, philosophical, theoretical — get away from them and pass into the hands of social scientists, literary critics, and historians" (1990:16).

It is no coincidence that Schechner — an experimental director, as well as a scholar — would take his environmental theater ideas onstage and apply them to theater scholarship, becoming one of the first to directly influence and formalize an emerging field of performance studies. Other scholars (Huizinga, Erving Goffman, and Austin, to name a few) were also starting to theorize the place of performance in society, and their texts would be co-opted into the performance studies paradigm. However, it was Schechner and his colleagues (Brooks McNamara, Barbara Kirshenblatt-Gimblett, the late Michael Kirby, among others) who were responsible for superseding the Department of Graduate Drama at New York University with the interdisciplinary Department of Performance Studies in the early 1980s. (Before the name change, the department was already shifting its focus in the 1970s.)

These scholars felt it was time to remold the intellectual ideas of theater into a paradigm of performance, applying it not just to theater productions and theater history but to any kind of social, cultural, and political behavior. Others outside their field were already practicing such scholarship. Sociologist Erving Goffman, for example, applied the theatrical paradigm to study social behavior in *The Presentation of Self in Everyday Life* (1959). In the 1970s anthropologist Victor Turner (a major influence on Schechner) also used the performance ideas of theater to help develop the theory of social dramas. What was becoming apparent to the faculty in the Department of Graduate Drama at NYU was that the theoretical underpinnings of theater — their field — were being developed by scholars in *other* disciplines, applying them in exciting new ways. They used performance as a model to understand events on a cultural and social scale outside the traditional purview of conventional theater scholars, who mainly analyzed plays, dramatic theory, play-texts, and theater history, in addition to training students in acting, directing, playwriting, scene design, lighting design,

and costume design. In order to make a distinction between conventional theater studies and the new application of theater being used by other scholars and
themselves, NYU's graduate drama faculty transformed their department into a
formal discipline of performance studies in an attempt to take back what they
believed was theirs in the first place: the rigorous and critical application of performance theories not only to avant-garde theater but to everyday life, popular
entertainments, ritual, folklore, and political and social movements — in fact,
to any human behavior where humans display themselves.

Later, other "schools" of performance thought developed that were not necessarily directly based on the theatrical paradigm. Northwestern University created the communication model of performance as expressed by Austin and
others. Judith Butler, in *Bodies That Matter* (1993), uses the idea of the performed body in an attempt to understand the social and cultural coding of gender. Many of the faculty and students at NYU and elsewhere have been slowly
shifting the focus of performance studies toward cultural studies, including gender and race studies. These other forms of performance analysis have their roots
in the late 1960s to early 1970s introduction of semiotics to the United States by
such French literary philosophers as Roland Barthes, Jacques Lacan, Jacques
Derrida, and Michel Foucault, among others. Semioticians analyze the connotations of language within the given context of cultural artifacts circulating
through society (especially as images of media). These examples prove the diver-
sity and interdisciplinary nature of the field, and in no way is one approach better than another. Performance studies is an interdisciplinary umbrella under
which all of these other disciplines provide a way to study social behavior in and
as performance. It is a fact, however, that performance studies did grow out of
the experimental performances of theater. It is my belief that if there were no
theater experiments breaking the nineteenth-century mold of conventional theater realism and naturalism inherited by the twentieth century, there would be
no formal scholarly field of performance studies today. (This is not to discount
the performance experiments of the early-twentieth-century Dadaists, for example, but the Dadaists failed to evolve an interdisciplinary field and were subsequently co-opted by art history.) Whereas the art world was able to accommodate
the predilections of its experimenters (even taking in the orphans of Dadaist performances), theater, for some reason, was unable to find a legitimate home for
its experimentalists until the 1960s, when it gained increased popularity. At that
time the conventions of science, culture, and society underwent an El Nino–like
shift spawning its own kind of haphazard storms.

Nonlinearity

Edward Lorenze studied and attempted to predict weather patterns in the
early 1960s by modeling them in "three coupled nonlinear equations" and discovered that "two trajectories would develop in completely different ways,"

despite the fact that the initial conditions were virtually the same (Capra 1996:134). This has since become known, in chaos theory, as the "'butterfly effect' because of the half-joking assertion that a butterfly stirring the air today in Beijing can cause a storm in New York next month" (134). Just as the butterfly effect challenges the notion that scientific patterns are artificially isolated, the field of performance studies claims that the divisions between humanities disciplines are just as artificial. That's why performance studies is interdisciplinary, easily absorbing aspects of semiotics, cultural studies, feminism, anthropology, dance, and so on. These become powerful tools when wielded under the rubric of performance by scholars trained in critical analysis.

Practitioners of performance studies (and other interdisciplinary fields) contend that to understand the complexities of our postmodern world in the midst of a mass information age, we can no longer study arts, cultures, and societies in isolation. A performance occurring in a cafe in Portland may not be as separate from a former war in Bosnia as we may think. The signing of a paper on the White House lawn not only has consequences in Israeli-Palestinian relationships, but it also affects the world stage and, in turn, is processed again at the microlevel as we see the effects of that signature appear in our homes on television screens. It is then further processed at work and at school. Artists process it further and regurgitate it in a new form of performance onstage, ad infinitum. Thus the micromovements of a pen in Washington, D.C., can create not only an assassination in Israel but an artistic "storm" in New York. Performances are not isolated. In order to "read" an event properly one needs to understand many cultural and social nodes surrounding a performance event. Performance studies is one such discipline, offering powerful tools to help explain a world becoming more and more multicultural and antilinear.

The age of modernism, with its binary hierarchies, low art and high art, the myth of masterpieces, which Antonin Artaud appropriately shot down in 1938 with his essay "No More Masterpieces," is over. A wide-scale academic evolution is taking place, and those academic departments that do not adapt and evolve will become stagnant if not extinct. This is not a mild hypothesis. The same adaptive scenario occurred in the sciences. From the time of the ancient Greeks until the Renaissance, geometry — with the absence of arithmetic — was applied to the science of astronomy. Aristotle, James Bailey argues in *After Thought: The Computer Challenge to Human Intelligence* (1996), believed that "arithmetic could never be used to demonstrate things geometric, or vice versa" (48). Copernicus's and Galileo's complex calculations were pure geometry. Regiomontanus, the person whose astronomical almanacs were used by Columbus, was himself leery about the numerically centered algebra: "When Regiomontanus first dipped into algebra to solve a specific problem, he never intended it as a general replacement technology for circles and lines [of geometry]. Much had changed by Descartes's time, however. Scientists had begun to wonder why the ancients had 'allowed almost no numbers other than integers; nor did they allow the material of arithmetic to be infinitely divisible like that of geometry'"

(67). A hundred years after Copernicus shifted the center of the universe from the Earth to the sun, Descartes developed his method of sequential thinking, placing linear human thought at the center of the cultural universe. It was during the Renaissance that algebra — with its linear formulations — was brought over by scholars from the Middle East and was later adopted by the sciences. Bailey believes that algebra dominated pattern-based nonlinear geometry because the printing press could cheaply promulgate algebraic formulas — geometric lines and circles were too expensive to reproduce. (Descartes would eventually meld geometry and algebra.)

Because of Descartes, Bailey believes, the human mind found linear thinking easier to process than the complex patterns of geometry: "'Order is what is needed,'" Descartes said; "'all the thoughts that can come into the human mind must be arranged in an order like the natural order of numbers'" (in Bailey 65). "Descartes drilled this methodology into the collective psyche of Europe," Bailey says. "Plato and Aristotle had divided science into astronomy and everything else. Now Descartes redivided it on the basis of whether the subject matter could be sequentialized or not" (65). And it is this sequential logic, Bailey contends, that allowed for the development of linear thinking so abundant in our schools of learning today.

Bailey identifies three major evolutions in science: 1) *Space*: during ancient Greek times the desire was to locate humanity's place in the universe through geometry; 2) *Pace*: with the invention of the mechanical clock and Newtonian physics during the Renaissance, our place in the universe was analyzed through velocity and time (with the tools of algebra and calculus); and, more recently, 3) *Pattern:* this is the emerging paradigm to help us understand our place in the information age. These scientific "revolutions" started off as isolated discoveries and eventually led to an encircling field of perceptual changes within culture. However, these changes did not occur naturally. They evolved through a person's desire to look through the "lens" of the evolving paradigm.

Thomas Kuhn, in describing the socioscientific process of scientific revolutions, explains how "at times of revolution, when the normal-scientific tradition changes, the scientist's perception of his environment must be re-educated — in some familiar situations he must learn to see a new gestalt" (1996 [1962]:112). Within the world of experimentation and discovery scientists' perceptions shift, and their views become "incommensurable with the one [they] had inhabited before" (112). Because of their training and particular learning environment, scientists begin to "see" through the lens of a particular paradigm. The consequence of "schools being guided by different paradigms," Kuhn contends, explains why they "are always at cross-purposes" (112). The theatrical revolution underwent a similar process. Rather than applying the scientific method to make new discoveries and develop hypotheses about nature, theater experimenters of the 1960s tested and broke the status quo of mainstream theater by challenging Aristotelian narratives and the conventional stagings of drama. They wanted to perceive the world differently from the one posited by the conventional theatrical paradigm. In the midst of social upheavals occurring in the world around them (Kennedy's and King's assassinations, the Vietnam War, the civil rights movement, even the Apollo moon landing), the perceptual field of the body politic began to change. While many held to traditional forms and proven methods as a way to cope with these changes, others *needed* to create experimental performances, for it was their way to interpret what was happening to the world around them. They believed the forms of nineteenth-century realism and naturalism were inappropriate models for their desire to experiment in an age of increasing technological advancement, political corruption, and social upheaval.

The Rise of a Nonlinear Humanities Discipline

It is apparent that the same nonlinear patterns occurring in the sciences occurred simultaneously in the humanities — one such site being theater. This is not to say experimental theater practitioners were conscious of changing scientific paradigms — many most likely were not. However, the fact remains that the scientific temper and the social milieu — if not connected — experienced parallel developments. At the time of Lorenze's weather experiments, which foreshadowed chaos science, the 1960s avant-garde theater tore down the conventional proscenium stage (metaphorically represented by linear-thinking processes) and placed the performers into the midst of the audience. Schechner's theater troupe, The Performance Group, was one of many that forayed into experimental performances. Schechner called his experiments Environmental Theater, a term loaded with systemic, nonlinear sensibilities: "environments ecological or theatrical can be imagined not only as spaces but as active players in complex systems of transformation" (1994:x). Schechner believes that performance — and everything within its space — is organic. The environmental staging of a performance is more than just shifting the action "off of the proscenium or out of the arena": it constitutes the entire "political," "scholarly," and "theatrical" body. "An environmental performance is one in which *all the elements or parts* making up the performance are recognized as alive," he argues. "To 'be alive' is to change, develop, transform; to have needs and desires; even, potentially, to acquire, express, and use consciousness" (x). As in the sciences, pattern became the attendant paradigm of the new theater.

Performance studies would say that in cultural and social systems there are only performances nesting within other performances. There is no high art or low art. These are but a critic's ethnocentric projection. There is, as Huizinga says, only "play." According to Capra, in linear-based disciplines people tend to analyze knowledge "in a hierarchical scheme by placing the larger systems above the smaller ones in pyramid fashion. But this is a human projection. In nature there is no 'above' or 'below,' there are no hierarchies. There are only networks nesting within other networks" (1996:35). The 1960s theater experiments reflected these changes occurring in the social and scientific fabric.

Bertolt Brecht believed that art must reflect the thought of the time, not just as an experiment or passing fad: "It is understood that the *radical transformation of the theatre* can't be the result of some artistic whim. It has simply to correspond to the whole radical transformation of the mentality of our time.... It is precisely theater, art, and literature which have to form the 'ideological superstructure' for a solid, practical rearrangement of our age's way of life" (1992:23). It is Brecht's belief that humans exist in a state of continual flux: "Changes in his exterior continually lead to an inner reshuffling. The continuity of the ego is a myth. A man is an atom that perpetually breaks up and forms anew. We have to show things as they are" (1992:15). Systemic, pattern-based nonlinear thinking forms the basis for today's ideological superstructure — whether it's occurring in the sciences or the arts. Our culture, our arts, our society reflect these newer patterns from which some of the most exciting and experimental performances grow. Much of conventional theater is stale, reproducing sensibilities found in the nineteenth and early twentieth centuries with museum-like precision. These productions fail to reflect an age entering into the twenty-first century.

Looking back at the experimental theater of the 1960s and 1970s, one can see how these performances foreshadowed the emerging scholarly field of performance studies in the 1970s and 1980s. The faculty and students in the Department of Performance Studies at New York University turned their back on conventional theater scholarship (developed from linear-thinking processes) and, in their own unique way, formally redefined the potential of nonlinear, systemic, pattern-based humanities in the process.

Conventional theater performances and scholarship, including their attendant college and university departments, could not and cannot survive in an increasingly interconnected, or systemic, world. Theater and other cultural and social events studied in isolation as entities separate from their constituent threads in history, politics, art, and literature become inbred on themselves. Isolated from the outside, the gene pool stagnates, and we continue to get the same old Broadway performances, textbooks on how to audition for plays, and another dissertation on Shakespeare's *The Tempest*. However, those educated to think in parallel, through multichanneled pattern-based, thinking can adapt to and understand an ever-evolving cultural, social, and political environment. Performance studies is one of the few fields in the humanities that can explain these changes, whether they occur at the macro level of the Nigerian executions (as looked at performatively by Abdul-Karim Mustapha in "Absolute Dictator/ Absolute Spectator") or the micro level, where a town's history was performed by its citizens in a production called *Swamp Gravy,* by Richard Owen Geer (both can be found in the summer 1996 issue of *TDR: The Journal of Performance Studies*). Performance studies is slowly redefining how we look at the humanities, and through this process we discover who we are as performers.

Brecht wanted actors to perform "for an audience of the scientific age." What follows is an attempt to use performance studies as a way to analyze performances occurring in a virtual age.

Overview

I have divided this book into three parts. In Part I: Imaginative Fantasies (chapters 1–3) I look at sites that require participants to use their imaginations to "see" the fantasy. Physical objects are used to reference something imaginary. An image on a card may represent a character who is part of a fictional world, or a wooden staff used by a performer may represent a magic spell. Or sound itself may represent an encounter with a UFO. In Part II: Physical Fantasies (chapters 4–8) I examine computer games, CD-ROM movies, theme park rides, and an immersive museum. These sites either physically exist or they appear on a computer with realistically rendered graphics or through digitized video. Not much imagination is needed to "see" the imaginary world they represent. In Part III: Social Fantasies (chapters 9–10) I describe how people have used such fantasies as the Heaven's Gate cult and *Star Trek* fandom to build communities and how Ronald Reagan attempted to build his Pax Americana from the tropes of *Star Wars*.

In chapter 1, "Aural Encounters of the Third Kind," I explore the nature of virtual fantasy by looking at the music of Michael Stearns, a musician who depicts electronically an aural encounter with a UFO in his work *Encounter* (1988). I situate this within the current frenzy of UFO culture and the scientific studies of the Search for Extraterrestrial Intelligence program (SETI), as well as scrutinizing the alien songs of the finback whales — who, long before UFO mythology, sang to each other across oceanic distances. If we have yet to hear signals from intelligent and technological life in nearby star systems, and UFO sitings are nothing but phantasms of the mind, as the late Carl Sagan believed, then perhaps through radio waves we can communicate across vast distances and encounter the Other. I use the themes of the alien and sound —finback whale songs and SETI radio— as a way to explain how Stearns applies his unique method of music composition to create a virtual encounter with an alien spacecraft, a fabled, but virtual, encounter of the third kind. I describe more of the social ramifications of UFO cults in chapter 9, "From Whitewater to Heaven's Gate."

I shift the work to fantasy games in chapters 2 and 3, in which I examine scene by scene a live-action role-playing adventure and describe a tournament of the collectible card game *Magic: The Gathering*. I describe the performance qualities and cultural basis of these kinds of games, investigating how people create virtual interactive fantasy stories. "Hack and Slash in the Woods," chapter 2, describes an actual live-action role-playing adventure that occurred in the woods of Boston some years ago. It chronicles what the gamemaster did before the players arrived and what happened during the day-long event, from the costumes the people wore and the adventures they had — including a hand-to-hand battle with the evil Mocker, a character who attempted to foil the characters' attempt to rescue Princess Arianne. After giving a synopsis of the adventure, I explain why role-playing games are a unique form of entertainment — looking at the three frames of performance that players operate in, as well as some of the game's historical roots.

In chapter 3, I give an overview of the *Magic: The Gathering* phenomenon — a game genre that outdistanced the popularity of role-playing games like a meteor flash. I describe the game within the context of a tournament held in New York City in 1995. Tournaments are places where dozens to hundreds of players trade, buy, and play fantasy cards. The next part of this chapter examines the nature of how objects of fantasy are a way to enter postcinematic fantasy environments. People were once satisfied with reading or watching fantasy — now they want to play with it. I posit an answer to the question of why people want to play with fantasy. I also examine why some people are afraid of these games by exposing the issue behind "dark play." Then I shift to Physical Fantasies.

This Path We Travel, described in chapter 4, was an exhibit at the National Museum of the American Indian in New York City. The American Indian museum explores environmentally how a virtual space resonates with certain meanings about Native American life from the point of view of Native Americans. It examines, among other things, how a replica of an old-style schoolroom built by the United States government is considered a "profane intrusion" on the Native American way of life. It examines how a large globe made of leaves and vines integrated with circuit boards, speakers, and television monitors questions the role of technology against cultures that respect nature. This museum ultimately breaks the rules of how to display traditional artifacts and, instead, offers an exhibit that has as many roots in virtuality as it does in the cultures it displays.

In chapter 5, "Traveling among the Lands of the Fantastic," I examine several science fiction tourist attractions where people can immerse themselves in fantasy environments. For some people, whether it's at Disneyland, in Vegas, at a bookstore, or online, Earth is just one stop on their travels among the lands of the fantastic. Instead of visiting previously constructed or natural objects of authenticity (such as the Statue of Liberty or the Grand Canyon), science fiction "tourists" create their own sites of authenticity by purchasing, constructing, or visiting artificial objects and environments whose predecessors are fictional media stories found in movies and novels. From Disneyland's Star Tours ride to the Babylon 5 space station online, people experience the simultaneous conflation of social reality and science fiction.

In chapter 6, "Cyberspace Performances," I describe some of the performance events occurring in cyberspace and how people mask their identities in order to explore such unique behaviors as having a virtual date or talking with

Vice President Al Gore online. It defines performance and what it means to visitors in cyberspace — where people can be who they are not: shy people become bold, the ugly transforms into beauty, and the otherwise handicapped are perceived as "normal." It does not matter what we look like or who we are on this side of the screen, for in cyberspace we can pretend to become nearly anyone we want.

In chapters 7 and 8 I explore the design concepts of interactive CD-ROM movies, looking at how interactivity can be modeled on a dramatic form and how an interface determines the dramatic structure of CD-ROMs. I examine the interactive experiments of the OZ Group at Carnegie Mellon University, where the departments of computer science and drama have come up with ways to explore how to make "intelligent" computer actions. I look at specific scenes in Roach's interactive movie *Quantum Gate* (1993) and show how its dramatic structure is related to Aristotle's model of classical drama. I also examine how users perform characters in *Passage to Vietnam* (1995) and *Star Trek: Klingon* (1996). I then shift my analysis to Social Fantasies in Part III.

In chapter 9, "From Whitewater to Heaven's Gate," I look at how science fiction fandom appears to intersect with UFO cults and explain the reasons why fandom offers people a community that attempts to fulfill a mythological need. I also theorize why some people look down on science fiction fandom because of the nineteenth-century invention of cultural hierarchy in the United States. Chapter 10, "The Pseudotragedy of *Star Wars* and Reagan's Pax Americana," gives me the opportunity to describe how former president Ronald Reagan appropriated motifs from Lucas's movie to help mythologize his furtherance of the Strategic Defense Initiative and the "New World Order." I also examine tragic elements in the *Star Wars* trilogy, specifically analyzing Luke Skywalker's confrontation with Darth Vader at the climax of *The Empire Strikes Back* (1980). In addition, I argue against the myth of *Star Wars* as a unifying moment of catharsis in United States culture, for it lacks the unitary nature of ancient Athenian dramas.

Although these essays are diverse, this book is not meant to offer an exhaustive survey of the many virtual fantasies abundant on the social and cultural landscape, today. Rather, they are particular sites of performances that I have either observed or immersed myself first-hand as a scholar/participant during the 1990s. The various connotations, analyses, observations, theoretical approaches, come from my own unique background as a performance studies scholar and a lifelong science fiction fan. Someone reading this book may have (or had) a different experience, approach, observation, or comment about these sites than me. If that is the case, we have to respect the fact that we are coming from different perspectives. The following essays describe the contemporary performances and popular entertainments developed at the cusp of a new millennium.

Part I
Imaginative Fantasies

1

Aural Encounters of the Third Kind: UFOs, SETI, and the Music of Michael Stearns

"For me this series of vignettes evoke very literal images of a Contact/Encounter, and a journey into the environments of what we call 'outer space.'"

— Michael Stearns

The Search for Extraterrestrial Life

Finback whales once sang to each other across the vast depths of oceans. The late astronomer Carl Sagan describes how, for over 99 percent of their own history (millions of years), "whales evolved their extraordinary audio communication system" (1980:272). Because of the low frequency, their songs would propagate across entire oceans. "The American biologist Roger Payne," Sagan writes, "has calculated that using the deep ocean sound channel, two whales could communicate with each other at twenty Hertz essentially anywhere in the world" (272). However, the technological revolution that placed motorized vessels on the surface of oceans interferes with the whales' frequencies in their communication with each other. Whereas before they could communicate with each other from a distance of 10,000 kilometers, now, Sagan says, "the corresponding number is perhaps a few hundred kilometers.... Creatures that communicated for tens of millions of years have now effectively been silenced" (272).

While whales can communicate across vast distances without any technological aid, humans need technology to hear the virtual presence of someone on the other side of the planet. We are no longer separated by hours, weeks, or months from people and news. On the other hand, whales, because of our technology, cannot communicate long distances. Their natural communication system has become subsumed into a post-technological state, where they are no longer part of a global communications network.

Radio waves allow us to communicate across large distances from the other side of the planet, across the solar system, and out into the galaxy. As part of the electromagnetic spectrum, radio waves travel at the speed of light. A being sitting on a hypothetical planet orbiting the star Vega (about 12 light years away), and who has a receiver set at the right frequency and a powerful enough amplifier, would be able to pick up old broadcast signals of *Miami Vice*. Not only are there artificial radio signals coursing through space like unheard whispers in the night, but natural ones, projected from stars and planets, constantly buzz forth electromagnetic radiation, of which visible light is just one small part of this spectrum.

Karl Jansky, a scientist working for Bell Labs, discovered that thunderstorms caused crackling interference in the transatlantic radiotelephone circuits. At the same time he discovered a hissing sound, which turned out to be cosmic radio waves from our own galaxy. Since that time astronomers have used radio telescopes to see what cannot be seen. Most astronomical objects are visible, but they also project invisible wavelengths (infrared, X-rays, ultraviolet) of the electromagnetic spectrum that must be received by radio telescopes and fed as data into a computer that digitizes this data allowing the astronomers to "see" these invisible patterns.

Coincidentally, around the same time that radio astronomy was being developed, people were beginning to see UFOs — so-called starships from other planets. Orson Welles's famous radio production (1938) of H. G. Wells's *The War of the Worlds* (1898), in addition to being entertaining, also caused widespread panic during the broadcast. A short time later the world entered the atomic age. Filmmakers fictionalized the idea that interplanetary civilizations would be concerned about Earth's own destructive capabilities. Robert Wise's classic movie *The Day the Earth Stood Still* (1951) was one such example, in which a human-looking alien visitor from a nearby planet warned Earth's inhabitants that if they took their destructive habits into space, they would be destroyed by a constabulary of robots. The aliens created these robots in order to contain the violent tendencies of other species. Since the beginning of the atomic age there have been thousands of UFO sightings; one of the most famous occurred near Roswell Air Force base in 1947. A television movie depicted the Air Force's cover-up of an apparent UFO crash about 35 miles northwest of Roswell, New Mexico, from which alien bodies were supposedly recovered. Many people believed the crash was a UFO; however, the Air Force said that the ruins were nothing but a special weather balloon (see Randle 1994). Ufologists have yet to be satisfied with the Air Force's explanation 50 years later.

UFO mythology, as I will explain in further detail in chapter 9, "From Whitewater to Heaven's Gate," has a strong presence on the World Wide Web. One site describes how an interesting UFO incident supposedly occurred during the first moonwalk, in which ham radio operators picked up uncensored NASA communications between Houston and *Apollo 11*. According to this account, a former NASA employee, Otto Binder, believes that during the famous Apollo 11 mission, where Neil Armstrong gave humanity a great leap during his first steps on the moon, radio ham operators back on Earth — using VHF receivers that bypassed NASA's own "censored" broadcasts to the public — picked up a conversation between the astronauts of *Apollo 11* and NASA:

> NASA: What's there? Mission Control calling *Apollo 11* ...
>
> APOLLO 11: These "babies" are huge, Sir! Enormous! Oh my God! You wouldn't believe it! I'm telling you there are other spacecraft out there, lined up on the far side of the crater edge! They're on the Moon watching us!
>
> (UFO Joe 1993)

UFO myths are not just mild hype. They have their roots in Orson Welles's radio production, which caused a regional panic in 1938. And, even more recently, "Spaniards flooded TV and radio switchboards with calls after news broadcasts reported space aliens hovering over New York. The alien invasion was in fact ads for the film *Independence Day*" (*Christian Science Monitor* 1996). Despite the fact that many people want to believe in UFOs and despite the fact that many witnesses claim to have seen UFOs, there has yet to be any scientific proof of encounters with aliens presented to the public. If there are alien craft here, then where are the radio signals that would accompany a highly advanced civilization?

Perhaps egged on by thousands of reports of UFO sightings from around the planet, NASA set up the SETI (Search for Extraterrestrial Intelligence) program, which uses radio receivers set at different frequencies in the hopes of picking up distant non-natural sounds — signs of technological civilizations outside Earth's orbit. This process was depicted in the movie *Contact* (1997), based on a novel by Sagan. In contrast to rumors of alien civilizations promulgated by ufology, Ron Brown offered a scientific approach for SETI in his opening remarks at the 1993 Bioastronomy Symposium, where he argued that statistical probabilities "lead to the conclusion that intelligent life, technologically advanced, exists in locations in the universe other than Earth. This is testable by seeking to detect decodable signals, which is precisely the basis of current SETI activities" (R. Brown 1995:10). The science of decoding electromagnetic radio broadcasts forms the basis for SETI's search strategy, and SETI scientists employ the same technology radio astronomers use to map the universe outside the visible light spectrum. Ufology, the gathering of rumors, stories, and folk myths about alien contact on Earth, was not included in this symposium. Sagan would argue that the intense growth of UFO sightings is no more than the phantasmatic images of a collective unconscious, much like the many sightings of ghosts and spirits near the end of the nineteenth century and demons in medieval times. In *The Demon Haunted World* (1996), Sagan debunks the myth of the existence of actual UFOs, even though he himself would have been the first to admit the existence of extraterrestrial life on other planets. (I examine this in more detail in chapter 9.)

Despite legendary UFO stories, word-of-mouth evidence, fuzzy photographs, and "alien autopsies," skepticism remains in the minds of most people because there has yet to be published proof from the scientific community or the United States government. Lacking scientific validity, these circulated stories have instead been surrogated into the performance of a UFO subculture — a mythos that includes claims of government cover-ups and press silence that's dramatized practically every week on Chris Carter's popular television series *The X-Files*. Scholar Joseph Roach says that a surrogate performance "stands in for an elusive entity that it is not but that it must vainly aspire both to embody and replace" (1996:3). The performed culture of UFO myth arises from the fact that there is yet to be conclusive evidence of alien visitations to Earth. This absence finds itself surrogated in myth, cultural artifacts, and performances.

Encounter *(1988): Constructing an Aural Encounter of the Third Kind*

If we have yet to hear signals from intelligent and technologically centered life in nearby star systems, and UFOs are at least nothing but phantasms of the mind, then perhaps it is through sounds, like those of the whales of an earlier age, that we can communicate across vast distances and encounter the other. So it's not surprising that musician Michael Stearns, who arranged spatial tones and sonorous audio wavelengths in order to take listeners into deep space with *Planetary Unfolding* (1985), would later create, entirely through sound, a virtual encounter with a UFO in his 1988 recording *Encounter*. Stearns places the listener in the midst of an aural painting that "pictures" alien contact. He produces music in the genre known artistically as *space music* and commercially labeled New Age. These kinds of musicians design aural landscapes. Through this method Stearns constructed a virtual encounter with an alien spacecraft, an aural close encounter of the third kind.

Like a radio astronomer, Stearns makes the invisible "seen." His music intersects UFO mythology and the SETI program (which is indirectly related to radio astronomy). The means of sending and receiving radio signals in space to determine the patterns of stellar matter outside the visible spectrum, as well as listening for artificial alien signals in order to make visible the invisible — signs of intelligent life outside the sphere of Earth's orbit — are virtually explored in Stearns's music. He shapes aurally what SETI is looking for and what many have claimed to have witnessed. A UFO mythos has already been textually and orally documented, produced for television, movies, and books. What writers have written about and what photographers and filmmakers have visually recorded and fantasized — fictional or otherwise — Michael Stearns creates aurally. Between radio astronomy, SETI, and UFOs, Stearns constructs a phantasmatic UFO encounter — an aural soundscape that attempts to make the invisible visible.

New Age music, known for its nonmelodic ethereal tones, is particularly suited for the atmospheric lonely flight through space that leads one to an alien encounter. Stearns opens the work (track 1, "Encounter: Awaiting the Other," 3:25) by mixing soft, gliding electronic tones with the evening sounds of chirping crickets, softly hooting owls, and an evening bird. In the background a faint but deep heart-thumping beats amidst electronic grunting. At about the three-minute mark, the sounds of footsteps walking on gravel can be heard as the tones stretch into a higher pitch. It eventually crescendos to a whine as the crickets get louder, and the work climaxes with sudden silence.

Track 2, "Craft: Dimensional Release" (6:23), begins with a humming sound mixed with an ominous gong. At 3:30 the spacecraft arrives with a dopplered whirring whine as it passes overhead. It lands with soft thunder and melodious tones, then crescendos to a higher pitch as it takes off again with a snapping thunder, followed by a melody of eerie loneliness and breathtaking vigor.

Stearns takes us on a journey through space, thematically naming the other tracks: 3. "The Beacon: Those Who Have Gone Before" (6:54); 4. "On the Way: Space Caravan" (3:48); 5. "Dimensional Shift: Across the Threshold" (5:16); 6. "Within: Choir of the Ascending Spirit" (3:50); 7. "Distant Thunder: Solitary Witness" (5:35); 8. "Alien Shore: Starlight Bay" (3:43); 9. "Procession: Sacred Ceremony (8:46); 10. "Star Dreams: Peace Eternal" (4:06).

If listeners were not given a thematic title of the work, would they understand that this music represents alien contact? Dennis Hall says that in New Age music, accompanying "album notes and titles," as well as pictures, provoke "[m]eaning and cultural utility" constructed, "as the occasion warrants, out of the transactions with the text" (1994:16–17). He explains that this kind of music "remain[s] much more open to the listener's construction of meaning and use" (15). The subjective experience of the listeners guide them into realms of the imagination through a technology governed by electricity. "Electricity transformed the very form of the imagination through which we discover our utopias and dystopias," sound scholar Allen Weiss contends (1994:4). This same electricity, he adds, buzzing at 50 Hertz (G-sharp) in Europe (30 Hertz more than the finback whale songs that once reached across the distance of entire oceans), "established a new, inexorable, unconscious tonal center which inhabits our every thought and underlies our every enunciation" (4). The finback whale's tonal center has since been plagued from interference by human technology. Our utopic technology is the whale's dystopia.

Sagan believes the same kind of aural interference that silenced the long-distance communication of whales will eventually jam the "interstellar channel," which is based on the "radio spectral line of hydrogen" at 1.42 billion Hertz: "the frequency band is being increasingly encroached upon by civilian and military communications traffic on Earth.... Uncontrolled growth of terrestrial radio technology may prevent us from ready communication with intelligent beings on distant worlds" (1980:172). I think Michael Stearns captures metaphorically what the whales once had. Stearns uses sound to create a communications system that reaches across vast distances within our minds — a music of the cosmos spreading its sonic tendrils through outer space, virtually.

Ufology claims many visitations from the Other. Scientists in the SETI program, using rigorous scientific methods in their search for signs of alien intelligence, have yet to prove the existence of any extraterrestrial intelligence. And through technology Stearns not only connects the listener to visions of space, but he also evokes the oceanic depth of unseen whale songs, the music of creatures who are all alone in the dark, not unlike stars lighting the deep night. Did the finbacks attempt to assuage this loneliness by trying to communicate with the artificial sounds of vessels on the surface of their ocean — and why wouldn't those vessels communicate back? Perhaps SETI is too preoccupied with artificial signals. What if life-forms — like whales in the ocean — glide through the depths of space or float in the atmosphere of alien planets? Are they being silenced by television broadcasts of *Bay Watch*? On track 8, "Alien Shore: Starlight Bay" (3:43), Stearns tries to touch us with a live intelligence guiding us through the depths of space to an alien shore. The music washes over us with electronic bubbles and wispy waves like the caressing touch of a nebula, interspersed between the increasingly melodic tonal beams flickering like a slow pulsar spinning in the lonely depths of space.

With track 9, "Procession: Sacred Ceremony" (8:46), Stearns climaxes his work, which, with casual listening, doesn't seem to have a beginning and end, as Dennis Hall says about New Age music: "This music is all middle; it starts and stops, it is turned on and off, but one does not get a distinct sense of beginnings and endings" (1994:14). (Perhaps Hall's complaint refers to individual pieces and not to the entire composition on the CD. Stearns often links all his tracks into the movements of an electronic symphony that does have Aristotelian structure.) Beginning this track, for about five minutes, Stearns builds almost choral tones (with occasional xylophone-like gongs) that shine with the timbrenic beams of a radiant dawn rising above the zenith of an orbiting planet. At this point (for the next minute and a half) the tone intensifies up to the vibrating intensity of a collapsing star going supernova, washing away everything in its path with an intense violent energy run amok. It softly fades and dims over the next three and a half minutes, leaving just a whisper of a low frequency tone overlaid with soft gongs like the fading pulses of an exploded star shredding away its cooling fragments of nebulous fire into the depths of space. This low frequency tone reminds me of the finbacks signaling their lost music in the ocean depths, like Artaud's actor signaling through the flames of a sacrificed self.

Timbre is one of the four characteristics of sound and is one of the salient features of New Age music. This, Susan Grove Hall says, lessens the "necessity for interesting melody, harmony, dynamic expression, and meter in music." For, she adds, "the tone colors, and their relative arrangements in duration and intensity, engage our primary interest" (S. Hall 1994:29). And this is the key factor in Stearns's work, especially in the piece described above. And it is this kind of music, space music, that puts us into space, as Stephen Hill, the producer of the syndicated radio program, *Music from the Hearts of Space*, defines it: "Celestial or cosmic music removes the listeners from their ordinary acoustical surroundings by creating stereo sound images of vast, apparently dimensionless spatial environments" (Hill 1988). Within these aural environments the "[r]hythmic or tonal movements animate the experience of flying, floating, cruising, gliding, or hovering within the auditory space.... The major effect of this music is to take the listener out of their body or at least out of their normal sound environment" (Hill 1988). In Stearns's music listeners may feel as if they are floating in space, buffeted by celestial energies. The chords of music act upon the imagination, and those who have an understanding or predilection for science fiction and UFOs can almost see within their imagination an encounter with an alien starship — no less so than if they were reading a novel.

Instead of words in a book that describes an imaginary trip through outer space, Stearns uses tonal structures to convey this journey. Part of my description of "Procession: Sacred Ceremony," comes from the understanding that New Age musicians use imagery as a creative basis for their music: "Some principle composers of New Age music trace the inspiration and form of their music to nature" (S. Hall 1994:24); "Few New Agers deny the highly visual character of their music.... If indeed New Age music is primarily functional in the sense of a 'mind movie,' one could expect the widest possible variety of visual interpretations, commensurate to the vast dissimilarity of compositions" (Zrzavy 1990:39). Stephen Hill says that space music artists "manipulate imagery as a variable of creativity. This was significant: imagery is the main thing in space music. As audio virtual reality develops, the possibility of creating imagery continues to grow" (Gerzoff 1996). Space music presents a virtual fantasy of traveling in outer space.

Brian Eno, who has put out some New Age titles, including *Thursday Afternoon* (1985) and the sound track to the documentary *For All Mankind* under the title *Apollo* (1983), agrees with this process, saying that he's trying to "paint" an "aural picture of some type":

> What I want to do is create a field of sound that the listener is plopped inside of and within which he isn't given any particular sense of values about things. It's much more like being in a real environment, where your choices are what determine the priority at a given time.... And as the piece developed, I'd get a stronger and stronger sense of the geography of that place and the time of day, the temperature, whether it was [a] windy or wet place or whatever. I was developing the pieces almost entirely in terms of a set of feelings that one normally wouldn't consider to be musical, not in terms of "Is this a nice tune? Is this a catchy rhythm?" Instead, I was always trying to develop this sense of the *place* of the music. (Milkowski 1983:16)

By means of sound, New Age musicians want to take the listener to a virtual place imagined in the mind. Novelists create similar effects with their stories.

Novelists paint imaginary pictures in the mind through words, not sound — although novels can evoke the sense of a sound, as in the following passage from Tolkien's *The Lord of the Rings*, which describes travelers fleeing the depths of the Mines of Moria after their leader, Gandalf, fell down an immense chasm while fighting a dreaded beast called a Balrog: "They looked back. Dark yawned the archway of the Gates under the mountain-shadow. Faint and far beneath the earth rolled the slow drum-beats: *doom*. A thin black smoke trailed out. Nothing else was to be seen; the dale all around was empty. *Doom.* Grief at last wholly overcame them, and they wept long: some standing and silent, some cast upon the ground. *Doom, doom.* The drum-beats faded" (1954:350).

In 1981 the BBC produced a radio drama of Tolkien's work. What's interesting to note is that for me the silence between the virtual notes of the written passage has more *sound* to it than the BBC audio production. I hear excellent Stanislavskian naturalistic acting, but it lacks the full cadence underneath the imagery of Tolkien's desperate prose. In the written passage, dissonant sound is poetically placed between sentences of the paragraph at three different locations. Within the silent emptiness of the vale, soft drumbeats of doom could be heard, the chapter fading into silence like the whisp of smoke rising out of the Gates, presenting a tableau, a pause for reflection, before moving on to the next chapter. The BBC production lacks this pause and moves quickly forward into the action.

Like a novelist, Michael Stearns tries to tell a story — not, however, through words but tones, musically painting an aural picture in the imagination. He wants listeners of *Encounter* to be taken out into space: "One of the musical dialects which has felt most natural to me is the language of Space," Stearns says. "Although many of my albums have been written and recorded in the flavor of Space, this is the first to focus on Space as a theme. For me this series of vignettes evokes very literal images of a Contact/Encounter, and a journey into the environments of what we call 'outer space.' We travel both linearly and dimensionally (obliquely) through this science fantasy, on a sonic voyage that is both very personal and yet familiar to all" (Stearns 1996). The familiarity to all is open to question. His music takes listeners on a sonic voyage that is more mysterious than familiar. Stearns's music becomes a technological but musical mediation between ourselves and the intelligence of an invisible Other: aliens and, perhaps, whales.

Philosopher Don Ihde uses phenomenology as a tool to explain technological mediation between ourselves and our world: our intentions are directed out into the world, and it reciprocates — what Ihde calls interactive intentionality. Technology is a mediation of this reflexive experience. On the one side there is, in this example, the listener of Stearns's music. On the other is the unknown intelligence whose sounds are invisible, if they exist at all. We can only experience the potential for an unmediated encounter with the alien through face-to-face communication. With *Encounter* we are not experiencing alien contact face-to-face but through a virtual aural experience. Using music of images, Stearns tries to represent an alien contact or encounter through sonic timbre. The "auralness" of Stearns's music is a symbolic representation of flight through space, including images of a mythological UFO contact. However, it must also include, by nature of their communication style, the whales as well. For their music, which we have taken away, becomes an inverse representation of SETI's hoped-for achievements of contact with aliens.

Stearns's music mediates these encounters sonically, and because it is a mediation, the music becomes not a magnifying glass allowing us to see the invisible intelligence (that remains unseen by those who do not live among the other) but a lens refracting what we hope to see when (or if) we do make contact. What we hear is an unresolved virtual image, bent or warped by the mediating lens of a visual musical style. This refraction is invisible. We're not aware of this mediation. We hear the virtual image (what Ihde would call the "irreal") and accept that as the real, and "if at the first level one may detect the irreal dimension of a mediated perception, at a second level one can also claim that this mediation has now been materialized and thus becomes part of reality. This is, of course, to say that media have a 'real' effect" (Ihde 1983:59). This could explain why Stearns's ride through space feels real. The virtual image, however irreal, can be felt, seen in the mind — playing on the cultural mythologies of the listener.

Like Duchamp's ready-made "Echo. Virtual sound"—a hidden noise in a ball of twine, which cannot be seen or identified, but contains the point source of a "virtual sound" (Adcock 1992:120)—Stearns's music becomes the point source for a virtual aural landscape of outer space. Perhaps unconsciously, Stearns taps into the psyche of virtual UFO encounters, as well as the silent listening of those astronomers who year after year await a signal that means contact with an intelligence outside Earth. Is this only a virtual hope? And yet, at the same time, the technological frequencies vibrating through the deep beneath the oceans are jamming the communications of an intelligence already here. Evocative more of the longing tones of whale songs than of rock, jazz, or classical music, space music connects us to our past and future as our television and radio broadcasts reach out to the stars across the vast depths of space. Perhaps an emerging intelligence out there has listened and, like the finbacks, has found what it heard wanting.

2

Hack and Slash
in the Woods:
Live-Action Fantasy
Role-Playing in Boston

"We accept our species as sapiens and fabricans: ones who think and make. We are in the process of learning how humans are also ludens and performans: ones who play and perform."

— Richard Schechner (1985:33)

The Game

Tugrath the Traveler, dressed in a green cloak and gray hood, appears to you in a dream as you sleep at an inn in the city of Dar of the kingdom Keldar. Warning of the return of the evil Mocker, Tugrath proclaims that "a great power will fall and a princess will die" unless you can help. In a ghost-like vision Tugrath directs you and your companions to rescue the princess from the Mocker, for she has the power to destroy him if you bring her the tablet containing a magic spell that will banish the Mocker from the land.

This was the opening scene from a live-action role-playing game held in a forest outside Boston on December 8, 1990. The players, like many other people around the country, dress up in costumes and drive for hours to attend outdoor live role-playing games, where ordinary people transport themselves to a pseudomedieval fantasy world of the imagination, becoming sword-swinging heroes for a day, performing such characters as knights and sorcerers. Role-playing games are an entertainment, although different from watching television, going to a movie, reading a novel, or listening to music. In the previous chap-

32

ter we saw how, through music, Stearns transports listeners into a virtual space composed of astronomical, astrological, and ufological tropes. Fantasy role-playing games, conversely, take players to a virtual world filled with tropes from such works as Tolkien's *The Lord of the Rings*, among dozens of other fantasy novels and movies. During the course of the game players are removed from their everyday environment. Theorist Johan Huizinga defines play as a "voluntary activity or occupation executed within certain fixed limits of time and place, according to rules freely accepted but absolutely binding, having its aim in itself and accompanied by a feeling of tension, joy, and the consciousness that it is 'different' from 'ordinary life'" (1955:28). Participants of a role-playing game actually perform a character. They are not watching a performance. They are playing a performance.

The live role-playing adventure called *Arianne's Terror* contains, as performance scholar Richard Schechner would put it, "certain patterns" found in a "unifiable realm of performance that includes ritual, theater, dance, music, sports, play, social drama, and various popular entertainments" (1988:257). Role-playing games are distinguished from, and yet similar to, other kinds of performances, including some historical folk events. They precede computer adventure games and CD-ROM movies. Computer games reflect in a limited way the interactive participatory storytelling capabilities of role-playing games.

All role-playing games — played orally around a table or as live-action outside — manifest several universal qualities. A moderator, called the gamemaster,* presents a step-by-step, plotted story to the players. These adventures, as they are commonly called, can take place in many different settings, ranging from a medieval fantasy world to starships in deep space. Players adopt a character that they use to interact with others as they progress through the scenario, everyone interactively creating and sharing the story. These characters — being individuals in a make-believe world — are unique, possessing qualities, skills, and occupations that may be far different from those of the players themselves, including cross-gendered characters. In the around-the-table version, the gamemaster plays the role of all the characters that the players meet in the story, but in live-action games other players perform these roles. The gamemaster moves the players through the plot by using these "non-player characters" (NPCs) in much the same way a novelist uses characters the hero meets in a novel. In the role-playing game, the gamemaster gives these non-player characters a purpose and adjusts their actions based on what the players do with their own characters. The choices the players make are open-ended but are influenced (or guided) by what the gamemaster says in response to a player's decision. The scenario is usually over when the players have moved their characters through

---

*Role-playing chronicler Sean Patrick Fannon lists some qualities of a gamemaster: "A gamemaster must have the Heart of a Bard, the Soul of an Artist, the Intellect of a Scientist, the Insight of a Philosopher, the Foresight of a General, the Memory of a Historian, the Will of an Umpire, the Compassion of a Priest, the Flexibility of a Diplomat, the Ego of an Auteur, and the Instincts of a Gambler" (1996:39).

the story and completed their goal, although this may last several sessions of play. The players may use their same characters in other adventures that the gamemaster creates. As they do this, the characters increase their reputation and power in the gamemaster's make-believe world.

In 1974 Gary Gygax and David Arneson published the first role-playing game, *Dungeons & Dragons*, also referred to as "D&D," which had a medieval fantasy setting. Both Arneson and Gygax played simulation war games like those published by Avalon Hill Game Company, which started publishing war games during the 1950s. Gary Fine theorizes that role-playing games evolved from war games through a series of transformations, as they became the privately published game, D&D, in 1974 (1983:14–15). About 1,000 copies of D&D were sold in 1974, and 4,000 copies in 1975 (Kellman 1983:34). The sales of the game increased. By 1979 TSR, Gygax's game company, grossed $2 million (DeWitt 1979:16). The profits multiplied in the following years, to $8.5 million in 1980, and an estimated $20 million in 1981 (*New York Times* 1980). TSR went on the edge of bankruptcy in 1997 and was bought out by Wizards of the Coast, the publishers of *Magic: The Gathering* (analyzed in the next chapter). Other companies formed during the 1970s and 1980s, publishing different kinds of rules and settings for role-playing games. Some of these games were based on fantasy and science fiction worlds as found in novels and movies — such as I. C. E.'s *Middle Earth Role-Playing* (1982) game based on J. R. R. Tolkien's *The Lord of the Rings*, FASA's *Star Trek* (1982) game, and West End Games' *Star Wars* (1987). Similar games, called MUDs (Multi-User Dungeons), can be found online.

As a likely result of the popularity of *Dungeons & Dragons*, in 1981 the International Fantasy Gaming Society (IFGS), based in Denver, Colorado, was formed, and it published a set of rules for an outdoor, fantasy role-playing game similar to the medieval-fantasy environment of D&D. As of 1990 there were five groups in the United States organized as chapters of the Colorado-based IFGS: The Denver-Boulder chapter was formed in 1981 and had organized 38 role-playing adventures as of 1987; the Colorado Springs chapter presented three adventures in 1987; the Dallas chapter ran four events in 1987; the New Jersey chapter put on one adventure in 1985; and the Boston chapter put on four events in 1990 (Toth 1989:119–122 and personal note).

The Scenes

On December 8, 1990, the Boston chapter of the IFGS presented the adventure *Arianne's Terror* at the Blue Hills Reservation, a wooded park outside Boston. Several players performing NPCs (the characters the protagonists would encounter) and the gamemaster arrived about 9:30 in the morning to set up the game. NPCs were set at various locations in the woods, and ten players, dressed in costumes, would encounter them at eight different sites as they were guided along the trails by the gamemaster. By 11:30 all the players had arrived. Most of the participants were from the Boston area, but a few people were from Maine and New York. Many of them came dressed in medieval-like costumes, and they looked out of place as they stepped out of their late-twentieth-century vehicles. One was dressed in a green cloak and wore a Robin Hood hat, and another person had a gray cloak, a staff, and a belt with various wizard-like items hanging from it. Another character, dressed all in black, wielded a six-foot sword. In all, there were five magic-users, a cleric, a ranger, a monk, a thief, and a fighter. Before the game started, many players talked to each other while others swung their swords for practice. Many of the players knew each other from participating in other game events earlier in the year. Most of the newcomers played NPCs. Everyone filled out a registration form and paid $15. NPC paid $5.

About 11:15 the NPCs were led up the wooded road, where they would wait in various locations and interact with the players. During the course of the adventure the players would try to rescue the kidnapped Princess Arianne from the hands of the Mocker and destroy him. The group would encounter various ambushes, traps, and so forth, until it reached the climax of rescuing the princess and destroying the Mocker. As part of the live-action role-playing game, players performed physical actions. They walked through the woods. During combat, they struck each other with handmade weapons made out of foam-wrapped PVC pipe. Magic-users verbally cast spells, whose effects were described by the gamemaster. When a character was hit by a sword, the gamemaster kept score. If a player received too much damage the character died and was removed from play.

ENCOUNTER 1: Around 11:30 the gamemaster (GM) led the players up the road about 20 yards. He turned to them as they spread out in a semicircle, and he told them that they were at an inn sleeping. The gamemaster, dressed in a green cloak with a gray hood, performed the part of Tugrath the Traveler, who told the players that he appears to their characters in a dream (as described in the opening of this chapter). He told the players that Tugrath is a ghost-like person who is known for giving council when the kingdom is in danger. He told them that Princess Arianne had been kidnapped by the evil Mocker and that they must rescue her. He gave them a magical gemstone (flashlight), incense of clear sight (two pieces of felt), and a tablet (cloth) to help them on their journey. After rescuing the princess, they were to give her the tablet and then go to a fountain and have the princess read the spell that will destroy the Mocker.

ENCOUNTER 2: Off to the left of the road, the party saw two NPCs fighting another NPC. Before the gamemaster could explain the scene, the black-clad fighter player charged into the fight, and the gamemaster had to call a hold — telling all the players to stop. The gamemaster, functioning as the storyteller, explained that the scene was an illusion created by a magic spell. As soon as the fighter player had run into the scene the illusion disappeared. The NPCs in the scene walked away. The players continued up the road. The whole structure of the adventure is similar to Tolkien's *The Hobbit*, wherein Bilbo Baggins, a party of dwarves, and the wizard, Gandalf, journeyed through a wilderness, encountering trolls, Orcs, and other beings that tried to thwart their mission.

ENCOUNTER 3: As the players ambled up the road, the gamemaster described how a mist was rising up around them, getting thicker and thicker. On a slight wooded mound on their left, five NPCs stood with swords and shields. The gamemaster said that what the players saw were five warriors overlooking the Crystal Falls of Zarnath. The scene again disappeared. The gamemaster constantly mediated the scenes. Where NPCs stood on a mound, his verbal description virtually turned them into five warriors overlooking a large waterfall. The players had to constantly use their imaginations to "flesh" out the details of the scene. The players continued up the road. Off the right side of the road they saw an NPC dressed in a gray cloak standing by a tree. The gamemaster said that the figure was a knight with a painful look in his eyes. A couple of players tried to talk to the knight, but he would not respond to them. Walking further up the road, they saw another NPC lying on a large rock, next to the side of the road on their left. The gamemaster told the players that the person appeared to be Arianne. When one of the players approached her, the gamemaster said that the princess disappeared — another illusion. The NPC got up and walked away. One of the players, in character, said, "This is a bad omen."

As the party walked up the road, some players talked about what had happened in previous scenes, sometimes joking among themselves. One person said, "The princess is already dead." As they walked, the ranger player talked to the gamemaster. He asked about other towns and villages in the area. The gamemaster, knowing the details of the world like he was a novelist, said that this was only a wilderness containing some aboriginal tribes. The party went farther up the road, and the gamemaster told them that the gem they received in the first scene led them to a trail on their left, which branched off from the main road. After a couple of minutes' walking along the narrow trail, the group stopped for a rest. The players asked the gamemaster questions about what Tugrath had told them in the first scene. A little while later, the fighter player asked if everyone was rested, and they continued in a single line up the trail. The rest stop was not necessarily for the players. It was part of the realism, conveying the fact that travelers on a road in the wilderness would stop and camp. It created the impression that more time was passing than actually occurred.

ENCOUNTER 4: The group walked into an ambush. Three NPC warriors hid behind trees off to the right, and another three hid behind a tree stump farther up the trail off to the left. Some of the players charged and engaged in sword-swinging physical combat. Three of the NPCs broke through the charge and tried to attack the wizard players in back. But one of the wizards cast a sleep spell on them. The gamemaster had to stop the action while he determined who was affected by the spell. The three NPCs were told to sit down where they were and "sleep." Two other NPCs were wounded and captured, and a third ran away. The captured NPCs where executed by the fighter when he discovered that they serviced the Mocker. The wounded characters were "healed" by a cleric casting a spell, and others were given first aid. Behind a tree stump, a player found some magical potions (which were containers of fruit juice). After they were ready, they walked to the next scene.

ENCOUNTER 5: Farther up the trail, the players saw three NPCs dressed in white standing back-to-back in a triangle formation. Red yarn hung over a tree limb above the trail. The gamemaster explained that the group stood in a large hallway. In front of them was a room with a pentagram on the floor with a wall of flame shooting out of it. The black-clad fighter player stepped into the doorway (an overhanging tree branch). As soon as he did this, the three NPCs threw beanbags at him. The beanbags represented magic fire balls. He parried one of them, and the other two missed as he retreated back down the hall (the wooded trail). The players gathered together and talked about how they were going to get around this obstacle. The ranger player looked through the "doorway" and another beanbag was thrown at him. He taunted the NPC: "You do that again and you'll be sorry." One of the NPCs chuckled in response. The ranger then took a canteen of water and splashed the three NPCs with it, making an out-of-character remark, "You wanted to be an NPC." Another beanbag/fireball was thrown, but it missed. The gamemaster told the ranger player that the water he threw on the NPCs had no game effect.

The cleric player suggested that they just go through the wall of fire. The gamemaster hinted that there seemed to be enough room on either side of the fire wall to squeeze around it. But other players complained of being ambushed by the NPC demons with the beanbag/fireballs. The ranger tried to taunt the NPCs by making faces at them so that they would throw more beanbags at him, using up the limited stock they had. Some of the players laughed at the ranger's taunting, but the NPCs did not throw any more beanbags. The group talked some more about how they would get through this obstacle, and the cleric suggested again that they just run through the room. After a moment the fighter, cleric, and thief players ran past the fire wall. The NPCs threw beanbags at them, but they missed. The other players eventually ran through as well, and some were hit by the beanbags/fireballs. The wounded characters drank magic potions that healed them. The gamemaster, chuckling, asked one of the players how bad the drinks were, and he said it tasted like cool-pops. The gamemaster gathered the players around, then gave a signal to an NPC hiding in the woods. It was the Mocker, who spoke a riddle. One of players yelled out, "That didn't rhyme. You'll be sorry." The Mocker player disappeared and the players continued up the path.

ENCOUNTER 6: The group took another side path on their left. The gamemaster told them that they saw three demon-like figures guarding a doorway (the space between two trees). In front of the NPC demons was a stick with a head on it, represented by a Halloween monster mask. They then heard screams for help from the princess, whom they could not see. The players advanced. The ranger, who was in the lead, fired his bow several times at the demon. This was done through a verbal description. He turned to the fighter and said, "Let's go in." They charged the NPC demons. One of the demon NPCs swung his sword at the ranger, stating, "Hit — 7," indicating that he had given seven points of damage to the fighter. His character wounded, the player backed off. Another player, a wizard wielding a staff, stepped up. The wizard placed an "electrify" spell on the staff so that when he swung it at the NPC demon, the character received six points of damage. The gamemaster, moderating the combat, told the demon NPC that the wound caused him to drop his weapon. The NPC player dropped his weapon and stepped back.

The rest of the players watched from behind, unable to join the battle because they were in a narrow corridor (represented by the wooded trail). One of the wizards behind the two players up front cast a sleep spell, hoping to cause the two demon NPCs to fall asleep. But the gamemaster said that he was so close to the two players up front that the spell caused them to fall asleep — whereas the demon NPCs were unaffected. The ranger and the wizard stepped up front and held their positions. The ranger player told the gamemaster that he would continue to fire his bow, saying, "They are not coming after me, so this seems like a good ploy." The gamemaster turned to the NPCs, stating in a polite tone, "Gentlemen, well, it's up to you — you want to stay in the room, or come out?" One of the demon NPCs rushed forward swinging his sword. The other joined him. The gamemaster had to call a hold when one of the players tripped and fell, but he was unhurt. There was a question about one of the NPCs receiving a blow from a sword, and the gamemaster had to ask him if he had indeed received a wound. He was told to limp back to the room he was in. The third NPC demon then charged with full force into the group of players, and the gamemaster had to call another hold, rebuking his rough play, saying "this isn't football." The players eventually defeated the NPC demons.

The players discovered more healing potions, and as the players were drinking them, the Mocker character stood some distance away in the woods and yelled out, "I will bathe you in blood!" then disappeared again. The players heard some yells for help from the princess, and they found her tied to a tree farther down the trail. She was leaning against a tree, but the gamemaster explained to them that she was really chained to the back wall. The fighter player said he would break the chains with his axe. The princess was grateful for the rescue and agreed to go to the fountain so she could cast the spell that would destroy the Mocker. The players gave her the tablet and gem (given to them by Tugrath in the first scene). They followed the Princess.

ENCOUNTER 7: She led them through a doorway marked by an opening between two trees. The Mocker turned to the princess and said, "Princess, come here." She replied, "I'm here, Master." The Mocker stood on a large rock (about six feet high and fifteen feet long). He turned to his six NPC henchmen and said, "Destroy the dogs." The players, tricked by an apparently fake princess, fought the henchmen. There were some long pauses in the mêlée in order for the GM to keep track of the combat. During one of these pauses the Mocker yelled to his henchmen, who were beginning to lose the battle, "Destroy them. Slaughter them! Cut their hearts out! Morons fight! You fools, burn them — take their souls!" Then he broke character and laughed. One of the NPC henchmen turned around and looked at the Mocker and laughed with him. The Mocker-player quickly turned to a video camera recording the event, and puckishly smiled, saying, "Hi." The players soon overcame them and freed the real princess, but the Mocker escaped.

They followed the real princess to the fountain, which was back up another trail. They were led to a small clearing containing large slabs of rocks rising above the players' heads. Players stood still like statues around the rocks and clearing. The gamemaster said that they were indeed statues. The princess stood beside one of the large rocks — which represented a fountain. The players guarded her as she read the spell from the stone tablet. Moments later the Mocker appeared on top of a huge boulder and the statues came alive. The players swung swords at them, holding them away from the princess as she finished casting her spell. The Mocker knew he was defeated. He spoke: "Well, Princess, your loyal guards have bested my minions once again. But I shall return and will meet you all before the Crystal Falls of Zarnath, where we will again contest the Rule of Keldar — farewell." The gamemaster told the players that the Mocker had been defeated.

Everyone helped pick up all the props and other belongings then walked back to the cars at the front gate of the park. They drank sodas and coffee and ate snacks as they talked about their adventure. The gamemaster handed out experience record sheets for players and NPCs to fill out. This would allow them to gain more power in later games. The event was over by 3:30 P.M.

Three Frames of Performance

There are three overlapping performance frames observable in role-playing games. At the center are characters who are part of a dramatic plot — the imaginary realm of the fantasy world; surrounding this are players participating in a game that has rules; and around this exists the real world. These frames exist simultaneously, feeding off of each other.

The real-world frame is the foundation for the other two frames. It is the daily frame that each of us lives in. People can easily escape this real-world frame at any time, "jumping" into another frame by reading a novel, watching a movie, or playing a game, among many other possibilities. Their imaginations become stimulated by participating in one of these many activities. They can become caught up in the imaginary world created by a novelist, or through the performance of actors in a movie, actually feeling for these imaginary characters vicariously. However, the real-world frame always exists around the imaginary world, and peoples' different personalities, attitudes, and histories will affect how they perceive and participate in the imaginary world. The middle frame, which exists between the real world and the imaginary world of the adventure, is the game itself, the rules providing the players the stimulation and the means to enter the third frame. The rules describe how to write the encounters in the adventure and how to create a character (including what kinds of character types there are), and they explain the importance of props and costumes, and so on — all creating a catalyst for the players to reach the imaginary world of the adventure. This middle frame is created every time an author puts down words on paper to make a story or a director holds rehearsals for actors, who will later enact a play for an audience.

The players participate in an event prepared by a gamemaster. In this adventure the gamemaster chose the locations on the trails where he would place the various NPC encounters. The second frame setup included placing props and explaining to the NPCs where they should stand. Huizinga explains how, before any kind of play commences, a playground boundary is marked. These boundaries, he writes, "are temporary worlds within the ordinary world, dedicated to the performance of an act apart" (1955:10). The setup of this playground occurs in the second frame, which helps stimulate the "performance" through the use of rules. Huizinga believes that "Play demands order absolute and supreme. The least deviation from it 'spoils the game,' robs it of its character and makes it worthless" (10). This was seen at one point when the gamemaster warned a player that he was getting too rough with his sword-play. The players' abilities to participate in the third-frame fantasy world are determined by their willingness to follow the second frame's order and rules. But at the same time the players' attitudes and histories carried over from the first frame affect how players follow the rules and how they role-play their characters.

The third frame, the imaginary world of the story, exists at the center of the role-playing performance. For this particular adventure, it is the world where the heroes are called to rescue the princess and destroy the evil Mocker. In this frame the creative, imaginary circumstances are the heart of a role-playing adventure, as they are with movies and plays. However, there is a large difference between role-playing games and these other performances. In conventional movies and plays, the third frame usually stays in focus, and it is kept in focus by the performers themselves. Stanislavsky, the father of naturalistic acting theory, states that for a performer to stay in character (to stay focused on the third frame), "we [as actors] must be aware either of the external circumstances which surround us ... or of an inner chain of circumstances which we ourselves have imagined in order to illustrate our parts" (1948a:60). The observers watching a play or movie need only sit back and watch the story unfold in front of them. But in a role-playing game the players, being more than spectators, participate in the imaginary world through their characters, but they are not necessarily absorbed into a role, as Stanislavsky hoped for his actors.

In role-playing games all three performance frames flux, varying in intensity, one dominating the other from moment to moment. The player, unlike the conventional actor, does not have to worry about staying in the third frame all the time, which is almost an impossibility in role-playing games. Players, more often than not, tend to exist "side by side" with their characters like the Brechtian actor who may suddenly (in the middle of a performance) shift a character from first person to third person, from, for example, "I don't like you," to "He says he doesn't like you." Performers of role-playing games don't have a script to help them become "absorbed" into their characters, but there are inherent events and behaviors in the adventure that the players react to and express while playing their characters. The stimulation, the catalyst, for these different behavior patterns exists in the second frame, and it is through this frame that the first and third frames are brought together: people playing a game and getting caught up in the illusion of a story.

First, in the real-world frame people get together at a remote park outside of Boston. Second, players have developed characters from a set of second-frame rule books; the gamemaster created an adventure located in the woods, away from as many twentieth-century objects as possible; and third, the gamemaster guides them to each encounter in the woods, where the players participate in the third-frame story. The second frame underpins and supports the third frame, and the real world exists by virtue of the players' personal behaviors and the environment around them.

At the fifth encounter, the players saw a wooded trail with three NPCs dressed in white, blocking the players' passage. Red yarn hung from tree branches. The real world, the physical environment, exists with the trappings of the second frame: the costumed players, the NPCs, and the yarn, all representing objects in the third-frame fantasy world. The gamemaster explained to the players what the second-frame visual objects were by using a third-frame verbal description: Their characters see a column of flame shooting out of a pentagram engraved on the ground of the passageway. When the players advanced, the NPCs, playing the characters of flame demons, threw beanbags (representing fireballs) at the players. If a player got hit, then the player would have to deduct six hit points from his character, a third-frame wound represented by a second-frame tally. At one point one of the players threw some water out of a canteen at one of the NPCs, hoping to squelch the fire demon. As he did this he remarked wryly to the NPC, "You wanted to be an NPC"— showing his first-frame personality by making a second-frame remark, hoping to create a third-frame effect from his canteen. This kind of simultaneous pattern can be seen throughout the performances of role-playing games. It's interesting that in a role-playing game, the plot is not "fixed." If the fire demon players had actually hit the players several times each, some of them would not have lived through the rest of the adventure. Or, if the henchmen had actually fought well in the final scene, they may have won, and the players would not have freed Princess Arianne. Their characters could also have been killed, at which point the game would have ended. In addition, it can by seen why it is not outside the scope of the game for a player to break out of character, as the Mocker did when he waved at the camera and smiled.

Six Points of Performance Contacts

In Schechner's work *Between Theater and Anthropology* he describes six anthropology-theater contacts, ideas which help explain the universality of performance events and the patterns that can be detected among them (1985:3–33). I apply these concepts to role-playing games in order to show how these games express moments of an aesthetic performance.

(1) *Transformation of being and/or consciousness.* Transformation is the process of change that occurs in the consciousness of the performer and/or spectator during a performance. In a role-playing game this transformation does happen, whether it shakes the boredom out of a player or simply gives the player a good feeling after accomplishing a difficult encounter in the adventure. Huizinga explains how a "player can abandon himself body and soul to the game, and the consciousness of its being 'merely' a game can be thrust into the background. The joy inextricably bound up with playing can turn not only into tension, but into elation" (1955:20–21). One player even mentioned how the game relieves a sense of frustration in his life. Part of this transformation is so engaging that some critics have complained that role-playing games become more real than reality (see Lancaster 1994).

(2) *Intensity of the performance.* According to Schechner, a performance fails if it doesn't cross "a certain definite threshold" which has "touched or moved an audience" (1985:10). The players are the performers and the spectators at the same time, and how well adventures move them depends upon how intense players role-play their characters and how forcefully they move the plot forward through their actions. At the end of this adventure the players encountered the Mocker and his minions. What should have been an intense, all-out climactic battle was interrupted by pauses and delays because the gamemaster had to keep stopping the action in order to keep track of five different pairs of combatants. However, one of the pauses didn't prevent the NPC playing the Mocker, who was intensely focused on his character, from yelling to the other NPCs, "Destroy them! Slaughter them! Cut their hearts out! Morons fight! You fools, burn them — take their souls!" But even this intense scene was interrupted by the player himself when he slipped out of character and started laughing and even smiling, saying "Hi" to the video camera recording the event. This is also a good example of how players shift performance frames during the game, thus making it a part of the entire event. This fact also helps explain how the plotted story of the game is not the whole game. It includes all the performance elements, whether players are in character or not.

(3) *Audience-performer interactions.* "Changes in the audience lead to changes in the performances," Schechner states (1985:16). As mentioned previously, players double as performers and spectators. Because each player is different, and clearly because there are no prewritten scripts, each performance of a role-playing game is totally different when different players play the game, even if they play the same adventure. The different character classes and per-

sonalities of individual players affect what kinds of decisions are made and how the players perform their different characters. The performance and the story flow of a particular adventure change with new players, as well as with different gamemasters.

(4) *The whole performance sequence.* According to Schechner, the following phases constitute an entire performance: "training, workshops, rehearsals, warm-ups, the performance, cool-down, and aftermath" (1985:16). Players do not go through any formal training to learn how to role-play a character — they tend to learn by participating and by picking up cues from experienced gamers. Some role-playing rules do provide tips on how to role-play, and Internet groups do discuss, in a workshop-type format, how to role-play characters. However, as with most games, there are no rehearsals in a role-playing game, and so the players do not know what will happen in the adventure from moment to moment. They improvise spontaneously as they interact with the gamemaster, NPCs, and each other. In this live role-playing adventure players warmed up by swinging swords, putting on their costumes, and determining who the party leader would be. The performance happens when players play the adventure. It began when the gamemaster led the players up the trail where they participated in the first encounter, and so on, until they rescued the princess and destroyed the Mocker. The cool-down phase included the gathering of all the props and equipment and walking back to the cars at the front gate of the park. At this time the players were awarded experience points that were placed on their character sheets. A character's increase of skills includes the aftermath phase, which is the long-term effect of the performance on a performer, observer, and critics. This chapter itself is another example of the adventure's aftermath.

(5) *Transmission of performance knowledge.* Players learn how to play role-playing games by buying rule books, generating characters, writing adventures, and participating in them. The knowledge of how to play a game is contained in the rules, and the execution of these guidelines helps create the performance event of a role-playing adventure. Word-of-mouth experiences and descriptions of adventures, as well as the adventure text itself, include the passing down of role-playing performance information.

(6) *How are performances evaluated?* Did the players meet their objective? How many experience points were awarded to the players? Did the players, the gamemaster, the NPCs all enjoy the game? Did players' characters survive? Did the players stay in character, the players' actions reflecting what the character would do in a given encounter? Did the gamemaster keep the game under control, and did he keep the game moving? Did the adventure provide a balance of action, character role-playing, and puzzle solving? Did the story have a beginning, middle, and end? The answers to many of these questions determine the success of an adventure. Some players may have been happy just to have their characters survive. Others may have wanted more action or more chances to role-play their character by interacting verbally with NPCs and not just fight them. One of the problems of a live-action role-playing adventure is the need

for the NPCs to clearly understand what they must do in an encounter, and they must have the ability to improvise within the context of the story. At some points in the game the NPCs were not sure what they were supposed to do, so the gamemaster had to remind them. In a regular, around-the-table role-playing game, the gamemaster role-plays all the NPCs and thus is able to keep the encounters under control, giving out any information to keep the game moving.

Historical Folk Traditions

Some of the performance aspects of role-playing games can be seen in the folk traditions of Halloween costuming and haunted houses, the English masquerade, and medieval tournaments. Below I briefly describe how these events relate to role-playing games and how the games grew indirectly out of preexisting performance traditions.

HALLOWEEN

Structurally, the encounters in "haunted house" mazes of Halloween are quite similar to a live role-playing game. A tour guide leads a group of people, usually dressed in costumes, through a maze in a building, where they are surprised by people dressed in monster costumes. This is similar to how the gamemaster led players along the wooded trail to each NPC encounter in the game. However, unlike the role-playing adventure — where players and NPCs interact among each other to move the story forward — the "monsters" in the haunted house do not interact with the people, other than, perhaps, momentarily scaring them. The encounters in the haunted house are mainly random, and the people going through the event have no dramatic objective. Certainly no skills or rules frame the event, other than walking through the entire maze. (Perhaps it's even considered breaking the rules to interact with the monsters.) There usually is no story to move them forward to the next encounter. Instead, "Halloween works for the individual as a public performance of a private persona, a personal participation in a group experience" (Santino 1983:17). Halloween is a social custom in which people walk the streets and attend parties as a costumed self. However, a live-action role-playing game is a private performance event giving the players a story to participate in. Like a Halloween event, they also wear costumes in helping to create a certain atmosphere.

ENGLISH MASQUERADES

Similar to the costuming of Halloween, the eighteenth-century English masquerade provided a social form of entertainment. According to one historian, the "pleasure of the masquerade attended on the experience of doubleness, the alienation of inner from outer" (Castle 1986:4). The mask, covering a person's normal self, allowed them to behave differently — as someone other than themselves — as during Halloween. At times, Castle continues, the masquerade mask "represented an inversion of one's nature. At its most piquant it expressed a violation of one's nature" (1986:5). A person such as a princess could socially play a commoner in a masquerade. In a role-playing game the rules allow a player who may be a computer programmer in the real world to become a spell-casting wizard or a sword-wielding hero who attempts to rescue a princess — certainly a "violation" of most players' daily natures or activity.

Medieval Tournaments

The medieval tournament combat events are similar to the combat in the game where players and NPCs use padded weapons to fight each other, but the padded weapons are much safer than the tournament weapons. Although the tournaments started as a means for battle practice, their popularity grew and became a part of the chivalric code in the literature of the day. Knights even adopted characters from these romantic tales, as Barker describes: "If tourney-ing occupied such an important place in chivalric literature it is not surprising that knights sought to imitate their literary heroes and thereby associate them-selves with some of the glamour and prestige attached to knights of romance" (1986:85). Barker supports this observation with historical documentation. In 1286, during the coronation of Henry of Cyprus as king of Jerusalem in Acre, "knights here were playing the parts of the most celebrated Arthurian heroes and enacting their adventures" (1986:88–89). In a similar way some players of role-playing games gain inspiration for playing their characters from contem-porary fantasy literature. Wizard players, perhaps, gain inspiration from Tolkien's wizard, Gandalf, from *The Hobbit* and *The Lord of the Rings*.

Playing a Performance

Role-playing games are performances. As such, they can be studied as per-formance. Performances, whether occurring in theaters, on television, or on the street, are a form of self-expression allowing people the liberty to emotionally touch others and themselves, to transport themselves and an audience into other realms of experiences. New forms of performances are not created from a vac-uum. Previous historical events, ceremonies, rituals, sporting events, and other kinds of performances have shaped and do influence the many new forms of per-formances occurring today. Victor Turner, an anthropologist, talks about Schechner's theory of "restored behavior," explaining that "the fire of meaning breaks out from rubbing together the hard and soft firesticks of the past (usu-ally embodied in traditional images, forms, and meanings) and present of social and individual experience" (in Schechner 1985:xi). Role-playing games have tra-ditional and historical roots in such performance events as Halloween events, masquerades, and medieval tournaments, among others. However much or little role-playing games share with these other performances, they are unique, having their own kinds of performance patterns and flavor. People are drawn to role-playing games because these games combine the innate need for people to interact socially, to observe, create, and perform stories. It allows them to play with fantasy. Already, new performance events can be seen as having their roots in role-playing games, including computer adventure games, and interactive CD-ROM movies, and the collectible card game, *Magic: The Gathering*.

3

Magic: The Gathering — Playing with Fantasy in a Postcinematic Form

"These cards are everywhere, and the language on them is taken straight from Satan."

— Mary Anne Di Bari

A New Phenomenon Created

August 1994. It is dark. Two hundred people jostle impatiently around the doors of a hobby store in Anchorage, Alaska. They've been waiting for several hours for the doors to open. In Denver, Colorado, an armored car drives up in front of a store. There is no money in this car. The owner of the store comes out and takes some boxes from the driver. Sacramento, California. Night. A person looks left, then right. No one is around. Taking the chance, the person breaks into the store, fills a bag with something that looks like decks of playing cards, leaves some money on the counter, then takes off (Zane 1994). Measured on a social barometer, these activities indicate an approaching storm front — cultural lightning flashes booming on the horizon, blowing in from the West Coast. The storm front gathered some years ago in Renton, Washington, during the spring of 1991 (Fannon 1996:156). It was the eye of the storm. Winds were calm. A young, boyish-looking Ph.D. math student named Richard Garfield from the University of Pennsylvania talked to Peter Adkison, president of a small fantasy game company called Wizards of the Coast in the suburbs of Seattle. Garfield pitched an idea for a board game, *RoboRally*, he had designed. However, heading a small company with only seven employees, Adkison turned the game down. "Come back with something less complicated," he said to the mathematician. He suggested that Garfield work on a card game that had artwork and was easy to play.

Garfield walked away defeated. He thought about the job offer he'd received from Whitman College in Walla Walla, Washington. A good solid teaching job. He put that in the back of his mind and thought about a new game. One that hadn't been done before. One that combined mythical fantasy creatures with playing cards. A week later the idea jelled. Garfield returned to Adkison, and sometime later they completed the prototype design for this new game. In fact, for a period of time the employees at Wizards of the Coast stopped their day-to-day activities, for they were too busy playing Garfield's new card game. They sent the design off to the printers and shipped it to stores across the country during the second half of 1993. In six weeks the company sold its entire run of 10 million cards. (See Fannon 1996 and Hauser 1994.) Lightning struck in the form of a collectible card game called *Magic: The Gathering*. According to game historian Sean Patrick Fannon, *Magic* was "[p]robably the *most* dramatic event in [role-playing game] history since the 1974 release of *D&D*" (1996:156). Garfield's patent on the game was approved in September 1997 (Slizewski 1997).

By 1995 the company had sold over 500 million cards (J. Brown 1995). There are over one million players worldwide (Smith 1995). In the second half of their first year in 1993, Wizards of the Coast made about $200,000 — a good amount for a small company. However, in 1994 that same small company made $40 million from Garfield's game! That figure probably doubled in 1995. Building off of *Magic*'s popularity, the company created and promoted an infrastructure of its game with such products as magazines, novels, comic books, a computer game version, and a World Wide Web page (with the latest tournament rules and comments about new cards and products). The Usenet bulletin board received 13,000 messages in just one month (July 1994). Using some of its profits the company spent $5 million in renovating a building in Seattle's university district and opened a game center where visitors can, on the ground floor, purchase hobby games and play video games and where downstairs they can play games on a network of computers or sit at one of the two dozen tables to play board games, role-playing games, and card games. A multimillion-dollar cultural phenomenon in the world of fantasy had begun. Armored cars indeed. *Magic* became so popular that, according to Fannon, during a period in 1994, role-playing game companies were scrambling to design their own collectible card games because they were not making enough money on their role-playing games: "Fewer [role-playing game] products were being ordered by distributors and retailers, who wanted to spend as much of their capital on obtaining as many cards to sell as possible. The initial crunch almost killed dozens of game companies (many of which are *still* struggling to recover) as their sales plummeted. A mad rush was on to create 'the next *Magic*'; RPG design came to a standstill ..." (1996:157).

Many other companies have since designed their own collectible card games, including *Middle Earth: The Wizards* by ICE (based on Tolkien's *The Lord of the Rings*), Decipher's *Star Trek* and *Star Wars* games, TSR's *Spellfire*, Steve Jackson

Games' Illuminati, to name a few, including an *X-Files* and a *Babylon 5* game. It is the biggest gaming phenomenon since role-playing games hit stores in 1974.

Controversy

Despite the game's popularity there are those who oppose it, reflecting the same antagonism felt against the role-playing game *Dungeons & Dragons* in the early 1980s, a controversy that has since faded. But during its height, *D&D* was actually banned in many schools around the country (see Lancaster 1994). Now *Magic* is the center of controversy. Some parents tried to have *Magic* removed from Pound Ridge Elementary School during the spring of 1995. One grand-parent, Mary Anne Di Bari, a lawyer from Bedford whose grandchildren attended Pound Ridge, complained, "The Devil has moved to Bedford, bag and baggage, and he is settling in. These cards are everywhere, and the language on them is taken straight from Satan," she said. She leads the opposition — a coalition called Concerned Parents, Citizens, and Professionals Against the Seduction of Children — for banning the game from the school district. The problem started when one parent organized a *Magic* club at Pound Ridge Elementary. When Ceil Di Nozzi's two fourth-grade children came home with *Magic* cards one day, she took a closer look. "I don't have to read into these cards, it's all there," she exclaims. "It's Satanic and demonic" (Lombardi 1995). She took her complaint to the superintendent of the school district, Bruce Dennis, who enacted a 30-day moratorium on the game. He spent time analyzing the game and seeking the opinions of professional psychiatrists. He also attended a *Magic* tournament proposed by students from Fox Lane Middle School and sponsored by the Bedford Presbyterian Church to raise money to purchase food for the homeless in New York City. Dennis, deciding that the game was not in any way dangerous, lifted the moratorium from the school and allowed the children to play *Magic* on school grounds but only under direct adult supervision. However Di Bari remained convinced about the harmful effects of the game and believed Dennis violated the First Amendment rights of the children, who should be allowed to worship freely without intimidation (from the game). With the support of the Christian Coalition she planned to fight it out with the school board in the courts. The case went before the court in 1997 (with no decision yet reached). Susan Clark, a parent, thinks the detractors are off base. "These are illustrations on a piece of cardboard, and a piece of cardboard isn't going to do anything to anybody" (Lombardi 1995).

A Post-Cinematic Game

Are these games just "illustrations on a piece of cardboard," or is there something else happening here? Why do certain groups of people resist fantasy cards while others embrace them, spending $40 million in 1994? What is the game's appeal? The rules say that "*Magic* is a game of battle in which you and your opponent represent powerful sorcerers attempting to drive each other from the lands of Dominia" (Wizards 1994:3). Despite this fantasy pretext, one player tends to look at *Magic* as an "overcomplicated version of rocks, papers, and scissors" (Zane 1994).

Two or more opponents use their own individually built decks to play against each other. Each deck contains cards of land, creatures, and spell enhancements. Players deal themselves seven cards, drawing one card at the beginning of each turn. They are allowed to play one land per turn. Lands are used, "tapped," in order to bring creatures and spells into play. The players line these cards faceup in front of them, the cards facing each other like the front line of an army. The players use these creatures and spells to attack and defend each other in an attempt to subtract enough points from their opponent so that he or she loses. Each player starts with 20 points, and when a player is down to zero, the game is over.

The game combines the fantasy appeal of the role-playing game *Dungeons & Dragons* (*D&D*), the chance of the deal and the luck of the draw of poker, and the strategy of chess. Good players will use what cards they have and play the game out, using careful strategy — planning several turns ahead as in chess. Although some people compare it to *D&D*, *Magic* is fundamentally a card game, a new version of an old form originating in India and brought to America "by way of the 15th-century French Court" (Zane 1994). Players do not really play characters as in a role-playing game. Why this fascination then?

What's of interest is how players of *Magic* have turned the game into a form of social behavior in which objects of fantasy are a means by which players enter a realm of fantasy and community. Typically, people enter fantasy worlds through movies and novels. However, people are looking for new ways to create fantasy entertainments. If the optical and mechanical forms of popular entertainments near the end of the nineteenth century (dioramas, peep slide shows, and so forth) were a pre-cinematic form replaced by a hungering for the realism of movies, then games like *Magic* echo in some ways these early forms of popular entertainment. However, the reasons people play *Magic* are not the same as the reasons people viewed pre-cinematic entertainments. Stories were told through the use of these objects, foreshadowing the development of stories told through motion pictures, and in both cases the audience remained physically (not necessarily emotionally or mentally) passive.

The phenomenon of *Magic* (and other fantasy games) reveals a symptom on the part of players desiring *post-cinematic* forms of entertainment. They no longer want to just watch images from a fantasy narrative; they want to participate as performers in the action. These performance-entertainments include such forms as movie theme parks, interactive environmental theater (murder mysteries, and so forth), karaoke bars, and role-playing games (see Lancaster 1997a). These post-cinematic forms allow people to transform themselves from physically passive audiences to active participants. People playing *Magic*, for instance, may have only read about dragons or seen images of them in fantasy movies, but now they can play with these mythical beings with other people who share similar interests and desires. Fantasy objects become the medium for active participation around which people build social communities.

The Convention: Space

Magic tournaments are one way players build social communities. Unable to build these communities in some public schools, where forces of antifantasy resist desires to express fantasy, players of *Magic* turn to other sites to meet people and play the game. The convention becomes a transformed public space, a place "safe" for fantasy. Here strangers meet other players who want to play *Magic*. On Saturday, September 30, 1995, I attended my first *Magic* Tournament and Convention in the Grand Ballroom of the Park Central Hotel in New York City. This convention was presented by New York Magic, a company that has sponsored tournaments nearly every month since November 1994.

From my observation of this convention, I have concluded that what people did at the *Magic* convention differed little from what they do with the game at home, in schools, and in small game stores across the country: (1) players show off their collection of cards; (2) they make deals by either trading or purchasing cards from each other; (3) they build and or modify their play-decks; and (4) they play the duel, the main part of the game itself. All of these activities make up the game's performance — not just the duel between players. The deals and duels, the exchange of cards and combat are where money and items of value exchange hands, where friendships are made and perhaps lost. The convention is a large-scale version of this social activity. The convention and tournament environment does not create this culture — it models it off of an existing form.

As I stood in line at the top of the stairs descending into the ballroom, all around me people — mostly white male teenagers and those in their 20s, some Asians and Hispanics, very few blacks and few women, many kids between 8 and 12 — were making deals, buying and selling individual cards. The air was filled with people talking about Shivan Dragons, Mox Rubies, Chaos Orbs, Alpha and Beta editions, Ice Age, and so forth. Deals were being offered, denied, and made all around me, despite the fact that the doors of the convention had not yet opened. For them the fantasy had already begun. Nearby, a man with long bleached hair set in a ponytail had a folder flipped open as two young teenagers looked at what he had: a notebook filled with many different cards, some valuable, some not. One of the kids gave the guy a handful of cash (several twenties) for a couple of cards. This is what would take place in the convention itself. When the officials let everyone downstairs, players paid the $15 entry fee and were given a tournament scorecard, which was essentially a numbered sheet of paper that indicated what seat players were to sit at when the tournament began and where opponents' names were to be written down.

The ballroom was roughly a large rectangle space, perhaps 100 feet by 80 feet, filled with over 80 tables covered with white tablecloths, six chairs per table. On the table, centered between each seat, was a number taped to the surface corresponding to the numbered score sheet each person was given. Along the west wall of the room stood about a dozen dealers' tables, where store owners sold their cards. By noon the entire room was filled with over 500 people who moved freely back and forth from the tournament areas to the dealers' tables. When they wanted to get away from the crowds, they stepped into the side areas away from the main convention floor, where they looked at their cards, made deals, played some games, and smoked. In a way the space was transformed into a fantasy festival, providing the mechanism, or support, by which players entered the fantasy game world.

The Convention: Deals

Part of this fantasy festival atmosphere at the convention included the deals, like the one described earlier occurring at the top of the stairs. Players love to buy and trade cards as much as they like to play with them. There were about 10 different dealers with tables set along the west wall of the main floor of the ballroom. Crowds of players shoved their way to the tables, where there were stacked boxes of starter packs, different editions of the game ($8 to $12), booster packs ($2 to $4), individual cards displayed in glass cases, as well as held in stacked boxes and binders — all for sale at various prices. Common cards cost as little as 25 cents, and rarer cards went for $5 to $40. One player pulled out $200 to buy one of the rarest cards (the Black Lotus). People tend to buy rare cards to help build what is called a "killer deck." "Like baseball-card collectors who must rifle through endless packs stuffed with David Seguis to find a Don Mattingly, *Magic* fans buy additional packs to secure that elusive potentate who will give them a 'killer' deck" (Zane 1994). A set of 1,000 to 1,500 cards is considered a modest collection compared to 30,000 to 200,000 cards owned by some players (J. Brown 1995). The professional store owners were not the only dealers, however. The players made deals among themselves away from the sales area, in the side rooms, and at the tournament tables. There were at least as many people playing duels with each other as there were people trading and buying cards among each other as they waited for the tournament to begin. Like what happened at the professional sales tables, these players would look through each others' displayed cards, find a particular card or set of cards, and make their pitch: either purchase with cash (guided by prices listed in the trade magazine *Scrye*) or trade with cards. A teenager at my tournament table said that she would sometimes get some good deals through trading.

The Convention: Tournament

Many stores hold their own smaller weekly tournaments with perhaps a few dozen people showing up. Every week, it was reported, over 200 people, ages 8 to 70, go to the Costa Mesa Women's Club to attend a *Magic* tournament (Smith 1995). The one in New York is unique in that it's an organization that rents space big enough to hold a large number of players and includes many different store owners. In many ways it's like a renaissance fair, with booths where craftspeople sell their goods alongside performance spaces where people meet and watch performance events. Some of these renaissance events have tournament duels of which the *Magic* duels are but a symbolic echo. At this convention there were a number of scheduled tournaments for the day, but all these activities centered around the Grand Prize tournaments: "Featuring a Grand Prize of either: The Big 10 (rare cards consisting of 5 moxes, Black Lotus, Time Walk, Time Twister, Ancestral Recall, and a Chaos Orb) or $1000 Cash."

At 11:45 A.M. an announcement was made that participants in the Type I and Type II tournaments were to take their seats. I looked for seat 108 and sat down. Two other people — one a teenage girl, the other a boy around age 10 — were at the table waiting for their tournament partners. I sat down and waited. The girl talked about how, if she won, she would take the prize of the Big Ten rare cards rather than the $1,000 cash. She believed the value of the Big Ten cards would go up and that they would soon be worth more than $1,000. I asked about some tournament rules, and she advised me that players needed at least 60 cards in the deck but that they were also allowed to build a 15-card "sideboard" that could be used to replace 15 cards out of the play deck after finishing a game. Other people arrived at our table and we began the tournament at around 12:25. The winner of this round would be the victor of two out of three games. My partner was a male teenager who had built a powerful deck of what I would call spell effects. My deck was built mostly as a creature deck. The first game I quickly lost because all I dealt to myself were large creatures that needed a lot of land before they could be brought into play. Because I couldn't get enough land out in time, my opponent was able to take advantage of this situation. The second game I was winning 20 to 10. However, even though it looked like I would win, my opponent pulled out a mirror universe card that caused the two of us to switch our respective scores: he was now at 20, I at 10. He used cards to destroy my lands so I could not get creatures into play to attack him, and then he played an enchant world card that caused any creature that I did bring into play to be removed from the game before the creature could attack. I needed a disenchant card to get rid of this card fast. But it was too late. By the time I drew it, my opponent had killed me. I was out of the tournament in the first round. We shook hands, and I congratulated him for a well-played game. To signify defeat I gave him my scorecard, and he went off to the next round. Many people would continue trading and buying cards, as well as playing "duels" among each other even after they had lost the tournament.

Fantasy

From the above description of the tournament, it would seem that this game is harmless. So why has it generated controversy? And why are so many people enamored by this game and by role-playing games? The answer to these questions lies in the nature of fantasy — which is the desire for the unattainable, a hoped-for but illusionary life or environment. Fantasy objects provide a way to enter fantasy environments. Fantasy is no longer just privately read about in novels or watched in movies. In the post-cinematic form people can now interact with objects of fantasy, causing hidden dreams to surface into reality. The fantasy phenomenon, including *Magic*, has its roots in J. R. R. Tolkien's *The Lord of the Rings*, which caused a renaissance in the field of fantasy writing in the 1960s and 1970s. During this same time the Society for Creative Anachronism was formed in 1966 as a way for people to perform in the romantic fantasy world of the European Middle Ages (Anderson 1984:167–172). But it was George Lucas's movie *Star Wars* (1977), visualizing an ultimate space fantasy adventure, that created a huge material culture of fantasy. (Just look at the number of science fiction and fantasy books published since *Star Wars*.) Through Tolkien and Lucas, people have become fascinated by alternate worlds of dragons and heroes, knights and demons, starships and deep space, aliens and laser pistols. Gandalf the Grey, the wizard of *The Lord of the Rings*, used Bilbo and Frodo Baggins as pawns to help overthrow evil in the land. In a similar way Obi Wan Kenobi and Yoda, the science fiction wizards of *Star Wars*, used Luke Skywalker and Han Solo as pawns to overthrow their enemy Darth Vader and the Emperor. How is this so different from *Magic*, where players perform wizards who use mythical creatures as pawns to fight their enemy? One form of fantasy supports and influences other forms of fantasy. *Magic: The Gathering* is just one more idea generated by the popular phenomenon of fantasy. The difference with *Magic* and role-playing games, however, is that now people are no longer satisfied to just read or watch fantasy — they want to play with it.

However, for some there is an inherent fear in the word *fantasy*. In the book *Imaginary Social Worlds* (1984) John Caughey writes that many people believe fantasy is "unnatural and pathological" and only a relatively few are influenced by it. However, he goes on to say that "Like psychotics, normal people characteristically live simultaneously in two different worlds, one of fantasy and one of reality" (157). In other words, there are those few who do blur the line between fantasy and reality to the point that they lose touch with reality, but he is also arguing that this is not necessarily limited to psychotics, but to people in general. Caughey contends that "television and film productions involve the enactment of an author's fantasy by a set of professional actors who temporarily 'become' the author's imaginary characters" — and it is in media that we find "formalized encodements of an author's culturally constituted fantasies. Media communications represent the mass consumption of such fantasy" (196). Most people would agree that very few people lose touch with reality by watching television.

However, can the same agreement be made for those who engage in fantasy games? It is the medium through which fantasy is entered that determines its acceptability (or lack thereof). One form of fantasy mediation, like television and film, can be seen as acceptable (people remaining in touch with reality), whereas other forms of fantasy mediation, like *Magic* and *D&D*, are seen as a negative influence on people.

A report from *The New York Times* would lead us to believe that "while the aggression in mainstream card games is seldom far below the surface, *Magic* is unabashed about its mayhem, allowing its participants to plunder, raid, and commit murder" (Zane 1994:2). Here the writer takes an extremely sensational (and ultimately irresponsible point of view) because he simply failed to describe the cultural mise-en-scène of a particular game. The reader is given no context for the social aspect of the game, and one may go away after reading this account and get the idea that perhaps this game *is* dangerous — and it would be if it really caused a dangerous form of psychosis in which players are induced to "plunder, raid, and commit murder." These games do allow players to engage in fantasy, but that does not mean the game causes players to be psychotic or demonic (as some might believe).

Caughey says that people live simultaneously in fantasy and reality (which is not necessarily a dangerous state). A closer look at Richard Schechner's performance frames will help us to analyze this phenomenon further. In this theory there are several concentric frames of references: (1) the outer real-world frame of the twentieth century is what Schechner calls the "indicative" (the world as it is); (2) the next frame in is the performance of the fantasy world, the "subjunctive" (the world as *if* it is); and (3) at the center is the "performance subjunctive" frame — the players' state of consciousness when performing in a game: "What happens is that the smaller subjunctive [center] frame temporarily and paradoxically expands, containing the indicative frame," Schechner writes. "Everything is 'make-believe' for the time being.... The indicative world is temporarily isolated, surrounded, and both permeated and penetrated by the subjunctive: on the outside is the environment of the performance, on the inside is the special consciousness of performing and witnessing/participating in a performance" (1985:92–93). This subjunctive performance is a fantasy construction of an alternate reality, a subjunctive mood that causes players of fantasy games to be as if they were someone and somewhere else but at the same time being who and where they actually are.

The fun and thrill of fantasy play transpires when this interior frame expands and envelops the real-world frame, transforming fantasy into reality. However, these frames shift during play. A good game occurs when this altered state is achieved and sustained throughout most of the game. When the game is over the indicative real world returns and the fantasy subjunctive fades. As Susan Clark says about her son playing *Magic*: "When the game is over, the cards are packed up and that's it. It's a game" (Lombardi 1995). What may frighten people about fantasy is when the fantasy "performance subjunctive" remains operating after the game is over. Fantasy becomes dangerous when the player's fantasy subjunctive transforms into indicative reality, where fun play becomes what Schechner calls, "dark play" (1993:24–44). However, in fantasy gaming this is an extremely rare occurrence, although people believe that it happens frequently — a myth arising from fear of fantasy. In *Magic* players do not necessarily get lost in the fantasy world of the game, but they do get caught up in the game play, concentrating on their moves and strategies like a player absorbed in a game of chess.

The controversy over fantasy games is a controversy about fantasy literature and play in general. In Ursula K. Le Guin's 1974 classic essay, "Why Are Americans Afraid of Dragons?", she posits "that almost all very highly technological peoples are more or less antifantasy.... Such a rejection of the entire art of fiction is related to several American characteristics: our Puritanism, our work ethic, our profit-mindedness, and even our sexual mores" (1989:35). Anthropologist Victor Turner mentions the fact that English Puritans introduced legislation to "force men to better their spiritual state through thrift and hard work" (1982:38). Turner goes on to cite Norbeck: "'play, the enemy of work, was reluctantly and charily permitted only to children.... The old admonition that play is the devil's handiwork continues to live in secular thought'" (in Turner 1982:39). Schechner explains that "[t]he reason why play [fantasy] — or, more properly, playing — is a rotten category is because the multiple realities of playing are situated inside a pyramidical hierarchy of increasing reality leading from unreal make believe to 'just the facts, Ma'am'" (1993:27). Fantasy remains a contested field. Hans Dieckmann attests that despite the argument of whether or not children should be told fairy tales, they "continue to be told; children hungrily snatch them up, usually leaving their fanciest technological toys lying there if they can hear a fairy tale" (1986:30). Today children (and adults) no longer listen to fairy tales — they play with them.

So why are the Christian Coalition and its adherents afraid of fantasy games? The answer lies in determining just what "play" is. Schechner makes a distinction between western forms of play, in which life is seen as rooted in work and play is separated, stigmatized, and framed off from it, and the Indian concept of *maya-lila* (illusion and play), in which life — including work — is seen as a continuing cycle of different forms of play: creation and destruction. There's the Indian story of Yasoda, who once asked her son, Krishna, why the other boys he was playing with told her that he had eaten dirt. Krishna denied this claim and challenged his mother to look into his mouth. When Yasoda looked into Krishna's opened mouth she saw a frightening site: an entire universe was in her son, including the earth, the village, and herself. She asked him to close his mouth, for knowledge of the absolute was too much for her. "But if reality and experience are networks of flexible constructions [in India], what then of 'ordinary play' — children manipulating their toys, adults playing ball, and so on?" Schechner asks (1993:34). His answer to this question gets at the controversy surrounding images and texts of mythical fantasy in *Magic* and *D&D*: "These [toys and ball playing] exist in India, as they do in the West, but they can suddenly, shockingly open to whole worlds of demons, humans, animals, and gods, as Yasoda found out when she looked into her son Krishna's mouth" (1993:34).

Di Barri and Di Nozzi (along with the right-wing Christian Coalition) literally raise hell about *Magic* playing in an elementary school precisely because they believe that people playing *Magic* and *D&D* will open "whole worlds of demons." Even a minister believes that "[*D&D*] books are filled with things that are not fantasy but are actual in the real demon world, and can be very dangerous for anyone involved in the game because it leaves them so open to satanic spirits" (Ivans 1980). For these people *Magic* is more than a fantasy described in a fairy tale because in *Magic* children (and adults) are *playing* with fantasy objects — making it more real and therefore as dangerous as the opening of Krishna's mouth. However, the players know that the images are not real. They may be entering into a fantasy world in which mythical creatures are "real," but it is just that: fantasy. Le Guin puts it this way; "Children know perfectly well that unicorns aren't real, but they also know that books about unicorns, if they are good books, are true books. All too often, that's more than Mummy and Daddy know; for, in denying their childhood, the adults have denied half their knowledge, and are left with the sad, sterile little fact: 'Unicorns aren't real'" (1989:44).

The question remains: Why do children and adults play with fantasy? Le Guin would say (and I agree with her) that it is a hunger for a childhood lost in a world filled with greedy postindustrial creative stagnation. I quote this beautiful passage in length, for it encapsulates and defines the desire for fantasy:

> Did you ever notice how very gloomy ... all those billionaires look in their photographs? They have this strange, pinched look, as if they were hungry. As if they were hungry for something, as if they had lost something and were trying to think where it could be, or perhaps what it could be, what it was they've lost. Could it be their childhood?
>
> ... I believe that maturity is not an outgrowing, but a growing up: that an adult is not a dead child, but a child who survived. I believe that all the best faculties of a mature human being exist in the child, and that if these faculties are encouraged in youth they will act well and wisely in the adult, but if they are repressed and denied in the child they will stunt and cripple the adult personality. And finally, I believe that one of the most deeply human, and humane, of these faculties is the power of the imagination....
>
> It is by such statements as, "Once upon a time there was a dragon," or "In a hole in the ground there lived a hobbit"— it is by such beautiful non-facts that we fantastic human beings may arrive, in our peculiar fashion, at the truth. (1989:39–40.)

I think Turner would also agree with Le Guin. He contends that it is in the subjunctive liminoid field of play and fantasy that people express feelings and desires and, in the process, reveal who they are as individuals, which is not necessarily who they are in the indicative world of work, their culturally formed persona

(1982:115). The teenager hoping to win the $1,000 grand prize in the *Magic* tournament, the kids who eagerly looked at and traded each others' cards, the adults who played many "duels" against each other, and those who sold and bought cards were not engaging in the occult or being violent with one another, as some would try to make others believe. Players of the game engage in a kind of performance that removes them from an ordinary day in their lives, the game placing them in a realm between the real world of the ordinary and the imaginary world of fantasy. By playing in such a liminal field people are connecting and communicating with each other in a post-cinematic way, and through this special process they arrive at some form of truth about their human condition. "Psst. Hey, how much for your Shivan Dragon?"

Part II
Physical Fantasies

4

Glimpsing "That Distant, Fleeting Star Stirred by Stories and Song" at the National Museum of the American Indian*

From Theatrical to Environmental

While looking at some clay artifacts in a glass case in the National Museum of the American Indian (NMAI) I noticed a flicker out of the corner of my eye. Turning, I saw black scrim — shaped like a letter-boxed movie screen — covering the back wall of this room. In the center of the display behind the scrim, a television monitor showed images of icy lands accompanied by a voice-over narration of Native American life in the arctic. A spotlight faded slowly in, focusing on a leather pelt jacket on the left side of the display (previously hidden by the scrim). The monitor presented black-and-white footage of Native Americans wearing similar looking jackets as they entered kayaks. Then the light focused on a kayak lying in the bottom of the display. The same effect was repeated as the narrator talked on another television monitor about making bead jackets as light faded in on an actual jacket on the right side of the display. The lighting effect here is similar to the way lighting is used on a theatrical stage — fading in and out as the mise-en-scene unfolds key moments in the narrative on stage.

At this moment I knew I was not in a conventional museum, for the NMAI

*A version of this essay was presented at the second annual Performance Studies Conference at Northwestern University in 1996.

eschews traditional means of archiving artifacts. Instead, objects are displayed in an almost theatrical way. It seems that performance theorist Richard Schechner is right: that theater, formerly "[c]hased from Plato's republic as nonrational and subversive but existing always, sometimes marginally, … is now showing itself everywhere: in social dramas, personal experience, political and economic interaction, art" (1985:150) — including museums. The theatricalization of museums is not new. The old tableau dioramas at the Museum of Natural History evince a mise-en-scene of a proscenium-arched stage. However, in NMAI's third exhibit, called "This Path We Travel" (1995), the museum stretches the boundaries of its theatricality into the realm of environmental theater, a term coined by Schechner (see 1994) to describe the effect when the 1960s avant-garde theater wrapped its entire mise-en-scene around the audience space like an environment found at Disneyland. Here the displays include a desert-like nature scene (in a couple of instances integrated with technology), religious objects, a schoolroom and home modeled from the United States government's view of how Native Americans should be educated and live, as well as television screens embedded in a globe-shaped vine-and-leaf sculpture. These environmental sites included objects, sets, lighting, and sound, creating a virtual environment that theatrically surrounds the senses and envelops the soul.

This museum reflects resonance and wonder, as Stephen Greenblatt defines these terms in relation to museum displays: One, an object can "reach out beyond its formal boundaries" and "evoke" a set of "complex, dynamic cultural forces"; and two, it can "stop the viewer in his or her tracks" (1991:42). The resonance of these exhibits in the NMAI, however, reflects not just a sense of Native American cultures but a conglomeration of these cultures and captures (at times unconsciously) the dynamic of cultural extinction caused by western colonization of the Americas.

The NMAI, housed in the old United States Customs House, opened its doors to the public on October 30, 1994. In addition to its American Indian Museums in New York and Maryland, the Smithsonian Institution will be opening a 260,000 square foot edifice near the Air and Space Museum in Washington, D.C., in 2001. The art displayed in the museum in New York was (and continues to be) selected by a 23-person committee made up of Native Americans. According to Richard West, director of the Washington, D.C., museum, "the guiding set of aesthetics in Indian art is inextricably tied to a shared concept of nature and a belief that life exists in things others might see as inanimate" (*New York Times* 1992:2, 53). Stephanie Betancourt, a "cultural information specialist," says that the NMAI is one of the first museums that broke away from a traditional type of museum, where there are exhibits of "well defined culture groups." In this way, she adds, the art is connected to the Native Americans in a cycle where the past is brought up to the present, and the present is brought to the future (Betancourt 1995). Artifacts are not frozen in time with labels pointing to a particular people as the creator of the work in past history.

Betancourt says the art represents the past, present, and future of how Native Americans view themselves. It is, in fact, how the artists and museum officials want the Native Americans to be viewed. This museum begins to realize Patrick Houlihan's statement about the future of Indian museums: where Native American artists will be used "to force us [curators] to rethink how we create exhibits or portions of exhibits that both resonate and reverberate in our viewers, bringing forth some sense of the essential meanings in Native American cultures" (1991:209). Native American artists designed the NMAI exhibits. Through symbol, myth, and art they express the values of life not from individual or specific cultural "tribes" but from a generalized Native American point of view.

The objects resonating with the spirit of Native American cultures clash when "mediated by the resonant contextualization of the building itself" (Greenblatt 1991:54). The central atrium in the U.S. Customs House depicts large murals of immigrants, an influx that was the genesis of Native American extermination. According to Betancourt, these issues, "the plight of the Indian," although "important," are not as important as showing the "good things that survived" (1995). The exhibits do not address current issues of poverty on the reservations, the problem of alcoholism, or the controversy of casinos.

The visitor is introduced to "This Path We Travel" by a television monitor sitting on the floor of a room whose contemporary earth-tone, rounded walls encircle a prehistoric sandstone-like cave floor, on which is painted a maze-shaped circular pattern. In this space one can sit on one of two cushioned benches and watch the monitor. Acting like an electronic guide,* with a slight virtual echo of the traditional shaman — an educator, spiritual guide, holder of secrets, and teller of tales — this monitor shows a four-minute video that includes narration and brief interviews with the 15 artists who spent two years together collaborating on a creation of contemporary Native American art. This exhibit is a partial outcome of that collaboration.

Whether these 15 artists reflect the multiplicity of Native American viewpoints (or if there is even any dissonance among these viewpoints and those that didn't even get a voice in the process) is an open question. In 1982 the University of British Columbia Museum of Anthropology was criticized when it invited Native Americans to carve and raise a totem pole at the museum. This Native American critic complained to Michael Ames that, "'[Y]ou haven't done a damn thing for Indians. We don't feel at home in your museums — any of them — because they don't tell us *our* story'" (Ames 1986:43). Ames went on to describe how this critic believed "some Indians eventually succumbed to the outsider

---

However, this guide is not interactive. You are free to watch, listen, or roam, but you do not "actively engage the site and those in it," as Barbara Kirshenblatt-Gimblett says about Plimoth Plantation — an interactive virtual site filled with actors who enact roles of pilgrims in 1627 — where "[t]he virtual world [visitors] are exploring 'pushes back'" (in Snow 1993:xiv). The exhibits in "This Path We Travel" may not necessarily interact with visitors verbally like the actors at Plimoth Plantation, but the environment does push back on the visitor emotionally.

views and incorporated" a "social science" objectivity as "their own" rather than preserving the Native American life as "derived from the memories of the elders" (1986:43). The art in the NMAI tries to come across as being opposed to the "objective facts of the social scientists."

Incorporated into this site are the areas of the Female, Creation, Male, Sacred, Profane Intrusion, and World View.

Walking Through Dreams on the Edge of Mythical Creation

The doorway from the introductory room leads to a short hall opening into a vestibule containing statements of artists and a list of their names and tribes they are associated with on the left and right walls. In front is a wall reaching about halfway to the ceiling painted the same color as the introductory room. In the middle of this wall is an archway with wooden poles spanning the length of the open doorway. To the left and right of the arch are two speakers issuing Native American music. I step through into a carpeted room and see, to the left and right of me, eight two-dimensional collage paintings of women. This room is labeled the Female. Looking ahead of me it seems — through a willing suspension of disbelief — that I am no longer in a museum. It feels like I'm immersed in a cave, or perhaps I have stepped out into a desert evening filled with rising mesa-like cliffs. Before me are not more paintings or artifacts encased in glass displays. Rather, a virtual wilderness of sandstone-like walls, the screech of a desert eagle mingled with Native American songs and the distant sounds of a thunderstorm "push back" against my soul, engaging my emotions at a primal level. Like Picasso's collage of 1912, when he placed a piece of oilcloth to his canvas and surrounded it with rope, projecting two-dimensional art into physical space, this exhibit is in essence a three-dimensional art form. This is no ordinary exhibit. This is a virtual reality experience.

In his essay "Hiding the Head of Medusa: Objects and Desire in a Virtual Environment," Edward Barrett talks about a museum in Dunquin on the west coast of Ireland. The museum is an "Interpretive Centre" of the people on Blasket Islands located offshore from the museum. The space is full of texts, photographs, music, and voices. A large window pictures islands outside. Barrett describes this site as an "interface for what lies outside of it, or a shield barring you from a world you will never really know" (1995:xii). He raises an interesting point that can be applied to the NMAI. Is this space I'm in an interface to what lies outside it — the essence of Native American cultures — or does it act as a shield against a way of life I will never know?

I move a couple of steps forward into the room. It is darker. Red sandstone-like molding shaped like a cliff protrudes out onto the floor, gripping the space like the trunk of a tree rising out of the roots of the earth. Off to the left and embedded in the cliff is a large clay pot with flickering blue light issuing from it. This sculpture is so large that a person could almost crawl into it. Projected above this are clouds aglow with the orange wash of light like the setting sun. To my right, a picture of a full moon rises behind the cliff. The space evokes a liminal dream-like state. Liminal moments have the potential to transform thinking. In the living museum Plimoth Plantation, performance scholar Barbara Kirshenblatt-Gimblett says, "We can see in the display history of the site a shift from ceremonial to virtual, from commemorative to exploratory, from discrete moments, objects, and scenes, to the waking dream of a virtual Pilgrim world" (Snow 1993:xiv). Here we feel the waking dream of Native American myths.

There is more here than the constructed order of art objects or artifacts created by ethnographers, where, as Kirshenblatt-Gimblett notes in her essay "Objects of Ethnography," "disciplines" detach artifacts from their source and "make" or remake them "and in the process make themselves" (1991:387). The artists, perhaps in an attempt to change this discipline-creating process, have shaped and built a virtual nature environment by combining the ethnographic process with art. They have constructed more than a diorama of craft collections so typical of conventional museum displays. The artists have created what the ethnographic object unconsciously represents: a virtual environment depicting the place where the object originated, so long hidden from the view of those only looking at an object — detached from its source — in a museum display case. Rather than recontextualizing an object, this exhibit places objects in environmental context where ambiance (not labels or texts) reveals meaning.

The technology of the museum mediates Native American cultures. The mediation is heightened not just by the artifacts (where they even exist) but by a virtual environment — a symbolic representation of the mythological and real world. This mediation is not a magnifying glass resolving previously unseen cultures into view by those who do not live in those cultures. Rather, it is a refraction of what Native Americans see — a virtual image, bent or warped by the mediating lens of the museum itself. This process is invisible. The virtual image, although mediated and illusory, becomes real through material actualization. Visitors interact with this as a reality by walking through the exhibit. scholar Tracy Davis argues that postmodern museums "activate the museum goer to perform the relationship between the artifacts and their setting" in an "interactive role that requires engagement with the subject matter and ideology" (1995:37). And this museum, like postmodern theater, may unsettle some visitors.

Cecile Fraquet from Brittany, France, wandering through this exhibit felt that it shows more than it explains. She would have liked to know more of the history and the culture of the people concerned here (Fraquet 1995). To her the interface did not provide what she was looking for or expecting. Perhaps she felt that this exhibit subverts Native American views because meaning is not realized in a conventional manner. No ethnographic labels explain to the visitor what these sites mean, what tribe created what and from where (even the brochure is rather vague in its explanations, and the video at the start of the exhibit doesn't interpret meaning). Instead, it contests the interpretation of conventionally displayed museum artifacts by allowing Native Americans to construct a virtual art form that provides an interface into their culture.

Standing in the room of the Female, I hear birds singing and women talking from the speakers behind and above me. In front of me a young woman kneels, peering into the video inside the large clay pot. Blue light flickers around her like a ghost, her head and shoulders a silhouette. Inside is a recorded image, but is this image the creator or the creation? It shows pictures of New York City and a Native American woman making bread. Is it one of the artists, or has an artist created this image of some other? It's a creation that uses present technology to convey past traditions, a ghost presenting a past way of life that reaches into the future by the permanent evanescence of a video image unconsciously passing down knowledge of itself to a future generation. Do I need ethnographic labels and biographies (or even textbooks) to interpret this tableau? Or is it enough that the environment pushes in around me trying to teach me its meaning, its history, philosophy, and myth, almost subconsciously? Here, a mythical view of the American Indian is actualized much in the same manner that historically restored villages like Plimoth Plantation "create, or re-create, or actualize, American history and imagination" (Schechner 1985:180).

Past the large clay pot, bright white light stabs straight down into a twilight darkness, casting a spiderweb pattern onto the floor. Looking up at the light I see a rope-like web stretched across the ceiling of this space. Is history or imagination being actualized here? This is the section entitled Creation, but it is not really a separate room. It is a liminal area linking the previous area, Female, with the next, Male — one large room delineated by changes from red sandstone to white in the stonework of the walls and floor, as well as by changes in atmospheric lighting and sound. This environment relies on metaphoric knowledge to fully reveal itself. This "metaphoric knowledge," as Schechner says, "is not inferior to 'realer' facticities but is a primary reality, one of several that braid into the human helix" (1985:150). The spiderweb on the floor and in the "sky" braids itself between reality and myth. It symbolizes and combines the trickster-creator of the Lakota tribe with the Navajo's Spider Woman, "who gave threads from her body to be woven into the earth" (National Museum n.d.).

Looking ahead, I see in the Male section a large woven, snake-like pattern on the floor. A stone cairn, its top lit orange, rises out of the center of the room. Still standing in the liminal Creation room, I see to my immediate left a square podium a little taller than myself. The podium rises out of a pile of smooth fist-size rocks. On top, a branch rises from the middle of it. On the branch are feathers and twigs, and set among the twigs is a white hand-size head that looks almost like a ghost. On one side of the podium is this inscription:

<blockquote>
We all search
<blockquote>
for the brilliance
that brings peace, healing
</blockquote>
Sometimes, we glimpse
<blockquote>
that distant, fleeting star
<blockquote>
stirred by stories
<blockquote>
and song.
</blockquote>
</blockquote>
</blockquote>
</blockquote>

The physical environment of the space, delineated by borders and yet not, comprises liminal environmental time zones representing birth, growth, and death — interfaces into Native American metaphors and spiritual beliefs. Like the museum visitor who, in the short movie "Crows," from *Akira Kurosawa's Dreams* (1990), steps into a virtual environment and mindscape of Vincent Van Gogh's paintings, we too can step inside the mindscape of Native Americans, actualizing their beliefs and philosophies in the imagination as we walk through this exhibit.

Because there is no taxonomy of tribal art in this exhibit — where one tribe's art goes here, another there — this museum not only reshapes the borders between ethnographic displays and art by opening up an environment that expresses the Native American way of life, but it also blurs the boundary of tribal borders as well. Betancourt, the cultural information specialist, said that the museum is designed specifically *not* to have defined culture groups, as would be the case in conventional museums. Rather, the museum chose a wide range of Native American artists to depict the Native American experience from the artists' point of view — from what they saw and from what they wanted the visitor to see. This perception is shaped by their art. In theorist Herbert Blau's terminology, "the agencies and instruments of perception alter the nature of what is seen. That is actually what we have come to mean by technique in a cybernetic age" (1995:57). This cybernetic technique does not allow for a separate spiderweb for each tribe, for it represents both Navajo and Lakota. In Walter Benjamin's terms — this is a "porous" exhibit.

The porosity of architecture reveals itself among art, tribes, and international cultures. Museum practices have traditionally separated the national identities of found cultures — along a wall here is one culture, in a corner there yet another. But this NMAI exhibit reflects the reality of history. The Native American nations' borders were "dissolved" with the arrival of Europeans. In 1820 there were about 120,000 Native Americans living east of the Mississippi River (Zinn 1990:124). In 24 years (1844) there were less than 30,000. However, Native Americans were not as soluble in the American melting pot as Europeans had hoped. Wars were fought and many Native Americans were killed; others were removed to the West in a wave of ethnic cleansing. As historian Howard Zinn notes, in an address to Congress in 1838 President Van Buren said, "It affords sincere pleasure to apprise the Congress of the entire removal of the Cherokee Nation of Indians to their new homes west of the Mississippi. The measures authorized by Congress at its last session have had the happiest effects"

(1990:146). This measure included the forced removal of 17,000 Cherokees westward in which an estimated 4,000 died en route. The tribes were eventually removed to reservations, where many lived in poverty. Even though reservations did contain tribes, they did not allow for a tribal way of life, for "[a]n Indian reservation is the most complete colonial system in the world," Zinn contends (514).

Museum taxonomy of the American Indian can be seen as a false border created by the colonizer. But in this museum Native Americans attempt to recreate their own borders — not between tribes, but between European and Native American cultures, an art that depicts their "identity and belief," as Betancourt said. For example, when I look at the spiderweb projected onto the floor by a beam of white light, for me it not only provides a connecting and discerning border between the Male and Female sites of the exhibit, but it also represents a new border, bounded by artistic and spiritual beliefs, between Western encroachment and contemporary Native American reidentification and pride — a border that everyone must cross in order to proceed into the next room.

Even the museum building itself — the United States Customs House of which the museum is but a part — is an icon representing Western power that exterminated traditional Native American beliefs. The building houses these beliefs attempting to resolve themselves in the midst of an icon that once dissolved them. The museum also stands in the midst of Wall Street (the Euro-American ideal of power), Ellis Island (another site where identity was stripped), and the Statue of Liberty (a symbol of freedom for all). As mentioned earlier, in the center of the museum is an atrium with paintings of European immigrants coming to the United States, initiating a large population move westward in order to attain America's Manifest Destiny — decimating the Native American population in the process. Although not directly explicated, the tug between these beliefs can be felt throughout this porous exhibit and is subtly seen in the space labeled the Profane Intrusion.

Waking the Historical Education in My Mind, Virtually

Stepping left out of the virtual wilderness of cliffs and moonlight and into a museum hallway whose left wall is covered with religious icons, I pass through the space entitled the Sacred. At the end of this hall and to the right, a doorway labeled Profane Intrusion opens into an early-twentieth-century schoolroom so realistic in detail that it looks like a movie set. There are rows of old-fashioned chairs lining the floor. A traditional teacher's desk stands in front of a chalkboard at the end of the room. To my left is a window lit with photographs of children in the school yard. Speakers fill the room with sounds of children playing. The next room off to the right is a family living space, complete with a sofa in the center of the room, a bed in the left-hand corner, a kitchen table along one wall, a television in front of the sofa, a refrigerator in a corner near the table, and commercial toys of cowboys and Indians along the back wall. Two windows, pasted with translucent photographs of a dog and a street, give the illusion that one is looking out into a yard. An American flag is used as a drape for one of the windows.

Getting over the amazement of these virtual replicas I remember that I am in the site of Profane Intrusion. Like Brecht's epic theater, which enacted his theories of the alienation effect, this space is designed to distance the spectator from being absorbed into the mise-en-scene. Spectators are meant to discern what is really going on in this scene. Despite the beauty of the artists' depiction of a 1930s-style classroom and a reservation home designed and built by the United States Department of Housing and Urban Development, textual and pictorial clues abound about how these two spaces are considered profane to the Native American lifestyle. These clues are placed about the space like Neher's visual projections commenting upon the "events on the stage" of Brecht's theater productions. Brecht had attempted to educate audiences about the nature of contemporary society through the use of alienation techniques (1992:38). The artists here used similar alienation effects. For example, on one of the school desks is a newspaper article from *The Ottawa Citizen* depicting how it was revealed that the school was abusive to children: "Brutal tales of Indian school finally get told" (1995:A5). In addition, a statue of the Madonna and a painting of the boy Jesus and his parents, are placed in the left-hand corner of the schoolroom. A picture of George Washington, one of the founding fathers of the United States, hangs on the right wall. Also, one of the toys along the back wall of the home is called "Cow-Boys of Moo Mesa. Geronimo Grade A Prime Beef. With Tomahawk Chopping Action."

If the previous spaces depicted the spiritual force of the Native American's view of nature, spirit, man, and woman, these two spaces are a social commentary of how the Native American way of life was stripped away by a Western concept of education, religion, and standard of living. Lexie Marsh, a former anthropology major and now a social worker in New York City, called these two rooms a "discontinuum" that snaps you out of the previous spaces that led to this particular site (Marsh 1995). The performance of the Profane Intrusion exhibit probably works as the artists intended, for the space intruded into my sensibilities, causing a jarring, Brechtian discontinuum from what I felt in the sacred, more spiritual sites in the previous rooms. Here there are no sounds of nature, no quiet chanting of an ancient song. This juxtaposition is a clash between the Native American way of life and Western education, as explained by one Native American: "'Oh, yes, I went to the white man's schools. I learned to read from school books, newspapers, and the Bible. But in time I found that these were not enough. Civilized people depend too much on man-made printed pages. I turn to the Great Spirit's book which is the whole of creation'" (in Zinn 1990:514).

The classroom and house stand out as something familiar, creating an almost nostalgic feeling for one who has been educated in the Western tradition in schools similar to the one depicted at this site and lived in houses that have a bedroom, living room, and kitchen similar to the ones replicated here. But that nostalgic Western feeling is out of place. A Brechtian alienation device hanging on a wall reads: "1819 Civilization Fund Act authorized the use of Indian schools as a way to 'civilize' Indian children." Currently the Federal Bureau of Indian Affairs oversees 187 schools. However, these schools are impoverished, needing $650–800 million worth of repairs. According to John Tippeconic, director of the Office of Indian Education Programs, "'In some cases we are probably putting some kids in danger, in unsafe conditions'" (*New York Times* 1995:17).

However, according to this exhibit, whether there's funding or not, the sacredness of Western education intrudes on the Native American's way of education and life. This site offers a harsh juxtaposition between what one may feel as nostalgic and what, on further thought, becomes profane. However, as Marsh said, there may not be enough here to reveal the profane (or it may be just hard to find the clues, or the clues may be patently ignored). For example, some kids and parents transformed these two rooms into a kind of playground. One child walked up to the teacher's desk, while friends and parents sat at the other desks and raised their hands, saying, "Teacher, teacher." Mr. Mow, a Native American security guard, stepped in like a Brechtian actor and explained to them that these two exhibits are a statement of what Native Americans did not like about Western encroachment on their way of life. Mow acted (unconsciously) in a "Brechtian" manner, for Brecht not only wanted a breakup of a pleasing wholeness of the unity of arts — through projections, jarring an audience out of a "hypnotic" narrative (1992:38) — but he also wanted actors to adopt a socially critical attitude, a role Mow, dressed in his blue uniform, provided. "In this way [an actor's] performance becomes a discussion (about social conditions) with the audience he is addressing," Brecht writes (139). If the space itself could not intrude on Western sensibilities, Mr. Mow would become the profane intrusion himself by alienating the visitors' almost sacred view of their own educational system that they were reliving. It was up to him to remind them that the artists intended this site to be a profane space — not a playground for the nostalgic.

In the Shadow of the Archway of Death: A World of Vines and Techno Chips

I step from the kitchen and living room into a space arched by a burial artifact. A statue of a "body," whose head is covered by 100 dollar bills and inset with a small television monitor depicting a horizontal "flat-line," lies on top of this arch. On the "body" is draped a leather rider's blanket with BMW, Lexus, and Mercedes symbols etched on it. On the left post is the top of a parking meter with antlers set on it. On the right burial post hang a couple of credit cards, enlarged five-dollar bills, and a box of Eau Sauvage aftershave lotion. Floating above this artifact is a Plexiglas triangle with a holograph of an infant in it. Through the arch is a space almost entirely filled by a large (5 or 6 feet in foot diameter) leaf-and-vine globe sculpture suspended from the ceiling. Four television monitors sit in the globe at its cardinal points. Circuit boards and speakers are entwined within vines and leaves. Each monitor has different images, some of war and destruction, one of technological growth such as the moon landing; another has live images from CNN's Headline News. A bench on the far wall allows viewers to watch and listen. Sounds of the reaction to the O. J. Simpson verdict are enveloped by other sounds of rockets launching and the machine-gun fire of war. The burial arch is a doorway depicting the spiritual death of humankind encompassed by greed, materialism, and destruction. The "body" has been killed by materialism — crashed into by credit expenditures financing expensive BMWs and Mercedes-Benzes. Its only eye is a TV monitor, flatlining the thoughts and care of a "civilized" people, whose desires are shaped by good parking spots, nice cars, money, and shallow television in the evening. The room is filled with the constant sounds of a heartbeat — a signal of life trying to be heard above the din of a world in chaos.

I am reminded of Mow's remarks about the often-told story of how Native Americans believed their souls would be stolen by the snapshots of cameras. This belief of technology stealing one's soul has evolved over time, changing into such devices as televisions, video games, movies, and other technological means for escape, Mr. Mow explains. Kids today do not know how to go out into the woods, take their shoes off, and feel nature speak to them, he contends. Mow complains about how children today remain indoors and fail to feel their environment trying to communicate with them, especially those that live in the city. The sites in these exhibits help to bring across that feeling.

Mow believes that the different rooms of this exhibit help to educate people (if not in real life, outdoors, then virtually through an environmental space) about how Native Americans view their environment. He also adds that it is designed so that one experiences the traditional spiritual values in a contemporary form. For one to understand the message of the artworks here, one must listen and feel the environment, he adds. Ironically, this room reveals the value of nature through the use of "soul-stealers." The artists ingeniously take recorded pictures of others' (non–Native American) "souls" and present them in an artwork that realizes Barrett's comment about how "digital technology is creating both a dialog and a mechanism for discussing itself" (1995:256). Marsh believed that this site was filled with "unbelievable, profound images" of world destruction, which to her reflect the devastation of the Native American by Western colonization (Marsh 1995). Mr. Mow explains that this room is a warning not to let this violence happen again. "Why are we killing people over this land when we should be nurturing it?" he asks rhetorically. Mow, acting as an unofficial spokesperson, knowledgeable about his culture, states that there are two worldviews: one, the Native American perspective based on the realization that no one can own land but may only borrow from it; and two, a world abused, filled with negative thoughts, toxic chemicals, trash, and atomic bomb testing that destroy the land. He adds that there needs to be a balance between humanity's desires and how people treat the land they live on. This room portrays these thoughts visually and aurally.

Where Do We Go From Here?

At the exit to this exhibit is a mirror in which visitors can look at themselves. Above it is the following statement, which perhaps sums up the purpose of this exhibit, "This Path We Travel":

> We're part of the dance, sisters and brothers!
> Given a chance unlike no other ...
> where do we go from here?

This mirror epitomizes how this exhibit acts as an interface into the environment of Native American culture. It tries to transform consciousness. Michael Heim says in *The Metaphysics of Virtual Reality* (1993) that the term *interface* is the same as the Greek word *prosopon*: "a face facing another face." There is a mutual interaction between this interface. "One face reacts to the other, and the other face reacts to the other's reaction, and the other reacts to that reaction, and so on ad infinitum. The relationship then lives on as a third thing or state of being" Heim explains (78).

Perhaps this third state of being is what the creators of the exhibit hope to show the visitor — a plea for change in the way Earth is treated and how people behave one toward another. But then again, perhaps I am just gazing at a vampire, as Allucquere Stone perceives Anne Rice's Lestat as a metaphor for the liminal cyborg: "a vampire for our seasons, struggling with the swiftly changing meanings of what it is to be human or, for that matter, unhuman" (1995:178). By weaving in and out of the different rooms of this exhibit, looking at video monitors melding with walls of fabricated nature, schoolrooms that once removed a native's way of life and imposed a new one, myself shooting pictures of the sacred and the profane with a camera, feeling the conditioned air pumping coolly through the space, as unnatural as the body with a television monitor set in a head wrapped in money placed on top of a burial arch, and finally to see myself in the mirror — I suddenly realize that I may have just received the "Dark Gift" of the vampire, and "there is no way back to a simpler and less problematic time," Stone says. "The gaze of the vampire, once achieved, cannot be repudiated; it changes vision forever" (183).

Can this exhibit enlighten people? Does it allow for an understanding into the Native American way of life? I read a recent newspaper article that talks about how high school athletes from Lakota Indian reservations in South Dakota "face derisive caricatures and gestures at nearly every competition. Taunts of 'dog eaters,' 'squaw,' 'dirty old Indians,' as well as war whoops and tomahawk chops greet the Lakota teams when they compete off the reservation. 'When one of our people was lying on the floor hurt,' I could hear people yelling, 'shoot her, shoot her,' recalls former Red Cloud basketball player Michelle Carlow" (Hamilton 1995). Would that these taunters could walk through this museum and look into the mirror. What would they see? Would they see Andrew Jackson (a hero in the Indian wars of ethnic cleansing), who hoped that Native Americans would one day "cast off their savage habits and become an interesting, civilized, and Christian community," as he told the United States Congress (Zinn 1990:139)? Or would their first racist impressions of fear be changed into Heim's third state of being something other than this? Or is racism that third state of being Heim talks about — a negative reaction against someone's action of a reaction? Or is there something more than this?

My thoughts lead me to think about an astronomer friend of mine, Laurence Doyle, whose research concern is to look for signs of extraterrestrial intelligence (Doyle n.d.). The first time I met him was when he was a guest lecturer in astronomy at my undergraduate college. He wore his hair in a long braid that reached well below his shoulders. After completing his second year of high school, he spent his summer working as a volunteer on a Navajo reservation, where he gained a sense of deep respect for the Navajo. When he came back to school in the fall, his principal told him that he would have to cut his hair short to stay in school. Disappointed, he returned home to his mother. He didn't know what to do because he wanted to respect both the Navajo and his principal. So he and his mother returned to the school, and they talked to the principal for a couple of hours. The principal turned to him and in essence said, "Laurence, it sounds like you're really interested in astronomy. I'm going to write a letter so you can enter a junior college this year, and you won't have to cut your hair." He skipped the last two years of high school by keeping respect for his Navajo friends. Perhaps the answer to facing the mirror's riddle lies somewhere there.

5

Traveling Among the Lands of the Fantastic: The Imaginary Worlds and Simulated Environments of Science Fiction Tourism*

To me, the science-fiction writers are our culture's most important original thinkers.... Mainstream literature replays again and again all the same old stuff, whereas the science-fiction writers try to imagine what would happen if our technologies and societies — and our minds themselves — were differently composed.

— Marvin Minsky (in Brockman 1995:160)

New Sites of Authenticity

You wake up with a start. The soft color tones of the room and the porthole looking out into the deep darkness of a starfield confuse you. The surroundings look familiar — perhaps something from the television show *Star Trek* has entered your dreamscape. But did you dream about losing a lot of money last night playing Domjack in Quark's Bar on the promenade of the space station *Deep Space Nine*? Perhaps the Dabo girl you saw eyeing you was here last night. You certainly remember her perfume, the glitter of lights, and the Ferengi running the bar. Then it hits you. You're not dreaming about being in the twenty-third century on board the starship *Enterprise*—you're in a hotel room

*A version of this essay appeared in the science fiction journal, Foundation #67 (Summer 1996).

in Las Vegas, circa 1998.* The Vegas *Star Trek* theme park, a resort environment, is just one of many simulations of fantastic worlds that visitors can travel to, whether in a city here on Earth or out in the nether regions of cyberspace, through computer games and online environments. Chris Roberts, creator and director of *Wing Commander IV: The Price of Freedom* (1995), an interactive CD-ROM movie/game with a budget of 10 million dollars, explains how players of these games desire to "buy into a universe" (Weiner 1995).

Some people want to be immersed in fantastic environments, in alternative universes and realities, such as the Star Tours ride at Disneyland, which offers immersion into a *Star Wars*–like environment climaxing with a flight simulator ride on board a shuttle. Online visitors can enter the concourse of the space station *Babylon 5* (from the television show) and see alien ships, download video and sound clips, interact live with other people, and jumpgate through hyperspace to many different *Babylon 5* Web pages. *Star Trek* fans, dressed in crew uniforms, were all set to travel to Los Angeles to take a $129 tour of the *Star Trek* sets at Paramount Pictures on December 2, 1995, until Paramount's last-minute cancellation. Even a bookstore in New York City, called Forbidden Planet, is in itself a science fiction environment filled with books, magazines, models, toys, games, posters, and life-size cardboard cutouts of famous science fiction media characters. These kinds of fantastic sites are what I am calling science fiction tourist attractions. Wanting more than just to experience the fantasy of science fiction by reading novels and watching television or films, many science fiction fans today desire whole simulated environments.

People who immerse themselves in different kinds of fantasy environments are figuratively traveling light years away, while remaining here on Earth. Science fiction objects (books, movies, toys, games, rides, and so forth) provide an interface for these kinds of voyages, offering a kind of mediated "panoramic perception" for the traveler. This phrase was applied to the nineteenth-century railroad traveler, whose perception "no longer belonged to the same space as the perceived objects: the traveler saw the objects, landscapes, etc. *through* the apparatus which moved him through the world. That machine and the motion it created became integrated into his visual perception: thus he could only see things in motion" (Schivelbusch 1986:64). These words of Wolfgang Schivelbusch — meditating on the changes occurring in travel, circulation of commodity, and the shrinking of distances as a result of the connection of communities by the nineteenth-century railway system — elucidates, to some extent, science fiction tourism.

The apparatus of science fiction objects becomes an interface for travels to alien worlds. For science fiction fans life is seen and experienced through the medium of science fiction — moving them through worlds — as scholar Henry Jenkins explains: "fans enthusiastically embrace favored texts and attempt to

*The planned hotel-room simulation never made it beyond the drawing board. Instead, for the theme park at the Vegas Hilton.

integrate media representations into their own social experience" (1992:18). By integrating "media representations" into their lives, fans realize, to some extent, that "the boundary between science fiction and social reality is an optical illusion," as biologist and feminist scholar Donna Haraway observes (1991:149). If there is no boundary between science fiction and social reality, then what kind of reality is created when these two realms become conflated in science fiction tourist attractions?

This question is especially interesting in relation to what tourism theorist Dean MacCannell says about sites of authenticity: "The rhetoric of tourism is full of manifestations of the importance of the authenticity of the relationship between tourists and what they see: this is a *typical* native house; this is the *very* place the leader fell; this is the *actual* pen used to sign the law" (1989:14). Walter Benjamin says that "[t]he authenticity of a thing is the essence of all that is transmissible from its beginning, ranging from its substantive duration to its testimony to the history which it has experienced" (1968:221). For an object to be "authentic" it must be an original (presumably not a simulacrum) and it must be historically grounded. When, as MacCannell theorizes, a visitor "unattached" to the mores of society visits sites of authenticity, he or she gains some sense of valuation and "construct totalities from his disparate experiences. Thus, his life and his society can appear to him as an orderly series of formal representations, like snapshots in a family album" (1989:15). Can tourists expect to find a similar level of authenticity when they visit the Statue of Liberty or the Grand Canyon as they would if they visited a *Star Trek* theme park or seemingly fly into the Death Star trench in the Star Tours ride at Disneyland?

My thesis is this: Instead of visiting previously constructed or natural objects of authenticity (such as the Empire State Building or the Grand Canyon), science fiction "tourists" create their own authenticity by purchasing, constructing, or visiting artificial objects and environments whose predecessors are fictional media stories found in movies and novels. When they visit these sites they simultaneously live in the conflation of social reality and science fiction. By looking beyond this boundaried optical illusion, science fiction fans, Jenkins explains, "build their culture within the gaps and margins of commercially circulating texts" (1992:35), building it from "raw materials the media provides" (49).

Most fans probably realize that science fiction offers "alternative and critical ways of imagining social and cultural reality" (Wolmark 1994:10). But does that mean science fiction tourist sites, being nonliterary, can have "utopian and radical possibilities" as Jenny Wolmark believes certain feminist science fiction literature imagines "these possibilities" (1994:11)? Jenkins believes that fans choose texts that suit their own ideology: "[f]ans have chosen these media products from the total range of available texts precisely because they seem to hold special potential as vehicles for expressing the fans' pre-existing social commitments and cultural interests" (1992:34). Fans' predilections are compatible with "the ideological construction of the text." It seems that the question of whether radical and utopian possibilities can be explored in such nonliterary sites as offered in science fiction tourism depends on the fans' desires and previously held viewpoints. Jenkins believes that "[r]eaders are not *always* resistant; *all* resistant readings are not necessarily progressive readings; the 'people' do not *always* recognize their conditions of alienation and subordination" (34). Social issues can be explored, but only if the cultural producers create them and the fans decide to examine them. These sites are not about fans being entrapped by capitalistic objects or any other dominating social structure as some may think. Rather than being played with, participants of these sites, play with them. By doing so fans express what they feel is important in their lives.

Science fiction tourist sites offer unique ways to explore these kinds of ideological manifestations — whether revealing social issues or reinforcing the tourist's ideological viewpoints — by providing "a space consciously explored," as Walter Benjamin explains how film optics shape perception: "With the close-up, space expands; with slow motion, movement is extended" (1968:236). To some extent Benjamin's statement can be metaphorically placed in relationship to Einstein's theory of relativity. As tourists travel at relativistic speeds to reach their distant destinations of fantasy at the following science fiction tourist attractions — the Forbidden Planet bookstore in New York City, the Star Tours Disney ride in California, the *Dark Forces* computer game, a *Star Trek* set tour at Paramount Pictures, and the *Babylon 5* space station located online in cyberspace — time and movement slow down as visitors consciously explore the physicalization of fictional narratives, what philosopher Don Ihde calls rituals of the technological age.

Forbidden Planet

Before the store Forbidden Plant moved north one block, a visitor could look through the window of the store on the corner of Broadway and 12th Street in New York City and see a large painting of an orange desert planet with a starship sitting on the surface of it. Around this mural were science fiction and fantasy novels for sale, as well as a flyer announcing the visit of a famous science fiction author (Orson Scott Card), available for a book signing that afternoon. The dioramic display promised me and other passersby that if we entered this store, alien worlds would open before our very eyes. And indeed they did, for a panoramic approach to displaying objects offers a "supreme vantage point," Barbara Kirshenblatt-Gimblett writes, where "the viewer is master of all that he or she surveys. The view is comprehensive, extensive, commanding, aggrandizing. As a prospect, it holds in it scenarios for future action" (1991:413). Entering the store I see "scenarios for future action" — possible ways to travel to alien lands. In front of me a glass display case houses dozens of miniature models of science fiction characters, including Yoda, Han Solo, and Boba Fett from the *Star Wars* movies (for sale as they are or as model kits one can build). Holding a comprehensive view, full-size cardboard cutouts of Klingons, Captain Picard, and other *Star Trek* characters look down at me from atop bookshelves. Mr. Spock peers out from behind the corner of a bookcase. A life-size Spider Man balloon hangs from the ceiling.

The visitors standing around browsing comic books, novels, and magazines affirm Michel de Certeau's words: "Far from being writers … readers are travelers" (1984:174). The visitors at this store are traveling vast distances in time and space in their minds — words on the page of science fiction and fantasy novels and pictures in comic books and magazines beckon visitors to tours of fictional worlds. And the physical media "artifacts" — models, posters, cardboard cutouts, *Star Trek* uniforms, masks of aliens, and so forth — prominently displayed about the room are created from the alien worlds visitors are reading about. These artifacts surrounding the browsers hint at the possibility that readers no longer want to just read about alien worlds as outsiders, but they may want to step into the fictional environments and go "native."

If a visitor wears a *Star Trek* uniform, it shows how much that person may want to be seen as a crew member of the *Enterprise*. Or if someone wears a stormtrooper helmet, putting on a rubber latex mask, they may be saying that they embrace the ideals of the Empire's philosophy and lifestyles as promulgated in the *Star Wars* movies, novels, and comics. Or someone just may buy a model of Darth Vader and build it, displaying an objectified screen villain at home. These different objects become a means for people to enact fantasy, to panoptically display oneself, which, according to Kirshenblatt-Gimblett, is a way "to show with respect to others what one would not reveal about oneself — one's body, person, and life" (1991:415). In normal life we live in our contemporary, everyday world. Most people will not show up to work in a Klingon uniform, but they may bring a *Star Trek* novel and read it during lunch hour — thus revealing who they are by displaying what they love to do during their free time.

Such displacements also, in some respects, corroborate what political scientist S. Paige Baty says about representative characters: that they are "cultural figure[s] through whom the character of political life is articulated" (1995:8). (I would, however, substitute the word *political* with *social*.) They are typically historical figures like Abraham Lincoln or Martin Luther King Jr., and in Baty's case she describes through an analysis of Marilyn Monroe how the body politic is articulated as a representative character: [t]hese figures convey the character of authority, legitimacy, and power in a culture through the vehicle of their lives and persons. The representative character embodies and expresses achievement, success, failure, genius, struggle, triumph, and other human possibilities: one representative character's story may be written as a cautionary tale, while another's may be erected as a monument to human achievement" (8–9). What happens when representative characters are fictional, when Luke Skywalker and Captain Jean Luc Picard convey social meanings as fundamental as those of John F. Kennedy or Ronald Reagan? The answer to this question helps explain why some people love science fiction, and it also goes back to the nature of authenticity. The social life depicted in some movies and novels, however fantastic, suggests an alternative way of life that some feel is better than the life they have in actuality.

Forbidden Planet, by its very nature, not only offers the means to enter fantasy worlds but is itself a fantasy world. When we enter this store, browse, and purchase the science fiction objects panoramically displayed about the room, it seems at times that we are no longer on 12th Street and Broadway. We enter this panoramic landscape and are intrigued by what it has to offer. Picking up an object we panoptically travel to an alien world, and it "offers the chance to see without being seen, to penetrate interior recesses, to violate intimacy" (Kirshenblatt-Gimblett 1991:413). These objects entice us to penetrate their secrets and enter their fictionally constructed social lives — like the life-size cardboard cutouts of two Klingon females displaying their cleavage from a window facing 12th Street. They seductively stand above *Star Trek* models, novels, and toys. These Klingon females are representative characters, reflecting for some fans a desire for sexual fantasy: "Would love to see those two do a photo spread for 'PLAYKLIN' Just Love that Klingon Kleavage ... K'Mel" (Kurkura 1995). These two characters, Lursa and B'Etor, were the first nefarious female Klingon characters on *Star Trek*, and they tried to tarnish Lt. Worf's name in the Klingon Empire. For one fan they are "the 2 most distinct female *Star Trek* characters" (Skywalk925 1995). However, they were killed off in the *Star Trek* movie *Generations* (1994) — but at Forbidden Planet they live on, and if you want them, you can take them home to your bedroom for $25. The real thrill isn't just watching these Klingons on television but seeing them in your house, where they embody the cultural memories of a television show.

This fantasy of cultural memories continues on the *Star Trek* forum at America Online, where fans discuss Lursa and B'Etor long after their "deaths." Knanna (AOL user name) complains that "Lursa and B'Etor are my heroes, ST lost its savor for me when they were murdered" (Knanna 1995). But Ricky exclaims with glee: "They finally died in [the movie] Generations! YEEEEEEEEEEEEEEEESSS" (Ricky 1701D 1995). Mahsja, offers a means of hope, "Al — Lursa and B'Etor are much valued among us. The two actresses do often appear at conventions. A leader of the Klingon Assault Group [a Klingon fan club] in Canada is determined to spearhead a 'Bring Them Back' movement. If you'd like to encourage him, e-mail me for his address:-)" (Mahsja 1995).

However, Magnus tries to reason within the story line for ways to bring back the two Klingons: "Picture this, the torpedo hits the ship, emergency doors (Yes Klingons have them!) shut, the bridge section, battered, no life support, air running out, they fall into the path of the Nexus Ribbon [a source for reaching paradise in the movie]. This of course means they CAN come back! Jah Doh!" (Magnus 1995). But WestStyle, who has been following the thread of how to bring them back, slams Magnus's theory: "They were destroyed way before the nexus arrived!! Steeerike Two!!!" (WestStyle 1995).

These fans are trying to write and rewrite alternative histories online. This is a form of what Michel de Certeau calls textual poaching (1984). Jenkins picks up de Certeau's theme and carries it further: "For fans, reading becomes a type of play, responsive to its own loosely structured rules and generating its own types of pleasure ... [the fans] who remake programs in their own image" (1994: 449–450). These people have, in essence, created a kind of performance, a performance textually inscribed in cyberspace but one that is inspired by the fantasy objects one can buy at Forbidden Planet. The fans' discussion about Lursa and B'Etor also confirms Jenkins's statement: "One becomes a fan not by being a regular viewer of a particular program but by translating that viewing into some type of cultural activity, by sharing feelings and thoughts about the program content with friends, by joining a community of other fans who share common interests" (451). In the eyes of some fans, these Klingons have become representative characters and therefore "exist at the intersection of cultural production and consumption, circulating in specific times and places where they are made to mediate values to a given community" (Baty 1995:90).

The online discussion reflects the larger mass media–produced values of *Star Trek,* and it is the memory of these characters as seen on television that is displayed through the physical objects that can be purchased at Forbidden Planet. As Baty says, "remembering is about creating what is real; it is about finding stories to tell ourselves about the past and present. These stories help us to think about where we have been, and in the process they help us to know who we are" (1995:31). As these *Star Trek* fans display their beliefs online they are reenacting the memory of their favorite episodes, stories, and characters — and it is here that it can be determined what they value and thus who they are. This construction is the foundation of a science fiction community. If there were no commodities, no sites of memories, then there would probably be no fandom: "When members of a community, whether a neighborhood or a nation-state, lose their common objects of memory, they have difficulty maintaining a common ground — a *present*— on which to construct foundations of mutuality, belonging, language, and knowledge" (Baty 1995:31).

Forbidden Planet is a "clearinghouse" for science fiction objects that allow people to enter worlds of fantasy, and these representations of fictional characters are "not simply available as shared stor[ies] but also for sale as product[s]" (Baty 1995:10). The merchandise purchased in this store becomes a means for branching out into other worlds (by reading and fantasizing)— the participants of which come together in a setting at this bookstore, online, or at a convention that "allow[s] for the development of a discourse in which community is realized, belonging becomes a possibility, and knowledge is circulated throughout the political [or social] culture" (Baty 1995:31). By discussing their encounters with the alien, the fans, these tourists, display who they are, where they have been, and where they are going. In science fiction travels there are many worlds to visit, many realms of possible exploration.

Star Tours

Whereas Forbidden Planet allows people to purchase books that take them into fantasy stories and objects that enable them to create a shared community of remembering these stories, Disneyland offers environmental sites where tourists can completely immerse themselves. One of these sites is Star Tours, a simulated environment that offers visitors an interface into the myth and legend of George Lucas's *Star Wars* (1977). Droids and aliens in an upper-level control room look down at "passengers" who walk into a hanger-sized room filled with control panels, walkways, beams, hissing steam, and a large video screen advertising tours of Hoth and the moon of Endor accompanied by scenes from *The Empire Strikes Back* (1980) and *Return of the Jedi* (1983), and so forth.* Visitors are literally immersed into a *Star Wars* environment that's more real than a movie set, for rather than just a wall and a floor where a camera films, this space has a ceiling, floor, and four surrounding walls. It's as if visitors are in the docking bay of a space station. A PA system announces arrivals and departures of passenger shuttles as visitors wait in line. They eventually are sent down a hall and through a doorway that leads out to the shuttle.

During the wait before the ride begins, visitors are immersed in an environment not made for a movie; it is not a set. It is a post-cinematic environment reverberating Benjamin's realization of the movie set: "in the studio the mechanical equipment has penetrated so deeply into reality that its pure aspect freed from the foreign substance of equipment is the result of a special procedure.... The equipment-free aspect of reality here has become the height of artiface" (1968:233). The equipment, the high-tech environment, is located in the Disney environment. It's just at such a height of artifice that it *appears* equipment-free.

Escorted by a Disney worker, about 40 people enter the shuttle through side doors and sit down on seats that fill the interior of the ship. A door slides open at the front left corner of the compartment, revealing a droid — a comic, C3PO-like character — who introduces himself as a pilot on his first flight. The droid presses a button and the viewscreen — spanning across the front wall of the shuttle — comes on, showing a motion picture projection of the shuttle launching bay as the ship takes off. The motion onscreen is matched by a kinesthetic motion of the shuttle: when the viewscreen reveals a right turn or a hard dive, for instance, the shuttle, sitting on a joystick-like rod, corresponds with the onscreen movement. The visitor feels the simulation of moving through space while staying in one place.† The passengers feel the ride as the ship launches out into space,

---

The science fiction (or space fantasy) images from the monitors showing the icy scenes of Hoth and the woods of the moon of Endor can be visited here on Earth, for the images are actually from the glaciers of Norway and the woods of northern California.

†*This ride, unlike other Disney rides, does not move through an environment. Instead, the projected image moves, creating the illusion of movement through an environment for the passengers. More like a computer game, you literally stay in one place. Universal Studios has a similar setup with their Back to the Future ride.*

travels through a comet, gets caught in the middle of a spaceship battle between Imperial TIE fighters and rebel X-Wing fighters, flies by the Death Star, follows an X-Wing fighter as it dives into the Death Star trench, accelerates away from it, and finally comes to a jolting stop as it careens through the landing bay of the space station. The doors open on the other side of the shuttle and everyone exits through a back hall that leads them into a *Star Wars* gift shop where they can purchase T-shirts, ties, toys, comic books, novels, scripts, and so forth.

The ride appears out of control. The passengers never reach their "destination" of Hoth or the moon of Endor as announced on the tourism advertisements projected in the entry area as they were waiting in line. They are given a ride that takes them not to an alien world but to the movies. The space flight scenes from *Star Wars* are experienced kinesthetically by the passengers, who have only previously viewed similar scenes in the passivity of a movie theater or on television. One may wonder what it is like to be a rebel pilot (like Luke Skywalker) fighting Imperial TIE fighters in *Star Wars*. At Star Tours, the visitor gets that question answered through an empathetic experience, as Brenda Laurel explains: "we experience *vicariously* what the characters in the action seem to be feeling. ... [T]he elements of 'real' fear and pain are absent. When we are agents in a mimetic action, our emotions about our *own* experiences partake of the same special grace. When I took my five-year-old daughter on the *Star Tours* ride at Disneyland..., she turned to me in mid-shriek and shouted, 'If this was *real*, I'd be *scared!*'" (1993:120). This simulated virtual environment is more real than the movies.

The greatest hope of the science fiction fan is not just to read about and watch other worlds on screen but to live in real alien environments and to converse with the alien. They want to "actively engage the site and those in it" (Kirshenblatt-Gimblett 1993:xiv). By staying in one place, visitors virtually travel light years and become kinesthetically immersed into a spaceship that takes them on a ride they have only read about or watched on a movie screen. Here one experiences immersion into the sensory world of *Star Wars*. "At the blending point of cinema and computer games are such new forms as super-arcade games like *Battle Tech* and sensory-rich amusement park installations like Star Tours. These types of systems involve the tactile and kinesthetic senses" (Laurel 1993:54). This tactile and kinesthetic environment is essentially an interface into the movie *Star Wars*, but it is also like a large video game where people are manipulated by forces outside their control — like when they careen through the icy tunnel of a large comet. Visitors become the game. Once the doors to the shuttle are closed, they cannot get out until the ride is over.

An interface (and this ride is one kind of interface), philosopher Michael Heim observes, "guides and even warps our visual imagination. People growing up today with films and television see things in video format. Our dreams and imaginings often occur to us as if we were watching television. We find it difficult to become aware of our own internal states without the objective representations of the interface" (1993:80). Here visitors are not traveling to other countries or cruising the Bahamas. They are touring a consumer product developed by the companies of Disneyland and Lucas film, an example of "a nationless space (the future) where companies replace countries [as sites of tourism], or a memory of or desire for travel to a country whose image is already so encrusted with fictionalization as to be no more real than a film or legend" (Project on Disney 1995:85). For example, the droid pilot is not C3PO but one who simulates his personality — his goofiness we have experienced in *Star Wars*. Even though we have never seen this droid before, the setting surrounding us and attitude expressed by this pilot droid creates the illusion that we have seen his image "encrusted with [the] fictionalization" of a *Star Wars* movie. The representative characters become a means of familiarity for an environment that was previously accessible only onscreen. The objects allow for this environment to become *Star Wars*–like, and it is no longer just watched but touched. Lucasfilm carries this interfacial illusion a step further in its computer game *Dark Forces*, which allows the user to walk through virtual sets and shoot up stormtroopers.

Dark Forces

The wind howls as you stand on a mountain cliff covered with ice. Taking a path that may lead you to the secret entrance of the Imperial base below the surface, you jump over a crevasse. Music tones ominously as you hear the digital crack of laser gunfire. You crouch and quickly turn to your right as you swing your blaster around. One of Darth Vader's Imperial stormtroopers, shouts, "Hey! You're not authorized here," as he pumps more rounds at you. You fire your blaster and he falls off the cliff with a scream. This game, *Dark Forces* (1995), is an example of how computer games are becoming more dramatic, realistic, theatrical, and cinematic. Allucquere Stone explains: "Computers are arenas for social experience and dramatic interaction, a type of media more like public theater, and their output is used for qualitative interaction, dialogue, and conversation. Inside the little box are *other people*" (1995:16). Some games, such as *Wing Commander III* and *IV*, are modeled after the fictional narrative styles of movies, in which elements typical of Hollywood production — scripts written by members of the Writers Guild, sets, live union actors, and so forth — are used to create interactive experiences. Inside the "little box" are actors, movie sets, alien landscapes. Other games use computer animation with the action modeled on a shoot-'em-up style of game play. However, even "computer games [like *Dark Forces*] can be seen to have evolved from the impact of dramatic ideas on the technology of interactive computing and graphical displays" (Laurel 1993:53).

Digital sound effects, like the sinister humming sound of a probe droid rising above the wall of a building (its sounds digitized from the sound effects heard in *The Empire Strikes Back*, when Han Solo shoots it down with his blaster on the ice planet of Hoth), pervade the game, *Dark Forces*, and provide a new level of realism never attained in the early days of 1980s Atari arcade games. In this game the users — unlike the visitors at the Disney Star Tours ride — get to visit, walk around, and explore the virtual landscapes of various alien worlds, as well as the interiors of several starships (one replicates the visual white panels seen on board Princess Leia's rebel blockade runner in the opening sequence of the first *Star Wars* movie, *A New Hope*). In Disneyland visitors are literally taken on a ride, but they don't get to fly the shuttle or walk into the control room or press buttons in the shuttle — they have to stand in a line and wait to be seated. However, in *Dark Forces* users actively participate in the action. They react to the aural and visual stimulation onscreen.

Star Wars is a mythic story of good overcoming evil. In the game *Dark Forces* players are given the means to expect "war to supply the artistic gratification of a sense perception that has been changed by technology" (Benjamin 1968:242). As players attempt to accomplish missions —finding information, rescuing a hostage, or committing acts of sabotage, and so forth — they realize that this "interface"— this computer screen providing a window into the "war" of the *Star Wars* universe —"is not simply the means whereby a person and a computer represent themselves to one another; rather it is a shared context for action in which both are agents. [An agent is] *one who initiates action*" (Laurel 1993:4). In Aristotelian terms: "Tragedy is an imitation, not of men, but of an action and of life, and life consists in action, and its end is a mode of action" (1961:62). The virtual environment gives people the ability to participate in actions unlike anything found in the real world but previously viewed in films. What they have only watched in a movie theater, or read in a *Star Wars* novel, players now get to directly experience through a computer character. They virtually stand on an alien world and shoot up stormtroopers as if they were Luke Skywalker or Han Solo, and when laser blasts streak across the screen and crack aurally through the speakers, players are moving that joystick around and ducking for their life. Players are imitating the action not of war found in real life but of the glorified war of a fictional movie.

Star Trek Set Tour

Cruise Trek is a company in Agoura Hills, California, that offers boat cruises for *Star Trek* fans and its stars to such places as the Caribbean and Alaska (essentially the cruises are specialized *Star Trek* conventions on a ship). Their motto: "CRUISE TREK: Boldly exploring our planet together; continuing to cruise where no group of Trek fans has cruised before!" (HorizInc 1995a). Tourist attractions for *Star Trek* fans are not new. Ever since the first *Star Trek* convention held in New York City in 1972 (Jindra 1994:27), fans have been organizing conventions, fan clubs, fanzines, and so forth. Fans, Jenkins says, "transform personal reaction into social interaction, spectator culture into participatory culture" (1994:451). Part of this participatory culture is experienced by getting close to the stars of the show. Fans want to experience or travel where the stars have gone before, namely the fictional worlds of *Star Trek*. Conventions and *Star Trek* cruises offer fans a way to experience and share live what they have all privately witnessed on television. The next-best thing would be to visit the place where the stars enact their Trek roles — the sound stages at Paramount Pictures where the *Star Trek* shows are filmed.

> On December 2, 1995, this wish almost became reality:
>
> Paramount Pictures presents
>
> STAR TREK TOURS
>
> An Exclusive Event offered by the Paramount Studio Group and the "*Star Trek*" producers
>
> Saturday, December 2, 1995
>
> Spend the day on the famous Paramount Studios lot in Hollywood, California, and visit the sets of "*Star Trek*: Voyager" and "*Star Trek*: Deep Space Nine"— open to the public for the first time ever! ... TICKETS PRICE: $129.00. (HorizInc 1995b)

Here fans had a chance not to just watch the bridge of *Voyager* or see the station of *Deep Space-Nine*, but to see and feel environmentally what they had only experienced two dimensionally on television.

This event was so unique that fleets of "starships," the crews from local *Star Trek* fan clubs, were prepared to go as members of Starfleet dressed in full uniform. One such starship was the USS *Atreides*, as signaled on AOL.* Here's one such communiqué from a "fleet captain":

> Subj: USS Atreides on the way
> Date: 95-10-21 18:49:17 EDT
> From: SF Unicorn
>
> Trek Tours,
>
> It took a little work, but we did it. As of now myself and three of my crew from our Chapter are shuttling (flying) down from Oakland Saturday AM, all in Uniform and makeup to take the tour and shuttle (fly) back home (San Francisco Bay Area) that night. Tonite is our Chapter monthly meeting and I'm sure more will be signing up to join us. Only 6 weeks to go. Time for the Uniform to head to the cleaners, start packing the shoulder bag of items to be signed, polish the boots.....point the ears >>BG<< Oh this is going to be major TREK fun for day. In Service to the Membership,
>
> ~ : { > .....

In World War II, naval ships would signal each other with spotlights and communicate through Morse code. In similar fashion Star Trek fans, as crews of starships, communicate with each other online on bulletin boards in cyberspace.

F[leet] Cpt. Unicorn Escobedo
CO, USS Atreides, NCC-60022-A
Interim Deputy Sector Chief 004, North
UFPI Presidential Ambassador at Large
SFAtreides@aol.com   (SF Unicorn 1995)

By dressing up in uniforms and wearing makeup, these fans, the crew members of USS *Atreides*, were going to have the honor of boarding the USS *Voyager* and the space station *Deep Space Nine*. In a way they were to become "guest stars" of the show. When Paramount suddenly canceled the event, fans were shocked and responded negatively to the company, as this one example shows: "Who needs Gingrich or THE Grinch, when Paramount can cancel Christmas!?!!" (CpowellRun 1995:).

More than a theme park attraction like Star Tours, the *Star Trek* set tour would have allowed fans to walk through the sets that physically represent where they have "traveled" weekly via television. It would have actualized what fans had previously experienced virtually. Like the Universal Studios theme park, which had a *Star Trek* set designed to film uniformed tourists who act out a simple plot (Jindra 1994:39), the Paramount set tour would have allowed for participation within an immersive setting. Going back to Benjamin's theory of how film explores space, he felt that "[o]ur taverns and our metropolitan streets, our offices and furnished rooms, our railroad stations and our factories appeared to have us locked up hopelessly" (1968:236). But film, by exploring in detail and in close-up the familiar, "extends our comprehension of the necessities which rule our lives" (236). And when people are allowed to explore environmental sets that have been previously viewed onscreen under "the ingenious guidance of the camera," they get to look at these environments, these "commonplace milieus" in hyper-reality close-up (236).

Those disappointed by Paramount's cancellation of the set tour have the opportunity to visit the *Star Trek* theme park in Las Vegas. This site includes the promenade from *Deep Space Nine*, a museum, restaurant and lounge, and a motion simulator ride. This tourist site will be *Star Trek* fans' dreams come true, for they will get to travel on a shuttle craft that takes them to the starship *Enterprise*, not as guest stars but as passenger guests. Rick Berman, the executive producer of *Star Trek*, describes how, while passengers are in the shuttle, they "are almost fully enwrapped above, below, and on all sides by a 70-millimeter film" projected around them. "The effect of warp speed and being in battle is extremely realistic" (Logan 1998:32). But will this *Enterprise*, as Benjamin said of film, "burst this prison-world asunder ..., so that now, ..., we [can] calmly and adventurously go traveling" (1968:236), seeking out new life and new civilizations?

Babylon 5 Online

From its money-saving production standards, its groundbreaking special effects, and its grand epic storytelling style —*Babylon 5* has made American television history. In 1995 the man behind the saga — the creator, executive producer, and author of 91 (out of 110) scripts during its five seasons — was the only person in the film and television industry to be named one of *Newsweek*'s 50 "most influential thinkers-innovators who will shape our lives as we move into the 21st century." The little-known writer named Joseph Michael Straczynski had his first play produced for his high school when he was 17. The following year a local theater produced one of his plays.

"Everyone told me to forget it, to take a regular job, and let the writing wait. But I knew that if I did this I'd never get out," Straczynski says. "It was all or nothing." It seems as a writer he has done it all. His output includes over 500 published articles, dozens of published short stories, 12 produced plays, two published novels, a number of screenplays (some TV movies, others unproduced), and over 150 produced television scripts. Writer's Digest Books published his expanded and updated best-selling classic, *The Complete Book of Scriptwriting* (1996).

Even though he has achieved a lot, he remains prolific. In 1986 Straczynski received a flash of inspiration for an epic science fiction television show. During the next two years he spent time writing out the idea that came to him. Next he tried to convince studio executives that he could do the series for a reasonable budget. For five years studio executives told him that his show could not be done, but his entire season of 22 episodes is paid for through advertising, with no overrun costs. An episode of *Babylon* 5 costs less than half of a *Star Trek: Deep Space Nine* or *Voyager* episode, and one-third that of Fox's canceled *Space: Above and Beyond*. He's able to cut costs by handing out three separate scripts to his production staff in advance so that the set, lighting, costume, special effects, and other teams can have enough time to complete their tasks without running up any overtime costs. The production team also uses high quality computer generated special effects created on Lightwave 3-D, a fairly inexpensive program that can run on desktop computers.

Unlike any other television writer in the United States, Straczynski has planned out five seasons for the show. The first season was the setup, and like some intricate novels, it can be a slow start as viewers get to know the characters, the setting, and the beginnings of a plot. Babylon 5 is a large space station five miles long, a rotational cylinder with centrifugal force providing artificial gravity, an idea reminiscent of Arthur Clark's mysterious ship from *Rendezvous with Rama* (1973), which was filled with buildings, meadows, and so forth along the inside of its hull. Like a United Nations in space, this large space station is host to many different kinds of alien species who live and interact among each other, a place where neutrality offers a medium for these aliens and humans to communicate their desires and needs in a galaxy of expanding commerce, discovery, and war. It was hoped the station would offer a chance for peace; however, in the evolving story line, it's mission has failed as the Great War of the Third Age of Mankind begins. Straczynski calls his show a novel for television, and it has been compared in its epic scope to Tolkien's *The Lord of the Rings*.

Breaking away from how stories are traditionally told on television, Straczynski strove for something new: "No one in American television has done a five-year story with a beginning, a middle, and an end, all written out ahead of time" (Holly et al. 1995:8). If Gene Roddenberry (the creator of *Star Trek*) was the Great Bird of the Galaxy, then J. Michael Straczynski is the Great Bird of the Universe. He is actually referred to as the Great Maker. It took him five years to convince networks to buy the pilot episode, and part of the show's success in the science fiction community comes from Straczynski's early encounter with science fiction literature: "When I grew up reading science fiction, what appealed to me the most was [the] sense of wonder that you got. A lot of science fiction, in television in particular, has lost [that] sense of wonder. You go to a different planet like you're going to the 7-11. Nobody says, 'What the heck is that?' And that's what I really want to bring out of the show" (Holly et al. 1995:13). This sense of wonder runs throughout the show as viewers see different aliens, starships, planets, and so forth. Designers have also attempted to create the Babylon 5 station online in cyberspace.

This *Babylon 5* site is similar to a science fiction convention, which, according to one fan, is "like being ushered into another world." Conventions offer a central auditorium where hundreds of people watch and listen to their favorite stars talk about their experiences on *Star Trek* and *Babylon 5*, among other science fiction shows. Conventions also show video clips from these shows and have space similar to Forbidden Planet, where dealers sell science fiction objects. American Online, a commercial online service, created the *Babylon 5* site in October 1995. It contains a virtual convention-style main stage area for guest speakers, video and sound clips, a public space to talk, and sales area. The "grand opening" of this site was attended online by Straczynski (JMS) and Bruce Boxleitner (BB), the actor who plays Captain Sheridan, the commander of *Babylon 5*. Like a convention, visitors got to ask the stars (moderated) questions:

> QUESTION: Bruce, all the best to you and Melissa on the arrival of your new son. What's your favorite role you've ever played?
>
> JMS at B5: Oops. sorry, Bruce, didn't see that was directed to you.
>
> BB at B5: Thank you from both Melissa and I. My favorite role.... Capt. John Sheridan of course.
>
> JMS at B5: (Memo to self: pay Bruce this week. Good answer.) (AOL 1995)

Many fans like to share inside information about their knowledge of stars as seen here from the fan's congratulations to Boxleitner and his wife for their son.

Aside from not being able to see the physical presence of the participants and viewers of this conference, there are some structural differences from traditional conventions unique to cyberspace "chats." One of these differences is that cyberspace allows for simultaneous conversations and parenthetical asides that can be viewed by all. This allows for users to follow more than one conversation at the same time, something that could not be done at crowded conventions where many people are spread throughout a large room and where noise levels may become excessive. In contrast, cyberspace allows users to talk to each other at the same time while they talk to the stars onstage. They can engage in multiple conversations simultaneously:

> QUESTION [TO BB]: What are your hours like? How much sleep do you get?
> CASADELARA [SPECTATOR]: Are you kidding … he has a new baby
> BB AT B5: Well with a new baby, much fewer. But work-wise, it's not bad, most days are around 12 hours.
> ELDONUNGOL [TO CASADELARA]: no s@$!! (AOL 1995 and personal note)*

Users can also exit the "auditorium" and go to other areas, such as the audiovisual section and download clips from the show. They can also exit the "convention" and go to other places on AOL, similar to the way a visitor at a convention will exit the building, walk down a street, and go to a mall, or visit a nearby shop.

Many AOL club sites are visual. When clicking the command to enter the *Babylon 5* site, the user sees a color picture of the space station with the following caption on the bottom of the page: "Click on *Babylon 5* to board the space station." The picture of the station is replaced by a picture of the station's concourse that has clickable panels that take the visitor to the following areas: Babcom Communication Center, Stellarcom WWW Jumpgate, Image Center, Audio Video, and Chat Area. *Babylon 5* online is essentially a way to travel in hyperspace. As Meredith Bricken observes: "Cyberspace participants interact directly with virtuality (rather than reality) to experience the embodiment of the application. This environment is 'as if real'" (1991:369).

Selecting the Babcom Communication Center, the user travels to another screen that includes another set of buttons: Message Center (bulletin board postings), Eclipse Cafe (live chat area), FAQ (frequently asked questions), and Fan Club. The Eclipse Cafe shows a picture of a solar eclipse with the following header: "Intergalactic Cuisine Volatile." This site is a precursor, a primitive blueprint of how, as Michael Benedikt says, "cyberspace architects will design electronic edifices that are fully as complex, functional, unique, involving, and beautiful as their physical counterparts if not more so. Theirs will be the task of visualizing the intrinsically nonphysical and giving inhabitable visible form to society's most intricate abstractions, processes, and organisms of information" (1991b:18). At AOL the architects have built a virtual Babylon 5 space station, but in a sense it is more "real" than the fictional television version because it allows users to "walk around" the virtual station. They can look out "windows" by downloading video clips from the Audio Video section, allowing them to see starships, aliens, and space battles occurring outside the station. This station is interactive. One can enter the Eclipse Cafe and talk to other people.

---

*It's interesting that the transcript of this conference does not include these sideline conversations.

A newer Web site was designed to allow users to join the *Babylon 5* fan club and shop on the station. But Straczynski wanted the site to be designed so that

> "When you come into it and you join the club, you get to hidden parts of the web page and you get your own quarters. You arrive at B5 through the docking bay, you are given an identi-card, you take a jpeg or gif of your face and put it on an identi-card, get your own quarters, a Babcom unit which you furnish however you want. We'll have a chat room set up so that you can go down to The Zocalo and hang-out. And have the face of the other person you are talking with on screen with you as you talk and some fun stuff. It will be virtually like arriving at Babylon 5. And we'll have some on-line tours. We discussed for a while putting up a camera hooked into the web page by the craft services table by the set, which is where the snacks are kept. And you could see Londo munchin' down potato chips. Which I think would be a hoot! We're talking to the actors about it. We'll see how that works out." (Bruckner 1996)

The technology that allows users to click on a computer screen and jump to different locations is known as hypertext. Hypertext, in the *Babylon 5* context, is metaphorically equivalent to hyperspace. Heim argues that "[t]he intuitive jump in hypertext is like the movement of space ships in futuristic fiction. When this fictional travel exceeds the speed of light, it becomes a jump through hyperspace. At such speeds it is impossible to trace the discrete points of the distance traveled" (1993:30–31). Hypertext allows visitors to travel to other worlds in cyberspace. In the concourse there's a button for the WWW Jumpgate. Clicking it, the user is taken to the Stellarcom page. At the left of the page is a picture of an active jumpgate digitized from an episode of *Babylon 5*. In science fiction terminology, a jumpgate allows starships to enter hyperspace, a faster-than-light means for traveling vast distances quickly. It allows them to "jump" to other planetary systems light years away. The *Babylon 5* jumpgate online takes the user to two different places: the Sci-Fi Link or the B5 WWW link. The B5 link is a connection to a series of World Wide Web pages on the subject of *Babylon 5*. One of the most popular sites is "The Lurker's Guide to *Babylon 5*" (maintained by Steven Grimm), which gives detailed information about the show, descriptions of individual episodes, including answers written by Straczynski to questions fans have asked about each episode.

People travel to other locations inside this virtual station, each one located in cyberspace: "We inhabit cyberspace when we feel ourselves moving through the interface into a relatively independent world with its own dimensions and rules," Heim says (1993:79). The dimensions and rules of the *Babylon 5* site and its cyberspace neighborhood on AOL are governed by non-Euclidean geometry. In 1854 Bernhard Riemann gave "one of the most important public lectures in the history of mathematics," author Kaku says, at the University of Gottingen, Germany. He broke away from the "confines of Euclidean geometry that had ruled mathematics for 2 millennia" by concluding that "electricity, magnetism, and gravity are caused by the crumpling of our three-dimensional universe in the unseen fourth dimension. Thus a 'force' has no independent life of its own; it is only the apparent effect caused by the distortion of geometry" (1994:36–37). In 1915 Albert Einstein linked Reiman's mathematical ideas to the physics of gravity in his theory of general relativity (Kaku 1994:93).

Hyperspace is a way to travel to other dimensions along the geometric curvature of space and time. Marcel Duchamp, experimenting with his "gap music" (the spaces between noise), explored the concept of a visual fourth dimension through sound:

> He spent a good deal of his energy writing notes that speculated about how a four-dimensional visual system might work…. The object in *With Hidden Noise* [a virtual sound sphere] is kept from view; it is secret, invisible, and can thus act as a metaphor in aural terms for the invisible directionality or the invisible virtuality of the fourth dimension…. In other words, a hidden echo or a virtual sound in normal space could possibly suggest that a four-dimensional object in a mirror — its virtual image — could stand for the virtuality of the fourth dimension, its "thereness" that cannot be specified. (Adcock 1992:121–122)

Metaphorically, travelers to *Babylon 5* enter a jumpgate, a hypertext link in cyberspace to another spatial, or dimensional, plane, where they can meet other travelers at the Eclipse Cafe, download images of Ambassador G'Kar, the Narn alien whose home planet was nearly destroyed by Centauri heavy battle cruisers. However, it can be argued that according to the mathematics of Reiman and the physics of Einstein, cyberspace architecture is a manipulation of multidimensional geometry. Hypertext is literally hyperspace, and users do travel through multiple dimensions of space to reach the Babylon 5 space station, "a self-contained world, five miles long, located in neutral territory. A place of commerce and diplomacy for a quarter of a million humans and aliens … a shining beacon in space, all alone in the night" (Straczynski 1994).

Railway to Outer Space

Like the nineteenth-century travelers who had their perspective shaped through a railroad interface, science fiction travelers' perspectives are shaped through the environments of science fiction, where they can travel to different worlds, meet others, and share their experiences. If these tourists cannot actually travel to other worlds and live permanently among indigenous aliens, they can at least purchase artifacts from their travels and bring them back to their own world. It is from around these artifacts that science fiction fans build fantasy environments, hoping to replicate and live in the sites of their travels, knowing that they must remain satisfied to only tour the lands of the fantastic. At these interfaces, fictional worlds, creators and cocreators of them, constructed artifacts from and of these worlds, technologies, and fandom intersect and create unique tourist productions.

By purchasing science fiction and fantasy objects at Forbidden Planet, people can travel to hundreds of different kinds of worlds in the imagination. Tourists are immersed in a three-dimensional *Star Wars* universe when they experience the kinesthetic Star Tours ride at Disneyland. Playing rebel freedom fighters in *Dark Forces*, players go on an adventure tour of *Star Wars* and shoot up Darth Vader's stormtroopers. In Vegas visitors play Domjock in Quark's bar on *Deep Space Nine*, boldly going where no tourist has gone before. The *Babylon 5* site on AOL is a virtual space station, where travelers jump through hyperspace and talk to fans and stars of the television show. In all of these events, the line between fantasy and reality overlaps, and the human-performer performs the performed-alien.

All these sites incorporate media-based fictional representative characters through which the values of the fans are seen and explored and from which fans build communities. Some may question whether the function of art (explored here as consumable mass market commodities) has a ritual, transformative function or if it merely offers a pleasurable aesthetic distraction. But if Benjamin is right, and "pure art" denies "any social function of art" (1968:224), then the communities that science fiction fans build and explore around objects of fandom are denied any kind of validity. It is under this kind of pretension that science fiction fans lose credibility, as Jenkins explains by summarizing an article from *Newsweek*: "'Hang on: You are being beamed to one of those *Star Trek* conventions, where grown-ups greet each other with the Vulcan salute....'" Fans are characterized as 'kooks' obsessed with trivia, celebrities, and collectibles; as misfits and 'crazies'" (1992:11). However, looking closer at Benjamin, it can be seen how the objects and environments of science fiction do have a certain authenticity: "By making many reproductions it substitutes a plurality of copies for a unique existence. And in permitting the reproduction to meet the beholder or listener in his own particular situation, it reactivates the object reproduced" (1968:221). Baty explores this theory through her development of representative characters, a site where social stories, events, lessons are activated through objects of these characters, whether Marilyn Monroe or John Lennon. I take her theory one step further by including within this domain fictional characters and settings that activate the world of the fiction through these objects and from which science fiction fans build communities.

Perhaps this desire for fantasy, this "[m]odern interest in science fiction," as Dean MacCannell theorizes, "is motivated by a collective quest for an overarching (solar or galactic) system, a higher moral authority in a godless universe, which makes of the entire world a single solidary unit, a *mere* world with its proper place among worlds" (1989:16). If the real world of Earth is not enough for science fiction fans to find meaning in life, then they may find it through tourism — their travel to and return from fantasy worlds. For according to one prominent author, Ursula K. Le Guin, "It is by such statements as, 'Once upon a time there was a dragon,' or 'In a hole in the ground there lived a hobbit'—it is by such beautiful non-facts that we fantastic human beings may arrive, in our peculiar fashion, at the truth" (1989:39–40). But perhaps the science fiction fan is a product of cyborg culture, where, as Haraway states, "Late twentieth-century machines have made thoroughly ambiguous the difference between natural and artificial, mind and body, self-developing and externally designed.... Our machines are disturbingly lively, and we ourselves are frighteningly inert" (1991:152). Or perhaps, according to novelist C. J. Cherryh, the desire for science fiction is a desire for "the world as it can be, ought to be—must someday, somewhere be.... Tale-telling is the most peaceful thing we do. It's investigatory. The best tale-telling always has been full of what-if" (1986:17). However, for the science fiction tourist there is no "what-if." Earth is just one stop on their travels among the lands of the fantastic.

6

Cyberspace Performances: Human Behavior Interfaced and Transformed on a Digital Stage*

End of the Industrial Age

The industrial age died when Alvin Toffler's Third Wave of the information age hit and washed over us like a great tsunami. As this wave recedes, what's left among the flotsam and jetsam are bits of electronic nodes. Around these cyberspatial fields of information people are connecting to their computers: building new kinds of communities and shaping binary data codes into coherent manipulative patterns ranging from interactive CD-ROMs to live chat rooms online. These objects, like a subway train, take us out of our homes and into the heart of a virtual city, where we find new sites, meet new people, go to movies, and play games — all this while sitting in front of a computer. The *virtual age* is upon us. How we interact with our computers and ourselves, the environments and communities we create by and through them is at the heart of the future growth of the virtual age.

Many performances occur in the realm of cyberspace — that location where, according to virtual reality pioneer Thomas Furness, "people come together in a virtual place, like a real place, only it doesn't exist anywhere" (Miller 1992:15) — by people who share what cyberpunk novelist William Gibson describes in *Neuromancer* (1984) as "a consensual hallucination." The performance can be one-way, as in interactive movies and games, in which audience-performers

A version of this essay was presented at the first annual Performance Studies Conference at New York University in 1995 and was subsequently published in Interactive Fantasy 1.4 (1995):21–31.

react to pre-recorded digitized actors as the virtual world unfold visually and aurally before them, or performers can respond and interact using text with other real users live on a computer network, such as with America Online. In addition, people can be totally "immersed" into a digital environment by wearing virtual reality equipment, which allows them to see, hear, and feel a virtual world. In any case, these kinds of virtual worlds are located within cyberspace, the digital architecture of a computer.

Computer Performance

But are these different computer activities "performance"? Are users performing? Performance is displayed behavior, whether people play a character who talks to and reacts to pre-recorded digitized actors, as in *Quantum Gate* (1993); have a cyberspace date by displaying themselves publicly inside the virtual, text-based room called "Romance Connection" on America Online; or have the illusion of being physically immersed in a digital, 3-D virtual reality world by wearing hi-tech visors and gloves. Performance scholar Richard Schechner theorizes that a performer "performs in the field between a negative and a double negative, a field of limitless potential, free as it is from both the person (not) and the person impersonated (not not). All effective performances share this "not-not not" quality: Olivier is not Hamlet, but also he is not not Hamlet: his performance is between a denial of being another (= I am me) and a denial of not being another (= I am Hamlet)" (1985:123). In the world of cyberspace, users are not necessarily performing the types of characters rehearsed and displayed on a stage like Olivier's Hamlet — however, those interfaced in cyberspace do share that performance quality of being "not" an *actual world individual* and "not-not" a *cyberspace identity*. For example, I, as a user interfaced into cyberspace, am not really me, for I am that virtual identity located in the cyberspace world of the computer, but I am also not-not that virtual identity, because some aspect of me is there, although it is not a physical presence. The user is a liminoid agent fluxed between the virtual and the actual.

Michael Benedikt puts it this way: "Egos and multiple egos, roles and functions, have a new existence in cyberspace. Here no individual is appreciated by virtue only, if at all, of their physical appearance, location, or circumstances. New liquid, and multiple associations between people are possible, ... and new modes and levels of truly interpersonal communication come into being" (1991a:123). In cyberspace, people identify and communicate among each other without the physical associations commonly found in the actual world. Through virtual identities new behaviors are liberated (or unleashed) in the users, and they may perform in ways not normally expressed in the everyday world.

The computer as a Mask

As a performer uses a mask at a carnival or in a theater performance as a license to get away with certain types of behaviors, so the computer is a mask that "disguises the conventional self and liberates the true personality" (Caillois 1979:21). In other words, even though the cyberspace identity is "me" interfaced in cyberspace, in Schechner's terms I may be "'behaving as if I am someone else' or 'as if I am "beside myself," or "not myself," as when in trance. But this 'some-one else' may also be 'me in another state of feeling/being,' as if there were mul-tiple "me's" in each person. The difference between performing myself ... and more formal presentations of self ... is a difference of degree, not kind" (1985:37). This is the essence of the performance nature of cyberspace. Users, like tradi-tional performers, have the ability to be someone else, but they are not some-one else — they are themselves performing behaviors they would, perhaps, not display if they were not-not performing in the virtual world.

Konstantin Stanislavsky, the founder of contemporary Western acting, believed that a character is a mask: "characterization is the mask which hides the actor-individual. Protected by it he can lay bare his soul" (30). Shomit Mit-ter explicates this statement:

> What Stanislavsky is unable explicitly to articulate in the system is that actors are able to "hide" behind masks because, when wearing a mask with an established expression, they cannot *look* intimidated or embarrassed and therefore do not *feel* those things. What takes place is not the deliberate concealment of an existing identity but the invol-untary obliteration of that identity through the physical incapacity of the body to express it. Actors lose their self-consciousness not because they are aware of being protected by the mask. They do so because, when their faces are concealed, they no longer possess the practical means by which to be "themselves." By the same measure, the soul, far from being "laid bare," is possessed to feel only and pre-cisely what the mask reflects. (1992:18–19)

By substituting the word *actor* with *user* we can see how the computer masks users. They almost involuntarily perform "characters" by expressing new kinds of behaviors in cyberspace that they would not ordinarily explore without that computer mask. The computer mask does not necessarily obliterate normal identity, but it temporarily transforms it. The question to ask is how the com-puter possesses one to feel only and precisely what this mask reflects?

The potential of a traditional stage performer to transform his personality, identity, and body through the playing of a character — the use of a "mask" — is clearly seen in the following description of an actor performing a role near the end of the nineteenth century:

> Under the strong impulse of a desire to perform his part, a noted actor was accustomed night after night to go upon the stage and sus-

tain his appointed task, walking about as actively as the youngest
member of the company. This old man was so lame that he hobbled
every day to the theater, and sat aching in his chair till his cue was
spoken, — a signal which made him as oblivious of physical infirmity
as if he had inhaled chloroform, though he was in the full possession
of his so called senses. (Eddy 1906:261)

If a traditional performer has this kind of performance potential to be "transformed, enabled to do things 'in performance' he cannot do ordinarily" (Schechner 1985:126), then certainly on the digital stage of cyberspace, users have
potential to perform new kinds of behaviors and identities. For example,
Matthew Deets, who is physically challenged, describes how, when he talks to
people in "real" life, the concrete material world, "a veil of intimidation or dis-
comfort descends on the conversation," but in the cyberspace community of
computer text-based communications, he says, "'I don't even have to mention
it'" (Shaw 1993:D6). Other users can only see Deets transformed as a text image:
they cannot see, hear, smell, or touch his physical presence. They can only interact with his virtual text-self.

This is the mask that creates a character that Roger Caillois believes liberates personality. For the virtual world of "cyberspace lets us dream that we can
build an inner frontier, a virtual reality, to our specs. So our culture is telling
itself sexy, glitzy, wishful stories about discovering alien territories right here on
Earth. About releasing ourselves from the burden of body and liberating ourselves
from sex and race and class. About acting out our fantasies in an electronic nether
world and tripping through that trapdoor in the mind that will let us, like Alice,
fall into a dream" (Porush 1993). Currently this "fantasy" of the electronic nether-
world, which frees users from inhibitions, is most pointedly seen in the conversations occurring in the text-based cyberspace "chats" with online computer
conferences. For example, in 1991 a class at McGill University, Montreal, Canada,
explored cyberspace in education. As part of the course, students participated in
online, cyberspace discussions, where communication was text-based. However,
the nature of the discussions involved with the online virtual classroom differed
so much from the physical, face-to-face discussions in the actual classroom that
"[t]o a casual observer, the online discussions would appear to involve a different
group of people than those in the class. To the informed observer, however, the
communication concerned a somewhat different aspect of existence — a kind of
parallel life" (Cartwright 1994:24). The students, while in cyberspace, were transformed into new kinds of identities in which they expressed behaviors different
from the ones experienced in their actual classroom.

The case of "Julie"

In a more extreme case, dating back to 1985, someone named Julie logged
on the Internet. She described herself as a disabled older woman who would push

the computer keys with a headstick. She made many female friends who shared their problems with her, and Julie would share advice back to them, advice that helped change some of the users' lives. However,

> "Julie" did not exist. "She" was, it turned out, a middle-aged male psychiatrist. Logging onto the conference for the first time, this man had accidentally begun a discussion with a woman who mistook him for another woman. "I was stunned," he said later, "at the conversational mode. I hadn't known that women talked among themselves that way. There was so much more vulnerability, so much more depth and complexity. Men's conversations on the nets were much more guarded and superficial, even among intimates. It was fascinating, and I wanted more." He had spent weeks developing the right persona. A totally disabled, single older woman was perfect. He felt that such a person wouldn't be expected to have a social life. Consequently her existence only as a net persona would seem natural. It worked for years, until one of Julie's devoted admirers, bent on finally meeting her in person, tracked her down. (Stone 1991:82–83)

Not only did the computer mask "Julie's" real-life identity, but it allowed "her" to communicate with and help people that "she" may never have met in the physical world. The psychiatrist wanted more open and vulnerable discussions he was not getting with other users, so he created a virtual identity, a masked character, who gave him the freedom to express communication behaviors he was unable to express without that persona. As Schechner would put it, the psychiatrist was not Julie, yet he was not-not Julie. Was "Julie" this psychiatrist's "true personality," as Caillois would say? The psychiatrist's disguise, Julie, certainly did allow him to help other people, for he gave advice that helped change people's lives, so in a way Julie was a cross-gendered psychiatrist.

Meeting the Vice President

Cyberspace is a "place of experimentation and exploration" (Cartwright 1994:24). Vice President Al Gore experimented and explored cyberspace through online text when he logged on to a computer conference using the CompuServe Information Service on January 13, 1994. The event was hosted by *U.S. News & World Report* and televised on C-SPAN, and it was the first time an official from the White House had ever participated in a public forum online. Some of the users, hidden behind the mask of the computer, were free to make such politically aggressive comments as: "'CONSERVATIVES RULE!!!'" and "'Bob Dole is awesome!!'" (Belsie 1994)—Republican statements directed at a Democrat vice president, which may not have been made if those same people were physically in the same room with Gore—a position many of them world never attain. Within the world of cyberspace there is no hierarchy, and virtual text-constructed "rooms" become places where people can vent political frustrations, or those with similar tastes, such as writers, can talk with each other about different ideas live, or some may even experience a cyberspace date.

Sex and Romance Online

Here's an example of an online cyberspace conversation. The scene took place on the evening of September 19, 1994, in the room "Romance Connection" on America Online:

> RICHY: hello alll
>
> TINKERBELL: 22/ a female fairy!
>
> MERRYLADY: :::watchin the RC spin around me:::
>
> RICKY: Hello Everyone! :)
>
> DEDEVVY: @}——}——-}————-}——————- for you Tink :-)
>
> MATTHEW: crky — rc? what do you mean?
>
> MERRYLADY: Howdee Richy!!!!
>
> TINKERBELL: {{{{{{{{{{{{{{De!!!}}}}}}}}}}}}}}}}}}}}}
>
> TINKERBELL: Thank you DE how sweet of you!
>
> RICHY: where r u from tink
>
> JOHN: One 20 year-old god for a 22 year old fairy.
>
> DEDEVVY: @}——}——-}———}————- for Merry becaws you are so sweet!!!!!!!
>
> MERRYLADY: How ya been Bratty Tink?
>
> MERRYLADY: Awww..thanks De….:::::tryin to focus on Rose::
>
> RICHY: {S Meow
>
> TINKERBELL: Been better! I have a pounding headache. How are you and work?

One feature of cyberspace dialogue in a "room" like this is its nonlinear, multiple parallel conversations, as well as its imaginative use of graphical character symbols to help support the text. For example, in the fifth line DeDevvy gives Tinkerbell a graphical rose, but there are so many people talking at once that Tinkerbell's response — "Thank you DE how sweet of you!" — doesn't appear until four lines later. Also, she may respond to multiple conversations about her simultaneously; for example, when John makes a pass at her, she ignores him but responds to MerryLady in the last line of the text. What usually happens next when someone finds another person he or she is interested in, that person will send an IM (Instant Message), which allows the two to talk privately. Here's an example of two people who meet, then IM each other with a series of questions and answers very similar to questions asked during an actual date. (They in fact later agree to meet in person.) I include the first couple of pages of the conversation:

MICHELLEY22: hi, Peterforu

PETERFORU: You have a cool name.

MICHELLEY22: oh … hold on one second … i have to step away..don't leave

PETERFORU: I'll wait.

PETERFORU: Are you there, Michelley22?

MICHELLEY22: I'm here

PETERFORU: Cool

MICHELLEY22: where are you in the city?

PETERFORU: Lower east side.

MICHELLEY22: I'm on 56th.

PETERFORU: You like it up there?

MICHELLEY22: yes … like the west side better, though

PETERFORU: This is what I look like: 5'8" 175 lbs, regular build, brown hair, blue eyes, clean shaven.

MICHELLEY22: 5'4, 115, short blonde hair, blue eyes, clean shaven….

PETERFORU: You don't have a picture online do you? I don't

MICHELLEY22: no….

PETERFORU: Do you like to go to movies?

MICHELLEY22: yes….

MICHELLEY22: what are you studying?

PETERFORU: Would you like to meet sometime at a movie theater?

MICHELLEY22: sure! at the Sony one on 68th street

MICHELLEY22: I have flu now

PETERFORU: That's my favorite one.

MICHELLEY22: saw Nixon there

PETERFORU: So, I guess you couldn't make it this weekend? Do you work during the week?

MICHELLEY22: yes…. I crawled out of bed for the first time last night … had to buy food…. I work midtown. editor/med. publisher

PETERFORU: Sounds like fun. How old are you. I'm 28.

MICHELLEY22: 26 next week

PETERFORU: What day?

MICHELLEY22: 12th

PETERFORU: I'll have to remember to email you, then.

MICHELLEY22: why, thank you!

PETERFORU: Do you want to try for a movie next Saturday?

MICHELLEY22: that sounds good … what sounds good?

MICHELLEY22: I mean, what movie?

PETERFORU: There may be some new movies out next Friday, so, we can check then.

MICHELLEY22: ok. did you see the Birdcage?

PETERFORU: Don't forget to set your clock forward one hour tonight.

PETERFORU: No, I haven't see that one yet.

MICHELLEY22: I won't!

PETERFORU: Here's a personal question. Do ever do cybersex online? Kind of curious.

MICHELLEY22: well, I prefer it in person with a nice boy.

MICHELLEY22: just my preference....

MICHELLEY22: I'm sure you could find someone around here though that would be into it!

PETERFORU: No problem. I was just curious.

The technology of the computer, the AOL interface, mediates the conversation, but it really doesn't change the structure of an actual conversation — with its starts and stops and sudden turns and leaps of thought. However, another kind of conversation can differ significantly from the one seen above, as when someone "scores," as in the example below.

In the privacy of IMs the conversations between two people can get quite sexual, as seen here in the following opening exchange:

JOHNBYE: Hi, Cathy, how are you doing? ;)

CATHYHOT: fine thanks and yourself cutie?

JOHNBYE: I'm fine. What color eyes do you have? I have blue.

CATHYHOT: brown

JOHNBYE: May I gently take your hand?

CATHYHOT: yes....

JOHNBYE: I look into your brown eyes, as my hands tug your hair and slide down your back resting on your hips.

CATHYHOT: and then what?

JOHNBYE: My lips press against your pulsing neck and slide down shirt, tugging on the buttons.

CATHYHOT: then?

This is the beginning of a sexual fantasy encounter. In cyberspace dating there is no hiding sexual motives, as may occur in a "face-to-face" date, or even a polite conversation, as could be seen between the two people earlier. This kind of encounter is closer to phone sex than a date. People, looking for safe sex (or any sex), surf for electronic flesh — technology mediating their virtual fantasies, which they may not even explore publicly without this masking by the computer.

Nonlinear Thought

Having the ability to follow nonlinear structures reflects a new way to process information. Gregory Ulmer theorizes that people absorbed in watching the nonlinear flow structure of MTV and the medium's "ability to simulta-neously present several different stories" are teaching people a new form of lit-eracy that breaks the "barriers of linear thinking — the logic of the written word in which one idea leads to the next" (Wheat 1994). In fact another professor, Roger Drury, thinks that students exposed to this kind of nonlinear structure found on MTV were able to comprehend the "abrupt shifts" and "juxtapositions" of T. S. Eliot's *The Wasteland*, whereas many of those from a generation earlier (who were not used to nonlinear thinking) found it "impenetrable" (Wheat 1994). In many ways cyberspace structures reflect the nonlinear pattern found on MTV, as well as providing, in some ways, shifting parallel thought-structures. This is a postmodern style of thinking, as Turkle explains: When people buy a computer, they are "getting an object that teaches them a new way of thinking and encourages them to develop new expectations about the kinds of relation-ships they and their children will have with machines" (1995:49).

In addition to online dates, people can enter cyberspace rooms transformed into fictitious stages for people to actually play characters in fictional world set-tings. On America Online people can "sim" — play a text-based virtual simula-tion of a character they create in a *Star Trek* world, for example. These performance events are called MUDs Multi-User Dimensions — "a form of social computer gaming" that "resemble[s] a parallel life, often with a completely different set of physical, social, and emotional attributes" (Cartwright 1994:24). Basically, these are role-playing games on a computer.

This kind of parallel cyberspace life was explored in Lucasfilm's online game, *Habitat*. Using a low resolution graphical user interface (instead of only text) this simulated, virtual world allowed users to "play games, go on adventures, fall in love, get married, get divorced, start businesses, found religions, wage wars, protest against them, and experiment with self-government." Within the virtual, "fictional" community of *Habitat*, the users had to decide what kind of society they wanted to make. For example, users debated whether murder should be considered a crime in *Habitat*. About half thought that within this virtual world it was part of the fun, whereas the other half thought murder should not be allowed. Shortly after this debate, one of the users went around and shot some of the other users' virtual characters. One of the other users (a Greek Orthodox priest in the real world) opened a church within the community, and members of this church were not allowed to carry weapons or use violence. The church became a popular part of the community. Later a sheriff was elected to help enforce laws. (See Morningstar and Farmer 1991:273–300.)

Some of the participants of the virtual world of the *Habitat* community used their philosophy and values of the real world to help order the virtual com-munity, whereas others welcomed the ability to create anarchy. Victor Turner, the late anthropologist and performance scholar, made an observation that fits here: "[w]hen we act on the stage, whatever our stage may be, we must now ... bring into the symbolic or fictitious world the urgent problems of our reality. ... And when we enter whatever theater our lives allow us, we have already learned how strange and many-layered everyday life is, how extraordinary the ordinary" (1982:122). The ordinary happenings within a cyberspace community become extraordinary because whether users are playing fictitious characters or not, they are displaying some aspect of their actual selves where human behaviors, wishes, and desires circulate within a virtual world, a world that allows them to explore their own nature and behaviors without, in most cases, an actual-world consequence.

Interactive Games and Movies

The next step of cyberspace performances will include realistic-looking worlds, in which users can see and hear the world environment all around them. Although the samples out in the market do not yet allow a shared virtual experience where one can visually see, hear, talk, or touch a real-looking virtual person in virtual rooms, there are examples that show the technology heading in this direction.

In the interactive movie *Quantum Gate* (1993) the user plays the character of Drew Griffin, who is never seen on the computer screen. Users see the virtual world through Griffin's eyes, and they meet other performers, who are digitized actors, and talk with them. Director Greg Roach employed over 30 actors to perform the characters in his movie. The actors performed in a studio in front of a blue screen and were later digitized into the computer-designed setting. A soundtrack was also added. The spectator is also the participant in front of the computer and "performs" the lead character, Drew. A linear plot unfolds, and there is one resolution to the story, no matter what users choose to say to the other characters. However, Roach designed the sequel so that "There are literally dozens of different endings'" (Trumbull 1994:4). The user experiences the virtual world visually and aurally. It certainly does not have the spontaneity and feel of a live online forum, where a user can literally say anything and try to do anything textually, but the interactive movie does explore the nature of pre-recorded interactivity, and it does allow the user to explore ways to relate to the other characters encountered in the story. It should be noted that the user, through the character of Drew, is "performing" a man. How would a female user interact with the other characters by playing a man? What if Drew was female? Would male users perform the character in the same way? I explore this CD-ROM movie in more detail in the next chapter.

In the game *Myst* (1993) the user plays a neutral, generic character, an explorer who needs to solve the mystery of an alternate world island. Most of the time users do not interact with other characters and are not forced into a linear plot. They need only to solve the mystery by finding clues and putting the pieces of clues together in whatever order they come across them. What is noteworthy about *Myst* is its eerie environmental ambiance: from its carefully structured back-story, its impressively detailed 2,500 rendered images, including atmospheric lighting and shadows, and its digitized sound, which includes waves lapping on the shoreline when the user stands on a dock — all of these elements combine to create a virtual world so realistic that users may wish they could step into it. According to one writer, the uniqueness of *Myst* set it apart from other CD-ROM games: "It was the only thing like itself; it had invented its own category" (Carroll 1994:70).

Virtual Reality

Future cyberspace performances will entail total immersion, where users can see, hear, and touch the cyberspace world and the virtual images of other people. "Instead of using screens and keyboards, people can put displays over their eyes, gloves on their hands, and headphones on their ears. A computer controls what they sense; and they, in turn, can control the computer" (Aukstakalnis and Blatner 1992:7). Through these different devices the user is surrounded by a three-dimensional, digital environment. All the other examples explained previously dealt with a user interacting with a world projected onto a screen — the user sits from without. With the head-mounted display the user sees the illusion of the virtual world from within. The sense of physical touch is created by wearing a special glove or bodysuit. One such design uses air bladders within the glove. When a virtual image is touched, air is compressed and released within certain parts of the glove, controlled by computer commands, giving the sensation of tactile pressure on the hands (Aukstakalnis and Blatner 1992:150-151).

One of the earliest "virtual reality" prototype machines was called the "Sensorama Simulator," entered into the United States Patent Office in 1962 by Morton Heilig. Looking like a "vintage pinball machine" the prototype allowed the user to "ride" on a motorcycle through the streets of Brooklyn. He or she could hear the motorcycle start, feel the vibration of it through the handlebars, and see the three-dimensional view throughout most of the field of vision. The concept never got off the ground. (See Rheingold 1991:49–50.) It wasn't until the mid 1980s that virtual reality began to gel — "when the right combination of sponsors, visionaries, engineers, and enabling technologies came together at NASA's Ames Research Center…. It was there that a generation of cybernauts donned a helmet-mounted display and glove input device, pointed their fingers, flew around wire-frame worlds of green light-mesh" (Rheingold 1991:128). Now users can go to such a place as DreamWorks SKG's GameWorks and pay money to wear virtual reality equipment that takes them into another world.

Watching a user wear virtual reality equipment from outside the performance frame, a spectator can see the performer expressing physical behaviors that can only be understood from within the frame of performance. The user is physically in two worlds at the same time. As Furness posits: "Virtual reality is an environment that you create using a combination of visual, auditory, and tactile images so that it becomes an alternative, sort of an artificial, environment or reality. We call it a 'reality' because you perceive it as if it is a world. It's just like you're walking into another world, and you're perceiving it as if it becomes reality itself" (Miller 1992:14). To be immersed in two worlds at once causes the user to become a paradox in space, for physically he or she is standing there, yet he or she is elsewhere.

Cyber-performances tend to reflect what Turner observed about the purpose of Jerzy Grotowski's experimental theater: "Let us create a liminal space-time 'pod' or pilgrimage center, ... where human beings may be disciplined and discipline themselves to strip off false personae stifling the individual within" (1982:120). Online text-based discussions, cybernetic helmets and gloves, and CD-ROM interactive movies all provide the means to create new modes of cultural performances, performances that will shape how individuals communicate, argue, make love; how they perceive and participate in politics, entertainment, friendships or enmities; and how they invent new fictional worlds or remake the actual one. The computer will not only become a pilgrimage center for users to find themselves, but ideally it will be where they will find others immersed in a new kind of community having no national borders, physical prejudices, ethnic cleansings, or refugees.

Pioneers on the Electronic Frontier

This is just the pioneer stage of performances occurring on the electronic frontier — as the technology advances so will the physical realism of cyberspace. Most likely these cyberspace worlds won't be the nightmare worlds of Gibson's cyberpunk visions, nor will they be placid worlds of tranquillity, but cyberspace will reflect the hopes, fears, dreams, aspirations, and fears of our own thinking, for in essence "[m]ortal mind perpetuates its own thought.... A mill at work or the action of a water-wheel is but a derivative from, and continuation of, the primitive mortal mind" (Eddy 1906:399). If humankind's evolving thought brought about the water-wheels and mills of the industrial revolution and thus the beginnings of the modern age at the end of the eighteenth and nineteenth centuries, then what is humankind developing into today, at the end of the twentieth century? In "All Good Things..." — the final episode of *Star Trek: The Next Generation* — Q, representative of a superior alien species, tells Captain Picard that humanity's future quests won't be found through mapping star systems or exploring nebulae but by exploring the unlimited possibilities of being. Cyberspace may reflect humanity's natural (and technological) evolution toward a new state or kind of being, and, in fact, the performances we are seeing today on the electronic frontier may be the genesis of a new kind of human being, a person whose primary future and identity lie in the realm of cyberspace.

7

Digitizing Aristotle: Directing the User in a Dramatic Experience in the Interactive CD-ROM Movie *Quantum Gate*

Playing with a Movie

The performer scrubs the side of a curved wall. His arm is tattooed and his head bald. Looking like a neo-nazi punk, he stares back at you from the computer screen. "Hey, can I talk to you?" he smirks, his expression as real as any seen on television or a movie. The computer flashes up a small box on the screen and gives you three options on how to respond to Private Michaels's overture. With the correct choice you send Private Michaels into a tirade of how not to trust the United Nations command at this military base. The plot unfolds as you walk around the corridors and rooms of the base and interact with other digitized performers. You begin to unearth a conspiracy that could mean the end of one civilization, sacrificed for the good of another. Meanwhile you get flashbacks of your girlfriend, who was involved in a serious accident, and your mother, who yells at you for leaving medical school and joining the military. These are scenes from Greg Roach's 1993 interactive movie *Quantum Gate*, contained on a CD-ROM and displayed on the digital stage of a computer screen.

One of the popular locations to experience entertainment in this increasingly virtual world is through the phenomenon of interactive CD-ROM movies — which offer a kind of performance that cannot be found in any other medium. Some interactive CD-ROMs are beginning to reach levels of Hollywood production standards of action movies, some have the feel of a game or an interactive novel, and some are more experimental in their approach to narrative storytelling. Despite their different styles, all CD-ROM movies share something in common: interactivity for the user, the spectator-participant. In these movies the director has not only directed the actors in the movie, but through the use of a subjective cinema language open to the interactive process, the user has also been incorporated into the movie as a performer. The other performers look directly into the camera, which gives the illusion that they are looking at the spectator-user. As Richards says subjective cinema language, "With the advent of interactive video, and the coming three-dimensional contact holograms, this language may find a power never known before" (1992:155).

Interactivity and Video Games

It's interesting to note how CD-ROM movies are not truly interactive as, say, a chat room online is — where users can engage in multiple conversations either privately with another person or with a group of people, where multiple consciousnesses harmonize and clash, whether one is on a virtual romantic date or chatting about the latest episode of *Babylon 5*. Multi-User Domains (MUDs) — somewhat similar to such role-playing games as *Dungeons & Dragons* — are fictional chat rooms, virtual online worlds where people can interact textually with each other through the use of virtual characters in an interactive story. In another example of interactivity, tourists can enter an interactive historical site at the restored village of Plimoth Plantation and talk to different pilgrims.

These different kinds of virtual environments are truly interactive. They are live, not pre-recorded. The spectator-participant interacts most of the time with a human being — there is a living consciousness on the other side of the screen in a MUD adventure or on that virtual date, and the pilgrims at Plimoth are performed by actors. This is different from the interactivity of CD-ROM movies, which are mainly linear in pattern and offer only limited actions for the user to choose from when interacting with the pre-recorded performers. This method is not much different from a video game in which users shoot up starfighters on a computer screen by interacting via a joystick. So what is the difference between today's high-tech, high-budget CD-ROM movies, where users manipulate actors to say or do something within a limited choice matrix by clicking a mouse, and the early 1980s video games, where users manipulated starships to shoot up others by clicking the trigger of a joystick? On the surface, besides the improvement of graphics, not much has changed. The real difference lies not in the level of interactivity but how the limited interactivity places the user within a fictional, narrative-centered environment.

The early video games of the 1980s (like *Defender* and *Space Invaders*) placed users in fast-paced shoot-'em-up environments, where hordes of oncoming ships came at them onscreen. If players weren't quick enough, the ship exploded, and then they were usually given the use of another ship to begin the game again. However, in today's CD-ROM movies, users are placed in a dramatic environment where there is a story, and they play the lead in an unfolding plot within a virtual environment. Some readers might say that this is not so different from the computerized version of adventure role-playing games, like the *Exodus Ultima* series and other *Dungeons & Dragons* variants designed for computers. These adventures certainly told a story, and they allowed the user to play characters. However, despite the fact that these games do narrate an interactive story, they are *not* the same as the CD-ROM movies coming out today. Computerized role-playing games combined the elements of random combat, storytelling, puzzle-solving, limited character manipulation, and a fairly loose plot within a typically low resolution environment. But some of today's CD-ROMs place users within hi-res virtual worlds, where they are talked to and can talk back to other real-looking characters within an unfolding story, which has a tight plot, a set beginning, middle, and end. These stories are more like movies than games. Participants learn about the world through exploration by talking and listening to other people and by responding to the environment, and as users do this they get caught up in the story. These CD-ROM movies have similarities to some environmental theater productions, which also have interactive capabilities (though limited) between the performers and spectators.

Environmental Interactivity in Tony 'n' Tina's Wedding

Environmental theater broke down boundaries between performer and spectator by removing the illusion of nineteenth-century fourth-wall proscenium realism. The audience was no longer placed within an auditorium — it shared the same space as the performers. In the Off-Broadway production of *Tony 'n' Tina's Wedding* (which opened in 1988) performers present a mock Italian wedding ceremony and reception, to which audience members are invited as guests. Tony and Tina have their wedding at Washington Square Church then pose for pictures on the steps of the church and drive off in stretch limousines to the reception — a simulated nightclub two blocks away. During the performance, characters talk with the spectators around the cash bar, the dance floor, and tables. Within the hour of the guests' arrival, the owner of the club comes out serving a baked ziti dinner.

However, the spectator-participant effects no real change in the production. The plot of *Tony 'n' Tina's Wedding* is set; the circumstances remain the same. What occurs outside the unchanging main plot is what different spectators do and say to the performers, who usually give immediate, improvisational feedback. Despite the actions of the spectators, the wedding goes on. Unlike the spectator-participant of *Quantum Gate*, who plays a character who actually propels the story forward, the spectators of *Tony 'n' Tina* are voyeurs, viewing and interacting with other characters. According to psychology professor Richard Atkins, the popularity of the show may come from the premise that people "'enjoy looking through the window at other people's lives'" (Benton 1990:5), allowing them in this case to discover that the bride's and groom's families have been feuding for generations. Participants, as they interact with the performers, also make other discoveries: Tina likes to "play around"; the maid of honor is pregnant, and the father is an usher; the priest gets drunk; the best man deals drugs in the bathroom; Tina's divorced parents have a fight; and Tony and Tina have a fight. Instead of affecting the plot, participants express their own values and beliefs that would not or could not be expressed at a real wedding.

CD-ROM movies do not reach this level of improvisational interaction. Instead of stepping into the environment of the performers, the participant presses onscreen buttons to manipulate the actors into performing certain predetermined behaviors, as if the participant were toggling a switch or checking off the correct answer on a multiple-choice test in an attempt to find ways to "win." Participants do not usually play themselves as they do in *Tony 'n' Tina's Wedding*. In *Quantum Gate* director Roach has the user play a character in a story that ultimately presents the moral question, Is it right to destroy an alien civilization in order to save your own? Instead of saying yes or no, or allowing the spectator-participant to say whatever they want to say within a given scene, they are presented with a predetermined response to what the user's character feels about the situation on the other side of the screen. This response is recorded, programmed by the director/writer, and does not necessarily reflect what the spectator-participant may feel about the situation. What CD-ROM movies do is give the spectator-participant an illusion of interaction between moments of cinematically shaped noninteractive scenes.

In *Quantum Gate* the user plays the character of Drew Griffin in first person mode. The character is never seen onscreen. What is seen onscreen is what the character sees. The user hears such pre-recorded thoughts as, "Jesus, this is big," when they listen to Dr. Marks's briefing on how the Earth is going to lose its sustainable ecostructure within five years. In these kinds of scenes there are no pre-recorded responses the participant can choose from. It's linear, which, according to Brenda Laurel's theory of computer-interactive design, should not be a problem because everything within the interactive movie doesn't have to be openly interactive, where the story branches off in many directions leaving the spectator-participant no sense of an unfolding plot. Instead, users are placed within the plot, like the spectators at *Tony 'n' Tina's Wedding*, and they can, in some scenes, just sit back and watch. But at other times the CD-ROM user has to interact to move the plot forward, which differs from *Tony 'n' Tina*, where a spectator could just watch without participating, and if they do perform actions, they don't influence the plot. Rather, when the spectator interacts in the play, it heightens their experience of it — there is a sense of involvement or inclusiveness. Because of its dramatic structure, similar feelings can be found in CD-ROM movies.

In her book, *Computers as Theater* (1991), Laurel provides the virtual-age architect with a theoretical framework on how to design human-computer experiences based on Aristotle's theories of the dramatic form. If a dramatic approach is used to govern design, then computer programs would engage the user in an aesthetic, pleasurable *experience*. Laurel turns to Aristotle's *Poetics* as a model for this potential.

Designing an Aristotelian Experience

This kind of experience cannot be found just by designing cute interfaces — slick graphics, digital sound, or even real actors that make up the mise-en-scène onscreen, (which was the problem with the 1980s video games — all about graphics and combat but lacking dramatic experience). "Thinking about interfaces is thinking too small," Laurel says. She doesn't want a better interface for the computer "desktop" but a way to create "imaginary worlds" that "extend, amplify, and enrich our own capacities to think, feel, and act" in the real world (1993:32–33). Laurel wants interfaces designed to give a dramatic and multisensory experience. In the early 1970s Laurel directed an environmental production of *Robin Hood* near a gothic tower by a lake. A minstrel on the stage invited the audience to follow this guide. She led the audience through the woods and around the lake where they watched different scenes unfold in action (197). This was a real-world virtual reality theater production providing 3D sensory immersion, and this is the kind of experience that Laurel would want computer users to enjoy. Current technologies may not offer such an immersive experience, but computer interfaces should allow for dramatic interaction between performer and spectator.

Laurel sees plot as a "flying wedge," where there are, at the beginning of the performance, many possibilities, but as the performance unfolds the many possible choices become a field of probable choices, until the plot narrows to a point where there can be only the necessary outcome of a given action. In an interactive "flying wedge,"

> the shaping of potential is influenced by people's real-time choices and actions, pruning possibilities and creating lines of probability that differ from session to session and person to person. The 'flying wedge' can be pointed off in different directions, thus increasing the program's potential for many whole actions. (Laurel 1993:72)

According to this logic, within a CD-ROM interactive movie there would be many choices at the beginning of the movie, and as the participant is thrust into the plot and chooses from several different possibilities, each choice is pared down to probable actions as she progresses over time through the story's potential.

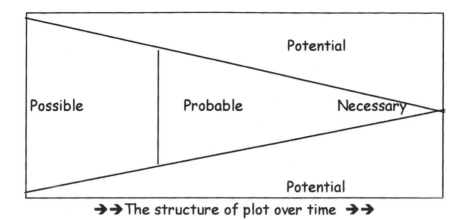

➜➜The structure of plot over time ➜➜

(Laurel 1993:70)

Laurel's model of plot over time is similar to Stephen Hawking's space-time diagrams given for his phenomenological explanation of how past events affect the present and how present actions affect the future as explained in his work *A Brief History of Time* (1988). His explanation of space and time is useful in understanding Laurel's model for plot. Hawking describes how cones of light intersect at the present, where the "absolute future of the event is the region inside the future light cone of P[resent]. It is the set of all events that can possibly be affected by what happens at P" (25). Laurel's "Necessary" point of convergence as necessitated by plot is Hawking's "Present" point as necessitated by time-events. Hawking's understanding of predictability when one knows everything on a particular timeline in the past is important in understanding the unfolding of plot in an interactive narrative. Let's examine Laurel's and Hawking's models by seeing how Roach lays out his dramatic scenes.

There are fifteen scenes that occur over a three-day game-time period (which takes about two to three hours to play). The scenes are linear and build to the climax on Day 3. Modeled on the "flying wedge" plot, the movie begins in Drew's quarters, where he has many possibilities to choose from. Each decision leads to further probable (no longer possible) actions. In Hawking's terms, past events will affect the present, and present actions will affect the future. For example, the user can manipulate Drew to access a message from his mother (who yells at him for joining the army) or read the news on the computer panel (which gives the user some background to the story, the UN's involvement in the Rangoon incident, and so forth). Later in the day, Private Michaels talks to the user about how the VR helmets used in combat could be altering what the wearer sees. This fear was foreshadowed in the news story that described the Rangoon incident. Is the news story correct, or is Private Michaels right in guessing that the UN is in the midst of a cover-up? The plot narrows as the user chooses different types of interactions, building toward the climax. An action taken in the "Present" will start the user on a whole new cycle of future probabilities directly linked to actions taken in the past. Part of the plot buildup is through computer manipulation (as programmed by the director), where the user is no longer given a choice to explore but is forced into a scene. This propels the plot forward, and within these scenes the user is given hints guiding her to explore different options during "free exploration" phases.*

After the user explores Drew's quarters during Day 1, the director forces the user into the orientation room by handing the control over to the computer, which locks out any "free exploration" by freezing the mouse control. The computer guides the user into the orientation room, where Drew is debriefed by Colonel Saunders and Dr. Marks. Before the briefing begins, the screen fades to black, indicating that Drew fell asleep while waiting. He dreams about his mother and his ex-girlfriend, Jenny. After a few moments Colonel Saunders fades in onscreen and forces Drew to wake up.

During Drew's dream the spectator sees in the upper left corner of the screen a panning image to Drew's mother, who slowly fades in and says that there's been an accident. That image fades to a pastoral painting of nude children dancing in a circle and the sounds of water from a running brook. A video image of Jenny fades in at each corner of the picture, one at a time, as Drew says, "Jenny, my angel, don't ever leave me," followed by the sound of a siren. Suddenly, Colonel Saunders's face appears in a close-up, laid over the upper-right-hand quadrant of the scene, saying, "Griffin, wake-up!"

This scene represents Roach's desire that the interface of his CD-ROM movie be presented in three layers. The first layer is the physical environment that the user walks around in, the one created from computer graphics. Over this, the second layer presents the digital video clips. It is in this layer that the user interacts with other characters and allows them some control over how the story unfolds. Roach says that each character the user encounters has "a unique,

---

*Breaking the 2,000-year-old Aristotelian hold on casual dramatic structure, the Critical Art Ensemble writes (in regard to video documentaries):

> Preferably, one should use liquid associational structures that invite various interpretations. To be sure, all imaging systems are mediated by the viewer: The question is, to what degree? Few systems invite interpretation, and hence meaning is imposed more often than it is created. Many producers, for fear of allowing interpretation to drift out of control, have shunned the use of associational structures for politicized electronic imaging. Further, associational films tend toward the abstract, and therefore become confusing, making them ineffective among the disinterested. These prompt the eternal return to more authoritarian [Aristotelian] models. The answer to such commentary is that the viewer deserved the right to disinterest, and the freedom to drift. Confusion should be seen as an acceptable aesthetic. The moment of confusion is the precondition or the skepticism necessary for radical thought to emerge (1994:51).

This model for associational video can also be applied to multimedia projects, which, because of hypertextual capabilities, are more open to a non–Aristotelian model.

abstracted background that expresses your feelings about that character" (Roach 1993). The third layer is what occurs in Drew's head — his thoughts, memories, and fantasies. Roach's sequel to *Quantum Gate*, *The Vortex* (1994), is designed so that what the user chooses early on will influence what scenes will develop later. "'Whole sections drop out depending on choices viewers make.... If you drive the character to a psychotic state, the soundtrack becomes psychotic to reflect that'" (Trumbull 1994:4). Whether this multilayered experience works well depends on how the computer appears to be "intelligent" — which ultimately is determined by the quality of the interactive dramatic design of the movie. Several groups have experimented with "intelligent" interactive designs by using different kinds of models to explore them.

Intelligent Interactions

Edward Barrett in *Contextual Media* (1995) uses a museum in Dunquin on the west coast of Ireland to provide an example of how an interface design fails to connect with the "user" (the visitor) in an interactive way because it lacks a human and dramatic feeling. The museum is an "Interpretive Centre" for the former people of Blasket Islands, located offshore from the museum. In it, Barrett says, you can "look at the walls, the texts, the photographs; hear music and voices. At the far end you can stand near a big window and look out at the islands. The Interpretive Centre is either an interface for what lies outside of it, or a shield barring you from a world you will never really know" (xii). However, Barrett adds, the local schoolmaster is "the only real connection to the world of the islanders." The schoolmaster is the "real" interface that allows visitors to interact with the dying world of the Blasket Islanders. Obviously, *Quantum Gate* is not a museum, but in a similar way director Roach provides in his CD-ROM movie an interface into the world of the movie through the mind and motivation of Drew Griffin. Participants actually see into Drew's mind — and for a time they share that mind in a dramatic experience, providing a level of psychology absent from most computer games. The images present the means by which users become connected to his world.

This CD-ROM shows how computer experiences are being designed from the basis of "*qualitative* interaction, dialogue, and conversation," a process that Allucquere Stone, in her work *The War of Desire and Technology* (1995), favors. In this way computers become "arenas for social experience and dramatic interaction, a type of media more like public theater .... Inside the little box are *other people*" (15–16). One can see how the Blasket Island museum provides the visitor with quantitative analysis, displaying artifacts as bits of cultural information, with no interaction with people. However, in order to really get to know the Blasket Islanders — what lies outside the museum — there needs to be an interface that doesn't bar one from a "world you will never know," as Barrett would argue. At the center of this kind of interface are other people — like the schoolmaster who speaks only a dialect of Irish, a real person visitors can interact with. Whether this interface design involves the use of real people (as in MUDs or chat rooms online) or Laurel's human-designed computational dramatic characters (1993:144–149)—like the characters seen in *Quantum Gate*—doesn't matter. Humanity has been situated into the heart of the computer. From this viewpoint computers no longer just store quantitative bits of constructed information like the Blasket Islanders' artifacts sitting in a museum glassed off from visitors, but computer programs will take these quantitative bits and make them come "alive," resolving them into sites of social worlds where meaning arises from dramatic interaction through the qualitative combination of people and objects. This kind of place is liminal, a place where we are no longer human, yet we are human. Stone says that we will "call into question the structure of meaning production by which we recognize each other as human" (1995:173). The virtual age sees humans interacting not face-to-face in the physical presence of others but with and through machines that seem "intelligent."

Experimenters at MIT explored this "otherness" of human-computer interaction within an "intelligent" virtual environment during the fall semester of 1992. Their experiment has useful consequences in the future development of CD-ROM movies. Here Davenport and Friedlander, in the chapter "Interactive Transformational Environments" in *Contextual Media*, write about how they collaborated with students to design and build an installation at the Villers Experimental Media Theater on campus. This was a walk-through installation where visitors encountered different rooms representing metaphorical environments of water, earth, and air. As visitors moved through each area they had to solve puzzles before they could move into the next room. In the water room visitors entered a large fishbowl-like structure, its walls made of scrim rising 40 feet into the air. Images of water were projected on the wall. In the center of the space was a 17-foot-long fabricated whale. The visitor had to talk to the whale and solve puzzles in order to get out of the room. From outside the room a guide operated a computer control console that gave the visitor hints to the person inside. The guide gave such clues as physical and audio signals, including a hand pointing "go left" on a monitor or a whispered voice from over a speaker. The designers' purpose for this exhibit was to experiment with the following question: "What would it be like to be in a world that 'knew' we were there, and that was totally responsive to our every move; a world that literally transformed itself as we traversed it?" (Barrett 1995:1).

The external guide was designed as a precursor to an intelligent machine that changes the environment depending on how people interact with the interfaces located in the environment. How would an intelligent machine behave within an environment of a CD-ROM movie? How would the user interact with something that responds consciously and intelligently? This MIT experiment in machine intelligence challenges the notion of computer cognitive intelligence — a "psychology for describing inner states in terms of logic and rules ... and the computer presence served as its sustaining myth," as sociologist Sherry Turkle says (1995:128). It is a precursor to an intelligent computer that will be able to engage the user at new levels of dramatic interactive experiences.

Laurel would argue that interactive metaphorical objects (such as those used in the MIT experiment) are usually "guided by the goal of representing *objects and relations among them* as opposed to representing *actions*" (1993:133). The question is, How does a scene, or object, prompt the user into action? An experiment done by the Computer Science's Oz Group and the Drama Department at Carnegie Mellon University in the spring of 1990, provided a plotted improvisation of a mediated experience based not on the relationships of objects but on the actions of people. A "user" wanted to buy a bus ticket and interacted with actors who wore headsets and were guided by a director backstage. A director oversaw the action and tried to guide the actors in an attempt to provide the participant (the interactor) a satisfying experience based on an unfolding sequence of actions that made up the plot:

MIN:SEC

0:00   Interactor enters bus station. He asks when the bus for San Francisco leaves and how much it costs. Clerk answers. Interactor says he wants to buy a ticket.

0:30   *Director tells Clerk not to sell ticket.* Clerk asks to see Interactor's money. He doesn't have two hundred dollars, but offers his credit card. Clerk says credit cards are no good. Interactor shows some money and asks if it is enough.

1:10   *Director tells Clerk to send Interactor back to his seat.* Clerk says she can't sell it for that much and that he should sit down. Interactor sits down and waits.

1:30   *Director tells Clerk to call her boss about credit cards.* Clerk asks for Interactor's credit card, announcing she will call her boss to see if credit cards are acceptable.

2:00   *Director tells Clerk to stall Interactor but eventually sell ticket.* Clerk calls her boss. Interactor waits.

2:20   *Director tells Tom to enter.* Clerk is still talking. Tom enters and sits down. Interactor watches Tom enter.

2:40   *Director tells Tom to buy ticket.* Tom gets up and walks to the desk. Clerk finishes call and tells Interactor to wait for her boss to come back. Tom tries to buy a ticket.

3:00   *Director tells Clerk to notice Tom is blind.* Interactor waits and observes conversation between Tom and Clerk. Tom has no money, and Clerk says Tom must wait for a credit card check as well....

6:00   *Director tells Punk to enter.* Interactor and Tom continue filling out the forms.

6:15   *Director tells Punk he wants money.* The Punk enters and asks Clerk about the next bus to Chicago.

6:40   *Director tells Punk to make himself noticed.* The Punk looks around and asks Tom if he's going to Philly. Punk asks the Interactor for a dollar.

7:20   *Director tells Punk to deal with Tom, not the Interactor.* The Punk turns his attention to asking Tom for money. Meanwhile, the Interactor is filling in the sheet....

9:05   *Director tells Punk to get the money.* Punk starts to harass Tom.

9:30–11:00   *Director tells Punk to build the intensity seven times, pumping him up as the tension of the scene builds.* The Punk increasingly harasses Tom. Tom appeals to the Clerk. Punk argues with the Clerk. Punk returns to harassing Tom. Interactor watches as the situation escalates around him.

11:15   *Director tells Punk to pull his knife on Tom.* Punk pulls his knife on Tom. He tells Tom it is a knife. Interactor tells Clerk to call the police. Punk violently pulls and disables telephone. Interactor jumps out of the way and sits on the other side of the station. Punk asks Tom for his wallet while Interactor watches....

13:00   *Director tells Punk to allow Interactor to go to desk.* Punk tells Interactor he can go to desk. Clerk gives Interactor itinerary. *Director tells Clerk to give Interactor gun.* Clerk gives Interactor gun. As Punk moves to Tom's dufflebag and searches it, Interactor returns to seat and reads itinerary, doing nothing about gun in pocket.

13:30   *Confused, Director asks Clerk if Interactor has gun.* Clerk nods her head yes. Done with Tom's dufflebag, Punk goes back to desk and asks Clerk for cash in desk drawer, his back to the Interactor.

14:00   Very slowly, the Interactor stands up, points gun at Punk and tells him to sit down and drop the knife. The Punk argues with the Interactor, not believing he will shoot. Finally, Punk turns his back, and then tells Interactor to go ahead and shoot.

14:30   Interactor points gun up in the air and fires it. Punk dramatically falls to the ground.(Kelso 1992:8–10)

This experiment helped the computer interactive designers understand what it is like to be "immersed in a dramatic interactive world" that the experimenters discovered heightened the drama for the participants — "causing immediate, personal emotions, not the traditional vicarious empathy for other characters" found in conventional drama (Kelso 1992:13–14). The Oz Group's research deals with how to design intelligent computer "agents" — the characters that the user interacts with — from the basis of artificial intelligence. Joseph Bates, head of the Oz

Group, felt that one of the best ways to produce this is to develop an "architecture for mind, called Tok, that exhibits some signs of internal goals, reactivity, emotion, natural language ability, and knowledge of agents (self and other) as well as of the simulated physical micro-world" (1992:2). This artificial simulation requires not so much the understanding of a software engineer but the knowledge of a playwright — one who knows how the characters in a play are motivated to action by desire. Laurel uses Aristotle's *Poetics* as a model to analyze the dramatic approach of the playwright and then explains how this same approach can be applied to computer software design. The computer program, she believes, must inherently represent a means for dramatic action.

In the 1970s to 1980s machines were considered primarily computational tools. Humans were intelligent, computers were not. They simply responded to programming. These ideas have evolved. Life is no longer a question of humanity versus machines, where the computer is just a number cruncher for a corporate world motivated by a work ethic, but, as Stone observes, the computer — thanks to hackers tapping into the computer's ludic potential — can now be seen "as arenas for social experience" (1995:15). Today directors and artists are designing new kinds of dramatic experiences on the computer. Turkle says, "These days, it is not unusual for people to say that they assume machines will learn how to behave *as if* they were intelligent and even alive" (1995:87). Part of the Oz project experiment was to "learn how to build convincing characters to populate these computer-mediated worlds," creating "dramatic frameworks for guiding the activities of both user and fictitious character" (Peterson 1992). The dramatic environment should effect the players as well as the onscreen artificial characters. Turkle, commenting on the Oz Group, says that they are not creating artificial characters who have real emotional desires, but they "generate behaviors that people interpret as expressing appropriate states of emotion" caused by how the AI agents "react to their environment" (1995:97).

The computer is programmed to simulate a physical environment, and several characters, guided by what Bates calls the "Drama Manager," influence the actions of the "drama" (Kelso 1992:2). It's important to note that 20 years before the Oz Group began conducting their interactive experiments, there existed and continues to exist an appropriate model for interactive engineers to learn about dramatic interactivity: the role-playing game. When I read Kelso's conclusion on the interactive bus stop experiment mentioned above: "interactors found interactive drama more powerful, easily causing immediate, personal emotions, not the traditional vicarious empathy for other characters" (1992:13–14), I couldn't help thinking that I have already experienced this in such games as *Dungeons & Dragons*, which was published in 1974. The Oz Group and others experimenting with and designing interactive movies and experiences will find interesting models existing in such games — which I examined in chapter 1. The role of the gamemaster, for example, who is in charge of guiding the overall narrative of a role-playing game adventure, parallels the Oz Group's "Drama Manager."

Richard Schechner foreshadowed interactive games and technologies in his environmental theater productions of the 1960s and 1970s. Aching to snap the pervasiveness of passive theater audiences, he placed them in environments where active participation became easier. He realized that "What is at stake is not the story being told but the telling of the story," and the only way to bring this back was through participation among the performers and spectators "not as a mechanical inevitability" but to "inject destiny," which "restores danger, excitement, and vitality" to the theater (1996:78–80). The "mechanical inevitability" challenges game designers and interactive movie producers to move away from interaction for the sake of having interaction and attempt to reflect more of Schechner's 1960s interactive theater aesthetics:

1. The audience is in a living space and a living situation. Things may happen to and with them as well as "in front" of them.

2. When a performer invites participation, he must be prepared to accept and deal with the spectator's reactions.

3. Participation should not be gratuitous. In participatory situations game structure replaces aesthetics. Instead of events worked out beforehand, there is a "game plan," a set of objectives, moves, and rules that are generally known or explained. The game plan is flexible, adapting to changing situations. (1996:78–80)

Granted, this game structure works more easily on live interactive sites like role-playing games, but it still challenges designers to create interactive games and environments that reflect more realistic interactions. This is what Bates is attempting to do. The agents would have to come alive through artificial intelligence. They would adapt and change, updating the game's database on the hard drive or recordable DVD drive.

Not only is environmental theater closely related to role-playing games (Schechner's book *Environmental Theater* was first published during the same period as the release of *Dungeons & Dragons*), but the idea that space — the physical milieu — can be alive is certainly a precursor to virtual and artificial environments, from Disneyland to such historical recreations as Plimoth Plantation. Most of the Oz Group's designs are text-based or use low-res graphics. Their live agents are modeled on Disney animation. Quoting such works as *Disney Animation: The Illusion of Life* (1981), Bates believes that AI researchers should turn to animators to learn how to simulate life. He writes, "If the character does not react emotionally to events, if they don't care, then neither will we. The emotionless character is lifeless, as a machine" (1994:2). The Oz Group has not only ignored environmental theater history and role-playing games, but they have not even touched the possibilities of interactive dramatic experiences found in CD-ROM movies.

According to Chris Roberts the director for the CD-ROM movies *Wing*

Commander III: The Heart of the Tiger (1994) and *WC IV: The Price of Freedom* (1995), there have been three generations of computer adventure games: "first text, then graphics, and now CD-ROM. It makes the story much more compelling because it has real people, with real emotion" (Frase 1995:185). And this fact — actors with video can deliver an emotional experience when placed within the context of a good story — explains why CD-ROM movies today challenge the Oz Group experiments in AI interactivities. CD-ROM movies like *Quantum Gate* and *The Price of Freedom* offer life-like environments and people who conduct intelligent actions within a dramatic context. The Oz Group researchers are stuck in the first and second generations of text and graphic computer adventures, with the exceptional goal of designing agents that are "thinking, feeling, living creatures, of creating at least the illusion of life, of building apparently autonomous entities that people, especially the creators, would genuinely care about" (Bates 1994:1). They want users to experience a virtual world by interacting with intelligent agents who can sense the user's presence and adjust their actions accordingly — all within a dramatic structure.

In the Oz Group Tok program, "Lyotard," the interactor plays with a text-based AI cat, who at first is afraid of the "user" and actually bites him or her:

Player:	(*GO-TO "the sunroom").
Lyotard:	(*JUMP-OFF "the chair").
	(*RUN-TO "the sunroom").
Player:	(*GO-TO "the sunroom").
Lyotard:	(*LOOKAROUND NERVOUSLY).
Player:	(*PET "Lyotard").
Loyotard:	(*BITE "Player").
	(*RUN-TO "the diningroom"). (Bates 1992:4)

Later, when Lyotard gets hungry, the player feeds him and the cat becomes friendly. Throughout this minidrama the user gets the feeling that the cat is intelligent, even though it decides actions based on a database of words that connote emotions and behaviors that give it an illusion of aliveness — especially when it behaves within the proper context of the player's inputs. However, do these AI character's actions differ so much from how Dr. Marks reacts to a user, depending on whether or not the user offers to light her cigarette in a scene from *Quantum Gate*? Users may be more impressed with Lyotard because they don't expect representations — text or graphics — to behave intelligently, but in CD-ROM movies they see human beings (recorded) whom they expect to respond "intelligently" to their own logical actions. The challenge is to take the level of reaction and intelligence within the Lyotard program into interactive movies: open architecture within a dramatic environment.

Bates would probably argue that CD-ROM movies and other adventure games are not truly interactive because the users do not get to input anything they want into the virtual world represented onscreen. A user can say or do almost anything to Lyotard, and the cat would probably react appropriately. However, in a CD-ROM movie a person may be given only two or three pre-recorded items to choose from. It's a measure of dramatic control and limited CD-ROM space. But even if their tools are different, the two models do have the same goal — providing an interactive dramatic experience. What will be interesting to see is the combination of AI research with digital video technology, when interactive computer movies will have AI models that open up the space to wider ranging interactions among the characters found in an interactive movie. Both Laurel's and Bates's theories are useful in defining the limits of current technology, and these theories can be seen working themselves out at some level in Greg Roach's CD-ROM production. His interactive movie becomes a benchmark for determining how interactivity was done in the past. It won't necessarily hold true for the future.

In *Quantum Gate* director and writer Roach guides the participant into certain logical and probable paths that will take them to the story's necessary outcome by layering clues that force the user into the dramatic action of the production. At the orientation scene described earlier (where Drew falls asleep and dreams about Jenny), Drew and the other soldiers get briefed by Dr. Marks, who warns them about Earth's failing ecosystem. At the end of her briefing she begins to emotionally break up, and Colonel Saunders tells her that she has said enough. We hear Drew say, "That's odd," clueing the spectator-participant to follow up on this observation at a later time. During breakfast the next morning Drew has the opportunity to sit with Dr. Marks and talk to her. In the scene she wants Drew to light her cigarette. However, depending on how the user responds to her — whether Drew gives her a light or not — will determine what she will say to him, whether she will give more hints about the UN mission, or whether she will give him the cold shoulder, if the user doesn't respond properly in the scene. Here is another example in which the user as Drew is "forced" to stay in character. The player may disagree about smoking and refuse to light Dr. Marcus's cigarette through the character of Drew, but this will cause the player to lose information crucial to the dramatic tension of the story. This situation is similar to Lyotard's (in the Oz AI program) virtually biting the user when they pet him, but if the user feeds him first, he'll purr. Roach, as the director, has forced the "audience" to choose between a moral stance and the dramatic need of the story. By combining Laurel's concept of the dramatic form as applied to interactive theories with the Oz Group's sense of artificial entities that respond to their environment and applying them together in a cinematic model — using digitized actors for his agents — Roach, in a way, has created an "intelligent" interactive CD-ROM movie.

His movie breaks down near the climax, when it turns into a low-res video game. During the climax the user fights what seem to be large alien bugs who are preventing the UN from completing its mission. During the Final Battle scene the spectator-participant enters a low-resolution early 1980s-style video game and shoots at the enemy. However, no matter what the user does, the enemy overwhelms Drew, causing the puncture of his encounter suite and the removal of the VR helmet. However, this reveals a surprise ending that confirms Private Michaels's paranoia of how the UN military command was manipulating its soldiers. According to Laurel's plotted "flying wedge," there can be only one conclusion to the story. But Roach places the user into a poor-looking video game and allows the user to keep shooting at these alien bugs until Drew is defeated. Whether Drew runs, fights, or tries to hide, there is only one outcome. Roach seems to want to give the user a means for "interacting" through the use of a video game, but because it is not required for the dramatic experience, the low-res combat takes away from the overall drama. It would have been better if he had stuck to a hi-res video clip, which may not have been interactive, but would have shown the "necessary" outcome in a more realistic way.

Past, Present, and Future of Interactive Design

A precursor to CD-ROM interactive movies occurred at the 1967 World's Fair in Montreal. A Czech cinematographer, Raduz Cincera, developed the Kino-Automat, an interactive movie experience that melded onscreen action with an actor onstage. The audience was asked during certain parts of the 45-minute film *One Man and His World* (1967) what decision the hero should make. The film stopped, and the actor playing the hero asked for help in making this decision. The audience pressed a red or green button and voted whether or not the character of Mr. Novak should be confronted with a moral and ultimately plot-twisting dilemma:

> … just before his wife was due home, he confronted at the door of his apartment a beautiful blonde woman clad only in a towel — somehow she had locked herself outside her own apartment next door. *Question*: should he let her in? *Audience answer* (every time): Yes. Later, when his wife (misunderstanding everything, …) ran away, Mr. Novak pursued her in a car. A policeman hailed him down. *Question*: should he break the law and keep driving? *Audience answer* (nearly always): Yes. Later still, Mr. Novak believed that a young man who could help him was in a certain apartment. *Question*: should he dash in and find the young man, even though the apartment tenant tried to bar his way? *Audience answer* (nearly always): Yes. Finally, a porter barred Mr. Novak's way when he was trying to put out what looked at that point like a minor fire. *Question*: should he hit the porter over the head and go about his business? *Audience answer* (usually): Yes. (Fulford 1968:128–129)

With the publication of *Quantum Gate* in 1993, CD-ROMs became cinematic, translating a 26-year historical echo of Cincera's World's Fair movie into computers, incorporating live actors within an animated virtual environment.

In 1977 George Lucas spent $10 million on his movie *Star Wars*. The same amount of money was spent on Chris Roberts's interactive CD-ROM *Wing Commander IV: The Price of Freedom* (1995). Both *WC III* and *IV* achieved a level of multimedia production that equaled Hollywood's production standards. The user is introduced to the main character through a 10-minute opening sequence that sets up the story. The participant in these CD-ROMs interacts with other characters on the ship by manipulating a character they can actually see (Mark Hamill). Between these scenes the user flies a ship on different missions reminiscent of video games, but in this case they are connected to the overall plot, and what occurs in the battles will affect how the user's character is treated by the other crew members back on the mother ship. At one point, as a player in *The Price of Freedom*, "your" captain, with whom you have served during the first part of this adventure and throughout the previous *Heart of the Tiger*, is replaced by a new captain. Your former captain suddenly decides to flee the ship in a shuttle, and you are ordered to bring him back or destroy him. At the crucial moment you are given a moral decision: follow orders or commit treason by joining your former captain. This is where interactors get to inject Schechner's destiny into their lives. No matter how some people may view this as trivial — millions each night watch inane television where their emotions are already predetermined. At least within this interactive movie experience we begin to see a new form of theater that restores some element of "danger, excitement, and vitality"— even through it is virtual (Schechner 1994:80). We have to think, and our decisions do have consequences within the movie.

Other CD-ROMs include such projects as *Steven Spielberg's Director's Chair* (1996), where users perform the role of a director going through an entire production cycle of a short movie. Rick Smolin's *Passage to Vietnam* allows users to experience a photojournalist's tour of Vietnam. There are hundreds of different products on the market, ranging from flight simulators to sexual stimulators, all averaging $30–$60 apiece. CD-ROMs are designed on a computer — where external files such as audio, video or film clips, graphic-environments — are edited and cut together on a hard drive. The separate components are stored as bits of data on the computer then accessed through programmed commands, using such languages as *Lingo*, Macromedia's *Director*, and other multimedia programming packages. Once everything is play-tested, the data is stored on a CD-ROM, which consumers purchase. CD-ROMs were given a technological and name overhaul with the release of Digital Video Disks (DVDs). DVDs increase the potential of interactive movie making. CD-ROM movie/game makers were constrained to a limited amount of video footage on a single CD-ROM. That is why many of the bigger productions comprise four to six discs, and they tend to take several solid days to complete. DVDs allow larger movies and clearer visual resolution.

James Cameron, the director of the *Terminator* movies and *Titanic* (1997), produced a new simulated theme park "ride," *T2 3-D: Battle Across Time* (1996), at Universal Studios in Florida. Priced at $60 million, the per-frame cost of this 12-minute environmental movie makes it one of the most expensive movies ever produced (Leydon 1996). The movie is an attempt, Cameron says, at "integrating film and the proscenium theatrical experience into the same project. We actually have characters jumping into the screen and back out of the screen, so we're breaking down that barrier between the audience and events in the picture" (Magid 1996:27). In Cameron's high-tech 70mm films the virtual onscreen image transforms into the real: Live actors come out of secret panels in the movie screen and onto the stage; when a frozen Terminator onscreen explodes into tiny drops of ice, mist sprays onto the spectators in the auditorium; and when the onscreen characters descend in an elevator, the audience's seats physically vibrate. Cameron's latest feat is a technological as well as a dramatic breakthrough and shows how the technology creates enveloping virtual experiences. The scene climaxes when the walls appear to rise around the audience, revealing a live computer projected on three 50X23-foot screens. Doubles for Arnold Schwarzenegger and Edward Furlong appear live onstage then meld into the onscreen actors during the scene.

Eventually, the designs of interactive CD-ROMs will attain a level of realism that will allow users to set themselves within an environment that will increasingly look like the holosuites from *Star Trek*. The closest this has come is in 3-D live chat rooms, such as Worlds Chat. Formerly chatrooms were all text-based, but through the evolving technology of VRML (Virtual Reality Modeling Language), users can choose an "avatar" (photorealistic virtual body) from a list and enter a fairly realistic imaged virtual room and talk to other avatars. With the right technology people could also have their face (or anyone else's, even an alien-like image from *Star Wars* or *Babylon 5*) scanned onto an avatar's body, creating a virtual masquerade. (See Li-Ron 1997.) Within a couple of years similar technologies will allow users to step into fantastic environments as themselves or others and perform role-playing adventures, dramatic scenes, perhaps guided by live or AI characters who oversee everyone's performance.

Chris Roberts's *Wing Commander III: The Heart of the Tiger*, starring Mark Hamill, placed the actors in front of bluescreens. As Roberts directed the actors, he looked at previously constructed virtual sets on video monitors, blocking the actors against the virtual backdrop — a technique used on *Babylon 5* and by George Lucas in the new *Star Wars* trilogy. In a *Playboy* virtual photoshoot users can click on a digitized model and have her stand and undress in different poses, in any combination the user desires (within the limits of the pre-recorded database). Each of Intel's new generation micro-chips focuses on the speed-up of video, sounds, and graphics on Pentium computers. This allows for faster frame rates for live-picture conferencing, as well as sharper images onscreen. It's only a matter of time before the actors will be scanned in and blocked by users with mouse-clicks.

When this technology fully arrives, one of the questions will be whether or not to place the image of a famous actor into a digitally made movie. Will the actors be able to copyright their image on the digital frontier? Or can a user scan an image of Arnold Schwarzenegger from a videocopy of *The Terminator* (1984) and place it into a VR chat room or into a homemade digital movie? Famous performers (and even nonactors) may become virtual actors: the director-writer-producer of the future could scan in the performers' images and, through advanced AI software, program them into virtual sets and export the movie out on the Internet for $20. This would allow nonactors to become virtual actors, as well. This is not a hypothetical issue. In an interview with George Lucas, the executive editor of *Wired*, Kevin Kelly (with Paula Parisi), asked him, "If somehow you had a 3-D digital Luke Skywalker, you could be putting him into movies for the next 100 years." Lucas responded, "That's what I'm doing anyway. I can put Yoda in a hundred movies."

The continuing conversation is revealing:

> *WIRED*: You can rent him out?
>
> Lucas: I can put him in the next Jim Carrey movie if I want to. I could work him just like an actor. Conceivably you can get to a point where you can create a character that anybody can use, and you can put him in any kind of an environment. ...
>
> *WIRED*: So how do you imbue them with spirit, and soul?
>
> LUCAS: It's no different than what Tolstoy did. You are going to be able to take Anna Karenina, turn her into a three-dimensional person, and put her into a particular environment instead of just a bunch of words on a page. The fact that eventually you'll have artificial intelligence that will be able to take on a particular persona is a whole other issue.... But we will be able to create the 3-D character. That's going to happen in a few years. The 3-D character is animated by a human being to make it react in a particular way, and that's Tolstoy. The real question is when the character starts to think for itself....
>
> *WIRED*: Who owns it? And who owns what it says?
>
> LUCAS: It's not a matter of who owns it, but what are you going to do with it? How are you going to relate to it? What happens if you fall in love with it? The question will be when do they start asking for their own rights? They'll say, "I have as much right to be here as you do, and the problem with these humans is that they are too dirty." And they will. (Kelly 1997:216)

For Lucas it's not a question of how it can be done or when the technology will arrive to do it. He's already doing some of this in his next *Star Wars* trilogy. What happens when digitized actors — based on the images of the real — start asking for SAG union rights?

Through interactive experiences spectator-participants are included in the action of CD-ROM movies and thus become cyborgs. Which is another way of saying that "the essence of technology is by no means anything technological," as Martin Heidegger said over 40 years ago (1993:311). It's an extension of human desire. The interactivity of cyborg pleasures offers new meaning to Laura Mulvey's observation in "Visual Pleasure and Narrative Cinema": "the mass of mainstream film, and the conventions within which it has consciously evolved, portray a hermetically sealed world which unwinds magically, indifferent to the presence of the audience, producing for them a sense of separation and playing on their voyeuristic phantasy" (1988:60). Through the dramatic experience of a CD-ROM movie and the potential of realistically imaged chat rooms and other online fantasy environments, technology no longer mediates our experience within the world. Will these entertainments of the future "hermetically seal" us off from the outside world, indifferent to our presence? Technology becomes the experience and we see not the world as we once knew it but step out of that world into a virtual reality of our imagination, a world dusted with phantasmatic images we can touch with a click of the mouse. And at some point in time we may no longer be able to tell the difference. The real world itself may become the mediation between ourselves and our virtual fantasies.

8

Interface as Performance: My Virtual Travels to Vietnam and the Klingon Empire

"But, Spock—They're Animals!"

The Klingons look at you from across a table. Your character's father lies dead on it. A dagger-shaped cursor, the size of a quarter, blinks onscreen — waiting for you to move it somewhere and click the mouse. Not sure of what to do you wait, hoping maybe the other Klingons will give you a hint. You perhaps think about how a Klingon would act here. However, as you pause in thought, the room and Klingons suddenly disappear as the simulation turns off. You now stand on a Federation holodeck like those seen on episodes of *Star Trek*. Gowron, leader of the Klingon High Council, standing in the middle of a black-box type theater checkered by yellow lines, glowers at you. He is not pleased. Acting as the stern tutor, he complains that you act too much like a human —*thinking* about decisions rather than *acting* upon them and dealing with the consequences later. He proffers an old Klingon proverb: "Act and ye shall *have* dinner. Think and ye shall *be* dinner." He allows the simulation to continue again, and this time you realize you don't have time to think — like a Klingon warrior you must act, now. On a hunch you move the cursor over the body of your father and click the mouse. The other Klingons place their hands on your father, lift their heads up and howl. You have just performed the Klingon death ritual, one of many cultural events you learn about in this CD-ROM, *Star Trek: Klingon* (1996), directed by Jonathan Frakes, a.k.a. the amiable Commander Riker from *The Next Generation* (1987–1994) (who also directed the last two *Star Trek* films).

Captain Kirk's assertion to his loyal friend Mr. Spock in the *Star Trek* movie

The Undiscovered Country (1991) reveals Kirk's prejudicial view of the Klingons, a warrior society enveloped by intrigue and revenge, attributes Spock was willing to overlook in order to make peace with a long-standing enemy of the idealistic and democratic Federation. Many fans have watched *Star Trek* for over 30 years, some perhaps wondering what it would be like if they could live in the *Star Trek* universe. With interactive media, fans gain some semblance of this universe by entering the fictional world of *Star Trek* and performing the part of a Klingon in this CD-ROM movie. In first-person view users perform the role of a Federation officer who plays a young Klingon warrior in an "immersive studies" holodeck program. The user learns about Klingon culture and customs during an investigation concerning the father's death. In this interactive movie the designers want users to "think like a Klingon." The underlying trope, "act and ye shall *have* dinner; think and ye shall *be* dinner," provides the thematic structure for the interface design. Users are not given time to think. It forces them to act instinctively. And it is this kind of interface — that surface tool which allows users to interact with onscreen characters and objects below the surface — that shapes (manipulates) how they perform their tasks, or roles, like a director fine-tuning an actor's performance: "more anger here, turn your head slowly this way, react to what your partner does," and so forth. All of this shapes a certain experience for an audience.

The kind of experience users have in interactive multimedia environments is determined by the kind of interface design they are confronted with. The story, actors, lighting, filmic editing, among many other factors that make up the content, do not alone define the type of adventure participants have. Rather, the interface — the mediator between us and the content — resolves the images of the content and shows users how they can interact with it. That is the core of interactive multimedia design. The interface is the medium by which users as spectators manipulate what they observe. It mediates how they will interact, participate. Multimedia is a kind of performance. It's like a two-dimensional stage production or cinematic experience incorporating actors, setting, light, sound, and so forth. As such, designers may want to think about different theories of performance when working on their projects.

What are the theories — not of drama — but of the theatrical mise-en-scene that can be applied to multimedia? When users interact with the onscreen interface, are they participating as performers? What kind of roles do they play? How are these roles determined — by a script or in other ways? What about lighting and sound design? What does it mean to navigate onscreen? Can navigation be seen as the equivalent to plot advancement and scene change? If clickable "interactive" icons are the tools to move around the "stage," how does blocking — the placement and movement of performers on stage — affect the aesthetics of the content? of the whole performance? Do interfaces need to change as the user advances through the multimedia application? Would this be a way to change the ambiance, the mood of a given adventure — as scenes change, so does the interface? What kind of roles do designers want users to play, and how are these roles manifested in the project? I don't offer complete answers here, but what I do examine needs to be thought about and eventually applied to multimedia applications if producers are to improve not just content but how users perceive that content through theatrical and cinematic elements.

By looking primarily at Rick Smolin's *Passage to Vietnam* (1995) and Jonathan Frakes's *Star Trek: Klingon* (1996), and somewhat at Chris Roberts's *Wing Commander IV: The Price of Freedom* (1995), I examine how interface design — and the theatrical elements that make up this design — determines how we experience multimedia. By doing so, I hope to articulate a poetics of multimedia interface design.

Ancient Virtual Experiences

Imagine yourself a student of Cicero. You have an oration to present to your fellow students tomorrow. He tells you, as he's been telling you and the other students all along, that the best way to memorize your oration is to walk through a building and picture different images on the wall. This mnemonic device allows you to remember your speech. Rhetoricians call this a "memory palace," which I see as an ancient forerunner of multimedia design. (I examine this to show that "multimedia" isn't as new or unique or as technologically mediated as we may think.) We normally think about interfaces as a means to interact (to control) technology. But I see them as the way our own consciousness interacts with the phenomena of our world. Our physical body is the interface enabling us to experience the world we perceive through a mind. We have eyes and hands to press buttons on a computer (a material outcome of thought), and thus we get it to do what we want it to do (most of the time). Mary Baker Eddy argues with philosophical logic that "Mortal mind perpetuates its own thought. It constructs a machine, manages it, and then calls it material. A mill at work or the action of a water-wheel is but a derivative from, and continuation of, the primitive mortal mind" (1906:399). Computer interfaces are simply tools allowing us to interact with virtual environments (constructed by people) on the other side of the screen, whereas in "real life" our bodies are the interface, the means of interaction in the "real world" environment. From Eddy's logic it would seem that virtual life is no more nor less real than the actual. From this point of view the phenomenological world seems to be a virtual reality of the mind.

Following Cicero's memory developments, the Italian missionary, Matteo Ricci, also developed a mnemonic device while in China. He placed ideograms and pictures around different rooms "as paintings in a gallery" (Woolley 1992: 139). In addition, medieval churches became a mnemonic device representing early Christian history. Through "strategically placed" objects and memorials "an entire cathedral became a metaphorical representation of the pilgrim's progress from birth through to death and salvation" (Woolley 1992:139). Images (perhaps even sounds and live events stirred Ricci's imagination) triggered —

like the click of a mouse on a computer-screen icon — stories, orations, and histories long since told. This "memorative art" process had its roots in the orators of ancient times, who prepared speeches by "symbolizing each paragraph by a properly chosen mental image," Bernheimer explains (1956:228). The orator would then walk through a building and place these images around different sections. "Each image had its 'set' on a column, in a corner or on an arch, where it would remain in store until it was recalled" (229). These virtual objects placed in the mind on actual architecture — like icons of a computer interface — were mnemonically activated by the orators, allowing them to complete their narration.

In a similar way to how "memory palaces" are constructed, Gregory Ulmer in *Heuretics: The Logic of Invention* (1994), applies hypermedia, or interactive thinking — "a method for writing and thinking electronically" (45) — to research done for "a follies performance in a simulated saloon of the 1880s" during Montana's centennial celebration in 1989 (54). He would like to see this kind of electronic thinking applied to liberal arts education: "hypermedia does for scholarship what photography did for portrait painting," Ulmer contends (29). He is not interested in technology per se but in how it creates a new kind of thinking process that would "entail a revision of the liberal arts *trivium* (grammar, rhetoric, logic) open to writing on a screen as well as on paper" (17). Ulmer sees interface as "another name for 'rhetoric'" (28), and like Cicero's memory palace, multimedia — without the technical components — become a tool for hyperthinking. Technology ends up reshaping how we think, write, and learn. An interface is but a new technological phenomenon for rhetoric.

We were (and are) satisfied by simple interfaces. We read words in a novel and are taken to past events, such as the Vietnam War, or we are thrown into a *Star Trek* future. Words on paper pages are an interface into an author's world, a way into the architecture of an author's imagination. Movies provide an interface into recorded and edited fictional and historical events. So why is it at this point in time that images, motion pictures, text, and sound converge onto a computer screen in the form of multimedia? Why is there a need for multimedia *interactivity*— button pushing and branching plot paths? The art of interactive multimedia design — as well as the accelerated growth and demand for new kinds of multimedia products — signifies that people (designers, artists, and consumers) are tiring of what museum curator and scholar Mary Nooter Roberts claims as the "ocularcentric bias [that] characterizes modernity.... Museums and exhibitions strive to isolate vision by creating a serene, hypothetically sublime, atmosphere in which the other perceptions are muted, even effaced" (Roberts and Vogel 1994:71). Ancient memory palaces and even traditional museums of our day are silent edifices filled out with our imagination. Multimedia leaves less to the imagination, layering the environment with multitrack images and sound.

Could it be that this desire for multisensory physicalization coupled with a daily inundation of multimedia cornucopia makes it so that some people simply *can't* accept just a static picture in a museum? Some people, like Roberts, think that the picture's missing something.* They want more than a one-track image encompassed by physical silence. Theater set designer John Conklin believes that once an object has been placed in a traditional museum it loses its original basis in performance. "Maybe it's frames," he states, "the gold frames drive me berserk.... Maybe that's the problem with museums: the stuff is always there. There is no event. We remove the work from a performance and set it in a static situation" (in Roberts and Vogel 1994:71). Conklin argues for the performed life of objects: "Life is performance, settings, costumes, scenes. Art is theatrical," he says (77). The power of a play (where Conklin is coming from) produced onstage versus one that is read lies in the fact that in the former an entire mise-en-scene is brought to bear on the senses of an audience to convey a story and in the latter the mise-en-scene must be created in one's own mind. This is what Rick Smolin does with his *Vietnam* multimedia project. He has taken a potential museum exhibit and layered it with theatrical techniques to create a "life-like" experience. "The experiential mode," says Donald Norman in *Things That Make Us Smart*, (1993) "leads to a state in which we perceive and react to events around us, efficiently and effortlessly" (Norman 16).

Interactive multimedia provide kinds of interfaces wherein the observer can "break the frame" between the users and their silent objects they're looking at and wherein these objects in one way or another react back through a selective saturation of a user's senses through many media. By this process a story is told or an experience is conveyed. But now, instead of Cicero placing subjective objects around the architecture to help trigger an oration, multimedia designers place sounds, pictures, and video in cyberspace to trigger their own kind of memory palaces for the user. The user manipulates pre-placed, pre-recorded, pre-scripted objects and see another person's tale, much as if Cicero had led a student around the walls of an ancient city, placing mnemonic devices in the student's mind so that he would never forget a certain oration. The adventure comes in experiencing someone else's memories, tales, or events. And by interacting with this system, participants learn something in a way that could not be learned without multimedia. Norman believes that a person with a technologi-

---

Others believe that museums are already interactive sites (like Cicero's memory palaces), where visitors pick their own path (or are guided through a certain route) that activates the space: "The Universal Survey Museum" (Duncan and Wallach 1980) and "Theatrum Mundi" (Bernheimer 1956). The paintings are clearly not static representations if, by their very presence, the space becomes transformed from a "white cube" to what Richard Schechner would call a "hot zone"— a space where performance heats up a space with the "aliveness" of spectators who are the performers (those looked upon by others) and spectators (those who look at the paintings and other people) of the museum space. The paintings — and the space they occupy — create the environment in which performance occurs. Museums, from this point of view, are interactive and clearly not static. Roberts and Conklin, looking at museums traditionally, miss this important point. What they appear to want is a multisensory environment in which sounds, lighting, and other theatrical elements become a part of the museum milieu.

cal device (like a computer) creates different "cognitive abilities" by which the "person + artifact is smarter than either alone" (1993:78). I see multimedia as a means for adventure and/or as a means for learning. Let's see how Smolin uses the interface in his virtual Vietnam.

Multimediating Vietnam, Smolin Style

Onscreen I click a small cube-shaped, dice-sized interface (down in the lower right corner of the picture) that has a right and left arrow on it. This is called the "Quebe," a navigation array, the interface that takes the user to another location in this virtual Vietnam. A camera-like clicking of the shutter is heard as I press the right arrow. The screen fills with a picture surrounded by a white border. Traditional, quick-paced Vietnamese music coarse through the speakers as I look at a meandering riverside filled with boats — a 5 × 7-inch still image of a water roadway. In the lower left corner of the picture are two half-faded dime-size icons side by side: one an image of curled film, the other a small "i." After I click on the "i," the entire picture fades slightly, and on the lower portion of it the following information appears: "Soctrang, Soctrang Province. Photograph by Michael Freeman, United Kingdom." (By clicking on the cube in the right corner, I find a map of Vietnam. Soctrang Province is southwest of Ho Chi Minh City.) I click the "i" circle again, and the picture reverts to normal. Next I click the curly film icon. The picture fades slightly and a 2 × 3-inch television-like screen appears. Six different video clips of river life fade in and out as I hear a Vietnamese man speak in accented English: "Many cities in this world have very, very beautiful rivers. But you know the Perfume River is unforgettable for the first time, and for the second time, and maybe one hundred times. Especially the life along the river." I see motion images in long shot of a child waving from a passing boat and a young man fishing. The screen then turns black with a sharp click and fades out with a white phosphorous dot like those seen on old television sets. The music comes back on, and the still picture fades back to its normal shade. By clicking on the cube, I can see many other pictures of Vietnam.

A world-renowned photographer, Rick Smolin headed the *A Day in the Life of…* book series, in which he and a group of professional photographers took pictures of people during a 24-hour period in different countries (Japan, Russia, the United States, and so forth). When he decided to do Vietnam a few years ago, the team spent a week shooting photographs and video. The book was simultaneously published with an interactive CD-ROM that offers a unique travel experience for the user. More than a museum photo display, the project takes the user on a photographic tour of Vietnam.

Smolin sets the stage for *Passage to Vietnam* with a letter inviting the user to join him and 70 of the world's leading photojournalists on a tour of Vietnam. From there the participant is taken on a multimedia photographic journey of

Vietnam that includes viewing a collection of photographs grouped together under the heading of different "passages": River Life, Street Life, History and the War, Cultural Heritage, Industry, Youth and Doi Moi. Within this "tour" are three kinds of side paths the user can take: (1) a branch into a group of more photos selected under the names of Rice, Salt, Weddings, Perfume Pagoda, Gao Dai, Buddhism, The Hmong, Faces of Vietnam, Silk, and Coal; (2) two different editing sessions to learn how editors choose a selection of photos for the River Life section and how a cover photo is chosen; and (3) a selection of four Virtual Galleries that include the virtual presence of a particular photographer who talks about his or her favorite photographs taken over the course of a career. The four photojournalists are Nicole Bengevino, Jay Dickman, Elliott Erwitt, and David Kennerly. Each "passage" is preceded by Rick Smolin, who enters the photograph in miniature and speaks about each section — acting like a "chorus" that comments upon the action in a Greek or Shakespearean play. This is the scenario, the framework, of Smolin's project, where all the computer's a stage on which all the users have their parts to play.

Passage to Vietnam recalls the ancient oratory device of subjective image placement. Setting photographs within a dynamic virtual architectural space, Smolin wants users to experience these photojournalists' Vietnam. At the same time, Smolin presents an interesting model for a technologically advanced museum, where users go through an immersive interactive photographer's gallery. As users view the different photographs simultaneously with audio of Vietnamese traditional music, they have the option of listening to a photographer's commentary about it, watching a motion video of a scene, scanning a map of Vietnam to find a picture's point of origin, viewing the photographer's photobiographical career, and so forth. Through many media, users reenact certain elements of Smolin's Vietnam experience like Cicero, who triggered certain memories by placing subjective pictures on the wall of a building. This is similar to the exhibit at the National Museum of the American Indian in New York City, where, from around several different kinds of displayed artifacts, artists speak virtually from multimedia kiosks about the actual displayed items.

Smolin's *Vietnam* is not a dramatic narrative with a Hollywood-size script as in Chris Roberts's *Heart of the Tiger* (1995), where writer's guild members Frank DePalma and Terry Borst were hired to write a multilayered action movie. Smolin's project is more like an interactive museum gallery than a narrative movie. This is an intriguing dichotomy, for even if it is not a narrative in the traditional Hollywood sense, *Vietnam* is somewhat cinematic. By taking the "tour," the user constructs a narrative, much like a museumgoer who chooses which galleries to walk through, which paths to take (a multimedia design concept). Ulmer explains how the designer of hypermedia "constructs an information environment" through which users travel (1994:28). Ultimately, this "hyperrhetoric" for audiovisual and print material will create "a new social machine" (Ulmer 1994:38). Rather than developing a linear argument — through thesis, antithesis, and synthesis — Ulmer wants the hypermedia artist or writer to develop individual scenes (or sets) that are not linearly developed (argued). Instead, each set is a node on a web that makes up this information environment. As readers or users move randomly through this environment, they will — through their experience of the random juxtaposition of texts, images, the nodes on the web — experience the choreographer's work of art. This requires people experiencing this environment to develop a memory of the links of their path through these nodal points.

Whether in interactive multimedia or at a museum, the process of ancient memory palaces is enacted. Performance studies scholar Barbara Kirshenblatt-Gimblett makes this point when she discusses "concept" or theme-park like museums. This kind of museum, she explains, is "more cinematic than it is artifactual and more immersive than it is cognitive, ... more experiential. That's the language ... of experience, not of seeing; [it's] more theatrical, where all the lines between ... world's fairs, amusement parks, and museums start to blur" (in Roberts and Vogel 1994:46). Because of the malleability of virtual-space architecture, the *Vietnam* project blurs these boundaries, and people buy into it because our technological society has become a place where electronic thinking is becoming more and more natural.

Smolin has taken a difficult subject, Vietnam, and placed its images (taken out of their location in Vietnam) into a computer-mediated environment, where he conflates tourist with photojournalist. This country has granted the photographers permission to take any picture they wish within sites heretofore inaccessible to foreign tourists. Smolin's team placed these photos not just within the context of Vietnam but within some of their personal lives as photojournalists. The galleries where photojournalists talk about their career take the viewer hypertextually out of the tour of Vietnam.

But users are not on a tour of Vietnam — they are on "assignment with the world's top photographers," as the subtitle to the CD-ROM states. The lines of government access, secrecy, tourism, and photography blur where users do not just see photographs but supposedly perform a mediated reenactment of the photojournalists' experience. Users are immersed in the virtual environment, where photographs are arranged like a gallery without an informative guide. Users get no detailed information about the pictures they see. They get a quick overview of what the photographer was thinking when taking the photograph, but they don't get a historical or cultural point of view. Here being immersive is in some ways more important than being informative. This strategy gives the user not just access to images unseen before by those living outside of Vietnam, but through the narrative frame of Smolin's project, users, in a way, learn what it is like to be a photojournalist. They would not necessarily experience this if they leafed through the book. However, under Norman's condition, when the *system* of the person + artifact perform together, then they supposedly have an experience that is enhanced — persons interacting with the CD-ROM will get more from that experience than if they just looked at the *Vietnam* companion book. That's the power of multimedia applications. And in Smolin's case, he attempts through this system to reshape our feelings about Vietnam, to "make us smarter," in Norman's vernacular.

In this project users do not get an Oliver Stone view of Vietnam. Smolin offers a subversive reading of this 25-year-old history of the Vietnam War. Less about war and more about the people living there today, *Passage to Vietnam* tells users that Americans are hanging on to memories of a war that many of the Vietnamese people the photographers met have long since forgotten. By circulating these "new" images of Vietnam, Smolin hopes, to some extent, Americans will create or build new memories that are not about war. This is what I mean about Smolin's being subversive. Many Americans have — through mass media — received a view of Vietnam that's mainly about how the war affected them in the United States. Political science scholar S. Paige Baty defines mass-mediated culture as that which "comprises the images, stories, persons — in short, the host of productions — circulated through the mass media" (1995:16). I believe that Smolin hopes to erase old memories in viewers by offering new authoritative images and stories. "Mass-mediated rememberings authorize public being while simultaneously eroding older forms of popular representation" (Baty 1995:17). Perhaps Smolin hopes to erode the past with his CD-ROM.

Smolin's hope is that the United States will open up trade with Vietnam. He wants tourists to visit Vietnam. To this end, Smolin places the user into a new narrative about photojournalists' memories of Vietnam. And Baty describes how technology and mass-media do have the power to shape memories: "Technologically reproduced, these mass-mediated rememberings insert the citizen into a virtual collective space often entered alone" (Baty 1995:19). This virtual space is an environment composed of memories transfixed by media objects: virtual images float in the ozone layer of human consciousness imbued by uplinked satellite media images and radio waves. Baty believes that "In this virtual realm of appearance, discursive acts and figures serve as the material of the 'real'" (19). This experience conflates the role of literal and figurative memory, she argues, so that people remember these representative characters "in relation to an event or historical era through the membrane of the media" (19). Baty's project is about the circulation of Marilyn Monroe through the American body politic, but her theories are valid for any circulating body (object, story, image) passing through the world's media.

Images of Vietnam have circulated throughout the United States, showing people as victims and brutalizers of a Third World country who lost 3,000,000 people (compared to the United States's 58,000) in a war never declared by the United States Congress. Smolin, whether he's conscious of it or not, through the *Passage to Vietnam* narrative, is creating new memories, which, as Baty claims, is a form of power: "remembering is about creating what is real; it is about finding [creating?] stories to tell ourselves about the past and present [and future?]." In this space of memory mediated stories become a "process" of discovering "who we are" and ultimately create a "community" — if they "lose their common objects of memory, they have difficulty maintaining a common ground — a *present* — on which to construct foundations of mutuality, belonging, language, and knowledge" (1995:31). Through this CD-ROM Smolin attempts to shift American memories focused on a lost war to a new set of Vietnam memories.

Passage to Vietnam eschews conventional narrative (a story with an Aristotelian beginning, middle, and end), yet it is still potently successful, for it is the compilation of images — alongside the "tourist-photographer" role, among its other elements — creating for the user an immersive *experience* — one that incorporates still and motion images, lighting, sound, and people. It gives the user new kinds of memories about Vietnam, memories heretofore shaped primarily by Hollywood movies and war news footage. A similar kind of experience can be found at a museum as well. In this case it seems that the museum is compacted into a CD-ROM that can be viewed on a computer. This kind of computer environment is shaped and mediated by the interface design.

From Clicking on Buttons to Clicking on Reality

Even though some may tend to think that only computers have interfaces, this is a misperception. Any time we view a work of art, visit a theater, or see a movie, we're confronted with an interface — sometimes invisible, sometimes not. Whether we're making toast, cooking bacon in a microwave, driving a car, flying in an airplane, reading a book, we are mediating our desires — cooking bread, getting from LA to New York, enjoying a good story — through an object that will take us from one state of being to another. How that interface is designed determines what kind of experience we have. Do we have to push four buttons to get bacon cooking in the microwave or just two? Are we flying in a single-prop plane or a 747? Is the novel a paperback or in hardcover, 800 pages or 400? These are not asinine questions. They are at the root of multimedia interface design.

Donald Norman, in *The Design of Everyday Things* (1990), presents a clear argument for simple designs so that people can naturally interact with everyday objects such as doors, microwaves, and so forth without having to feel stupid when an object cannot be manipulated without the use of detailed instructions. "Designs should," he writes

- Make it easy to determine what actions are possible at any moment (make use of constraints).

- Make things visible, including the conceptual model of the system, the alternative actions, and the results of actions.

- Make it easy to evaluate the current state of the system.

- Follow natural mappings between intentions and the required actions; between actions and the resulting effect; and between the information that is visible and the interpretation of the system state. (188)

These four bits of advice, he contends, are nothing more than keeping the design and interface clear and simple in order to "make sure that (1) the user can figure out what to do, and (2) the user can tell what is going on" (188). This is an important credo for multimedia developers, but despite the obvious advice, one interactive CD-ROM movie, *Silent Steel* (1995), fails in this regard. The user plays a submarine captain in third-person mode. Because the interface doesn't capture the essence of what kind of role the user should be performing, it is not, in Norman's words, "easy to determine what actions are possible at any moment." After attempting to play it several times I had to give up because I didn't know what to do. It failed all of Norman's criteria. It also failed my premise that the interface should place the user into a character role. Therefore, I never got the feeling of playing a submarine captain.

Before examining interface design more thoroughly, I want to look at some definitions of *interface*. Interface design finds its current history in technology. Michael Heim, in *The Metaphysics of Virtual Reality* (1993), explains that interfaces once referred to power plugs, then to video, and now between the human-machine connection and "the human entry into a self-contained cyberspace" (79). He claims that "An interface occurs where two or more information sources come face-to-face. A human user connects with the system, and the computer becomes interactive.... Interface means the human being is wired up" (77). Figueroa-Sarriera would agree with Heim and defines an interface as a "surface forming a common boundary, a meeting-point or area of contact between objects, systems, etc. This view of interface as a common boundary implies an inexorable machine/human connection" (1995:129). Many people may continue to think of an interface in terms of how they interact with technology. But this was not always the case. Heim explains how "In ancient times, the term *interface* sparked awe and mystery" (1993:78). He examines how the Greek word *prosopon* (one "face facing another face") was equivalent to today's use of the word *interface*. Through mutual interaction the two faces continue to develop as they react to one another until it's clear that this development evolves into "a third thing or state of being" (78).

I contend that interface design becomes dramatically interesting when *prosopon* is invoked as a model for getting at multimedia content — when a third "state of being" arises out of interactivity with the objects through the interface. This is also closer to Cicero's memory palace and Ulmer's hypermedia thinking. Clicking buttons is not enough. Game designer and theorist Brenda Laurel believes that "[t]hinking about interfaces is thinking too small." Rather, she believes it's more about "creating imaginary worlds" that attempt to "extend, amplify, and enrich our own capacities to think, feel, and act" rather than just creating a new desktop window (1993:32–33). The live theater model offers some useful models, but thinking about interfaces is never too small, despite Laurel's claim. Imaginary worlds cannot touch users without interfaces. The two examples provided so far, *Klingon* and *Vietnam*, prove that her statement about imaginary worlds amplifying and enriching "our own capacities to think, feel, and act" is achievable. It is time to think about how interfaces shape the user's experience in these imaginary worlds.

The Theatrical Interface

Long before cyberspace, performers on the stage interacted with the set, props, and each other. For the audience the stage is an interface into another world. However, the proscenium stage offers only a limited interface for spectators. "Feedback from the house to the stage is limited," Richard Schechner says about conventional theater (1994:37). He lays out a dichotomous comparison between the proscenium stage and auditorium:

Stage	*Auditorium*
bright	dark
active	passive
giving	taking
noisy	quiet
irregular arrangement	regular arrangement
costumed	everyday dress
magic space	plain space

(1994:38)

This conventional model, which has gripped the popular stages of Broadway and regional theaters since the nineteenth century, has changed. The environmental theater of the 1960s and 1970s lifted spectators out of the auditorium and placed them within all-encompassing environments, breaking the fourth-wall illusion of the proscenium in the process. The space proffers collaboration between spectators and performers: the "areas occupied by the audience are a kind of sea through which the performers swim" (Schechner 1994:39). It is through the cooperation among participants that this process works. "The design," Schechner adds, "encourages participation; it is also a reflection of the wish for participation. There are no settled sides automatically dividing the audience off from the performers" (39). Environmental theater provides a good model for exploring and designing interactive multimedia products.

As explained in the previous chapter, Laurel believes plot is the key for shaping interactive adventures, which include murder mystery dinners and fantasy role-playing games. She explores interactive designs through dramatic theory in her work *Computers as Theater* (1991), explicating the Aristotelian model. She shows how plot is a convergence of many possible events that narrow to a necessary outcome over a period of time. In multimedia projects the user is given several choices, which allows the plot to branch off in different potential directions, leading to more than one necessary outcome:

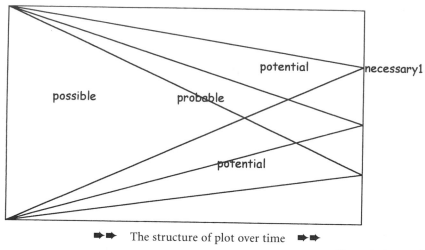

➡➡   The structure of plot over time   ➡➡

(Laurel 1993:72)

"The 'flying wedge,'" she writes, "can be pointed off in different directions, thus increasing the program's potential for many whole actions" (72). This is similar to "plot tree" designs found in choose-your-adventure novels, which were based on role-playing games. The flying wedge, however, is not the model for projects like Smolin's *Vietnam*, which, as Michael Kirby says about Laurie Anderson's performance works, "have little or no relationship to drama" (1987:105). Smolin creates instead an art that is theatricalized by the layering of theatrical elements (performers, virtual sets, lighting, and audio) onto a photojournalist-like gallery. His interactive multimedia project co-opts theatrical elements and places them in a miniature virtual environment. And this reveals a weakness in Laurel's book.

Laurel, by focusing mainly on Aristotle's concept of drama, excludes other dramatic forms. Even more pivotal, however, is Laurel's lack of a full theoretical discussion about the placement of an interactive mise-en-scene (the entire performance space, including sets, lighting, sound, performers, spectator-user-performer) within multimedia projects. What could happen, for example, if multimedia designers applied Appia's theories of lighting and set design to their projects? Appia (an early-twentieth-century theorist whose play designs, especially his ideas on lighting, still influence theatrical and cinema lighting design) stepped away from the Renaissance-born practice of staging scenes in front of realistic-looking painted flats. In contrast, he saw the stage "as plastic and dynamic spaces, constructed to meet the needs of the actor as he expresses and realizes a work of dramatic art" (Beacham 1987:95).

By studying some of Appia's theatrical productions, the multimedia designer can learn how the emotional importance of setting and atmospheric lighting can affect the user. Appia is only one example of many theater practitioners whose ideas could be explored by multimedia designers. In the introduction to the "History and the War" section of Smolin's *Vietnam*, he virtually places himself into a photograph of a Cu Chi tunnel. From the photographer's view, users look up to a man holding a door open to the tunnel, filled mainly with darkness. Light surrounds him, shafting down into the darkness below to a moving virtual image of Smolin, who sits in the still darkness with some of this light virtually added, as he talks about the war. Compare this to Beacham's description of Appia's production of *Orpheus*: "Amor was represented — much to the spectator's surprise — by a single strong beam of light, the performer sang from behind the set. After the god departed, and Orpheus accepted his challenge, the upstage portion of the curtains parted, to form an opening out of which streamed a strong, and, as it seemed, 'other-worldly' glow, at the same moment as the downstage light faded. Orpheus approached and entered, climbing the steps with his arms raised above his head, to form a silhouette against the lurid illumination" (Beacham 1994:100). When a scene, lighting, or sound change occurs onstage, the audience subtly notices a dramatic change.

Interface design needs to include within the environment of the multimedia world the theatrical elements of lighting, set, sound, and costume design. Light and shadows determine the kind of atmosphere a designer wants to bring to the user. Sound creates an aural ambience that the designers of *Myst* (1993) were able to convey so well. It was not just the pictorial representation that brought the user into the world of *Myst*, where "our world will become your world," but the ambience of sound — from the lapping of waves on the ocean shore to the eerie music in the dentist office–looking planetarium. In the same way that changes in lighting affect how audiences feel about a particular scene, interface design should take the user from one dramatic state to another, determined not by drama alone but by how the user interacts with changing content through the alteration of interfaces. To change a scene, mood, or atmosphere, the *interface must change* in order for the change within the user to occur.

The Poetic Facade

The interface design determines what kind of experience the user realizes — change the interface and the user will experience the content differently. When the content of a scene changes, the interface should logically change with it. Navigation by means of this interface structures how users perceive content. Designs have come a long way from the interfaces of computer video games. Sociologist Sherry Turkle believes that the video games of the past are over. "In today's game simulations," she writes, "people experience themselves in a new, often exotic setting. The minds they meet are their own" (1995:31). The crude video games of the past allowed users to guide spaceships through two-dimensional environments where they dodged and shot up asteroids and spaceships with a click of a trigger button. Today, the click of a mouse takes users into photographically real environments and cultures of foreign countries, or as in *Klingon* they live the experiences of a *Star Trek* character in the far reaches of space.

Interactive multimedia designers have to determine how they want users to experience their projects. The interface in many ways is the form, the shape, the gateway into the content perceived and interacted with by users. It is the means for performing a role. It is the trappings of character: the costume, props, and script for an actor to perform a character. It is the equivalent of character sheets found in fantasy role-playing games. It is an extension of the user's body in the environment of foreign lands and alien worlds by which the user can interact (*prosopon*) with people, characters, and universes on the other side of the screen. It is their way to participate in the multimedia world. Multimedia designer Ben Davis calls an interface a "poetic facade" (1995:248). Multimedia must not just offer the "surface" of its subject, but it must be enveloped by a cultural depth that is aware of historical and social nuances. There "must be a close relationship between the form of the product (its metaphors, interactive functions, visual design, intuitive navigation, etc.), its content ..., and the form of production" (1995:252). These issues described by Davis have much less to do with worrying about whether an interactive multimedia story or scenario has open architecture or closed architecture, branching paths or side paths, and more to do with what kind of role the designer wants users to perform. For that determines the kind of interface and navigational array needed for the content or story. Once that is determined, the other issues will fall into place. The Klingon CD-ROM provides an interesting example of this.

To Be Klingon

In this interactive movie users play, in first-person view, a Federation officer who acts the role of a young Klingon warrior in an "immersive studies" holodeck program. The user learns about Klingon culture and customs as their character's father is assassinated and the young Klingon is thrown into the midst of an investigation. The designers want the user to "think like a Klingon." The narrative places the user into a Klingon home, and the camera style — cinéma vérité — and the first-person perspective (where the performers onscreen look into the camera) give the user an illusion of walking around the environment listening to and being addressed by other characters. The user watches the unfolding full-screen-sized movie,* and at various points the quarter-size cursor shaped like a Klingon dagger appears, indicating the user is to choose an action, whether interacting with other characters or objects. However, unlike *Wing Commander* or

---

*The Duck Corporation has designed full-screen motion video compression for 8-bit and 16-bit graphic capabilities. The old Macintosh business card–sized QuickTime motion video compression found in Quantum Gate and Passage to Vietnam (among too many others) is a thing of the past. The power of grand scale cannot be underestimated when a video window goes from less than a four-square-inch area to an area close to 75 square inches. The change in scale is no less than Wagnerian.

Quantum Gate, there is no menu offering a list of decisions or actions (and the character speaks very little dialogue). Users either make an action in the three-second time allotted, or they don't. At one point, after the death of the character's father, the "interface" cursor appears as other characters in the scene wait for the user to take action. If the user fails to act within three seconds, the holodeck program shuts off, and Gowron (played by Robert O'Reilly, reprising his recurring *Star Trek* role), the "tutor," appears and screams: "Act and ye shall *have* dinner. Think and ye shall *be* dinner."

Although there is not much interaction within this Klingon universe, the designers have clearly defined the role the user is to experience in this interactive CD-ROM. The interface meets the expectation of how they want the user to interact with the Klingon culture. Using the same content, a different interface would have given users a different experience. But in this case the interface doubly conveys a fast-pace, action-style movie within a fictional cultural immersion experience — if users take time to think through their options within the movie they will be "dinner" (fail to act like a Klingon). I like Ben Davis's description of interfaces. For the type of "poetic facade" designed reveals how the user sees and interacts with the content — whether it's a story, tour, or training simulation.

If two different poets were to write about the same subject, their forms, word choices, meter, and so forth would cause the reader to experience the same topic differently. Similarly, interactive designers must decide what kind of emotional experience they want the user to have — whether journeying to Vietnam as a photographer or to Klingon space as a cultural student. Both of these examples, by the way, offer similar content: a way to learn about a foreign culture — one teaches what it is like to go to Vietnam as a photojournalist, the other what it is like to live as a Klingon — by framing the experience within an Aristotelian narrative event.

Interacting with Miniature Universes

Unlike environmental theater productions, fantasy role-playing games, and murder-mystery dinners, there are no live personas on the other side of the screen to help shape the users' experience in CD-ROMs. In the near future, evolving technology will have users interacting with live actors, playing characters like the Klingons or talking with live Vietnamese people, and they will be able to respond to what users say, as opposed to the current limited array of pre-scripted actions found in CD-ROM movies. At this point in time, artificial worlds remain tightly scripted, and users interact within these constraints.

So interactivity occurs in artificially created worlds that reflect, in some way, aspects of the actual world. In Chris Roberts's *The Price of Freedom* (1996), he has designed a universe of future Earth in a state of near civil war with colonized border worlds. The user's character must discover and stop the cause of this strife. Mark Hamill is the user's link. He is the interface. Users interact with other characters through him. They fly starfighters in combat with enemy craft, and they walk on the decks of starships as Hamill's Colonel Blair character. But these people are not "live"—they are pre-recorded, and their experiences are preshaped by a director.

Instead of interacting with live people, users interact with carefully constructed alternate virtual worlds—in Smolin's case, a hidden Vietnam revealed through pictures and video clips of real people placed within a miniature tour of Vietnam. Users enter Vietnam by means of an artificially created environment, and this representation becomes a doorway into a symbolic, simulated Vietnam (and a simulated photojournalist's experience). Users may perceive this simulation as the whole of Vietnam. Writing about the Renaissance, "The Age of Curiosity," in *Collectors and Curiosities*, Krzysztof Pomian describes how certain kinds of art "depict the major categories of beings and objects which together encompass the entire contents of the universe" (1990:49): "It would seem that the aim was not so much to create a faithful portrait of a particular room on a particular date, but rather to convey the very essence of such a room, showing it as a place where the universe, considered as a whole, became visible through the intermediary of objects intended to represent the major categories of beings and things.... In other words, it is here that the universe became visible as a single entity, for although it retained every single constituent part, it underwent a process of miniaturization" (50). Instead of a memory palace, where virtually-placed objects trigger an oration, here, in one location, are multimedia objects that trigger memories of an entire world.

Within these miniature universes we begin to realize what Allen Weiss says about Marcel Duchamp's theory of art, in which the "artwork is completed by the spectator" (1994:117). Through an artwork-spectator dialectic, "the spectator's ego ... is split and reinstated in the work" (117). Perhaps the desire for multimedia—where all works of art appear in one location, a miniature universe—is really a multifaceted desire for our split postmodern selves to appear whole again. This occurs through the mediation of an interface. In the age of cyberspace we find less and less *prosopon* interactions and more and more multimedia interactions. Through interfaces we explore entire universes, and within these universes we find our phantasmatic selves mirrored in virtual phosphorescent images onscreen.

Part III
Social Fantasies

9

From Whitewater to Heaven's Gate: Performing Rituals of a Technological Age

"Mortal mind sees what it believes as certainly as it believes what it sees."

— Mary Baker Eddy (1906:86)

Science Fiction and UFOs

When an amateur astronomer photographed comet Hale-Bopp in November 1996, he believed his telescope resolved a second object flying near the comet: a UFO, an interstellar spacecraft. Astronomers disproved this belief. The second object was a star. The damage, however, had already been done. Rumors shot across Internet lines at the speed of light. And many, sadly, believed the rumors — including 39 members of the Heaven's Gate cult led by Marshall Applewhite in San Diego. In March 1997 they decided to kill themselves in a moment of supposed apocalyptic self-enlightenment that would traject if not their bodies then their souls to that same supposed UFO cruising behind this comet, its tail glowing in streaming grandeur, which would not be seen again until its next revolution around our star.

Thirty years after the airing of the first season of *Star Trek* (since regurgitated into several spin-off series), Barbara Adams, an alternate juror for the Whitewater trial in Arkansas, decided to do something different. She showed up for jury duty in a maroon and black Star Trek uniform, complete with communicator, tricorder, and phaser props, which are a normality at countless science fiction conventions. In the courtroom, however, this simulacrum resonated with something more. According to her, *Star Trek* promotes "inclusion, tolerance, peace, and faith in mankind. 'If it helps to make people think a little bit more what those ideals are, then I'll keep wearing this uniform,'" she said (Associated Press 1996).

Many equate science fiction fandom (of which the above is one of the more extreme examples of fandom intersecting "real" world events) with UFO phenomena. This equivalency grounds itself on falsity. I believe that UFO myths are an irrational reaction against, or indications of a latent fear of, a mysterious future — our advancing technological age. In contrast, science fiction (sf) reflects a reasoned mythological construct of the imagination in an attempt to point out where we are going and what we are doing as a society. Science fiction fandom attempts to build communities by circulating these tales (novels, short stories, comics, and movies). UFO cultists believe in alien encounters of the third and fourth kind. They perceive these folk myths as realities. However, it can't be denied that some could also see Adams crossing the line from reality to fantasy in the Whitewater/*Star Trek* courtroom example — which on the surface appears to be the action of one not fully in her right mind. She certainly seems to be living in a fictional world. This shallow view of Adams agrees with much of what the mainstream press thinks about science fiction fandom. Fans are those who, for lack of a better word, play with and build communities around the art of science fiction objects. (For the sake of argument I'm considering sf as art and sf fans as consumers of this art — more about this later.) So, was it really a surprise when reporters and experts reacting to the 39 suicides of the Heaven's Gate Cult postulated how science fiction influenced this cultic event, arguing how such shows as *The X-Files* (narrating a UFO mythos) have garnered a "quasi-cultic following" (Marquand and Wood 1997)?

David Reed, professor of pastoral theology at Wycliffe College, University of Toronto, states that such cults as Heaven's Gate have been "drawn from a generation fed by *Star Trek* and *Star Wars*." He adds that the cultists — and by association, sf fans —"have had their world view altered. They have reconstructed a spiritual world that draws from popular culture" (Marquand and Wood 1997). To equate the Heaven's Gate fiasco with science fiction fandom is to argue against logic. UFO cultists believe in the reality of their myth. Science fiction fans know that their myths are stories. As I will show, however, there are similarities in how the two groups reconstruct mythic or fantastic worldviews.

A similar pattern emerges among cult groups and fandom: the attempt to create a mythical environment that they can live in. Science fiction fans and UFO cultists construct shared mental worlds from what Daniel Mackay calls an "imaginary entertainment environment"— essentially an interactive milieu created from the symbiotic relationship among novels, comics, movies, role-playing games, and so forth and evolving into a shared universe. *Star Trek* is an example of imaginary entertainment environment. I contend that UFO cults have constructed their communities around another kind of imaginary entertainment environment created from an entire UFO folk mythos perpetuated by such events as Roswell, Project Blue Book, men in black, and countless other government cover-up conspiracies. This mythos created an environment for creative fiction (like *The X-Files*). There is certainly a feedback loop between the two, as authors (through their fiction) comment upon and perhaps perpetuate UFO folk myths. From these environments fans and cults perform roles — similar to, but not exactly in the same way as an actor plays a character. The environment, the fantasy milieu, performs its role on those who live or play within its realm. Let me explain.

Performing in Imaginary Entertainment Environments

Embedded within these various sites are potentials for performance. When participants engage the components built into these imaginary environments, they do so by means of an interface (like a *Star Trek* uniform or a photograph of a comet). The interface allows the participants to tap into the virtual milieu, and, symbiotically, embedded "strips of behavior" within the milieu perform on them. In "Restoration of Behavior" Richard Schechner explains how performers, during the rehearsal process, "get in touch with, recover, or even invent these strips of behavior and then rebehave according to these strips, either by being absorbed into them ... or by existing side by side with them" (1985:36). During rehearsals actors construct a performance score from the selection of various strips of behavior garnered through life or passed down from teacher to student in a classroom.

Interfaces are the mediation between the participant and these strips of behavior. A play is an interface into an author's imaginary environment. Performers rehearse at "living" in this milieu. Their behavior, as well as the lights, sound, and costumes, constitute the mise-en-scène, which, in its entirety, represents the author's imaginary world of the play. The audience perceives the author's imaginary construct through the interface of the mise-en-scène on stage. In contrast, sf conventions and UFO cults are imaginary environments constructed from bits and pieces of stories and myth. These environments do not necessarily offer a cohesive story. Rather, the spectator-participants circulate their own desires, or narratives, within the fantasy milieu — which contains embedded bits of behavior. People may express, or perform, these bits through a material object, the interface into the imaginary environment. However, they do not "discover" strips of behavior during a rehearsal process; rather, the strips of behavior embedded within these environments perform on them through the interface. When people enter these sites they cause the strips of embedded behavior to come alive (activated by the participant engaging the interface). The interface object allows the strips of stored behavior contained in the interface to

transmit the imaginary environment to them and through them. Thus spectators become performers.

The picture of the Hale-Bopp comet and the attendant second object, as
broadcast on the Internet, became the interface into the imaginary environment
of UFO folk myths. The followers of this mythology believed the second object
was a UFO because the picture activated strips of behavior that fired the viewers' imaginations, giving them needed "proof" to valuate their belief system.
Because the object was perceived as a real UFO (they could "see" the picture for
themselves on the Internet), the final strip of behavior they would perform was
the ritual suicides. This, they hoped, would take them into the physical presence of their heretofore imaginary or virtual environment, a hope that eventually led them down a path of ruin.

Conversely, instead of seeing Adams — or any other Star Trek or sf fan as
representing a dysfunctional state of mind, I see her performing one of Baty's
representative characters. These kinds of characters "exist at the intersection of
cultural production and consumption, circulating in specific times and places
where they are made to mediate values to a given community" (1995:9). She
adds, "The mass-mediated representative character operates as a figure through
whom multiple meanings, references, and roles are remembered" (11). Essentially, Adams was "playing" a character, but not so much a character an actor
portrays.

By placing Star Trek into a U.S. district courthouse, Adams created an intersection between the multiple meanings of American jurisprudence and Captain
Picard's just Federation law. Through her the Trek universe became reality within
the world of this courtroom. She was the interface into the imaginary Star Trek
environment. Adams probably received press attention because many, including William Shatner, thought her a bit strange. However, from her point of view
she represented the many meanings of Star Trek values, a future projection of
law created to perhaps make a statement about today's often wanting legal system (lacking in many cases quick or fair resolutions). The Whitewater came
after the O. J. Simpson trial. Those familiar with Star Trek would identify with
those values, and those who didn't would know Adams's reason for wearing her
uniform after she was interviewed by the press. However, she was dismissed
from duty after faithfully serving nine sessions, for the judge forbade jurors from
talking to the media.

What made her Star Trek desire so interesting to the press was not that people didn't agree with Star Trek utopia, nor that her uniform was an iconographic
representation of this utopia, but the "excessive commodification that accom-
panies, and is made possible through, iconographic rememberings of representative characters" (Baty 1995:10). For a time Barbara Adams sat in that courtroom
not as Barbara Adams but — because her uniform activated strips of behavior
formerly embodied by the actors who played Captain Kirk, Captain Picard, Lt.
Uhura, Mr. Spock, Commander Data, and other characters on Star Trek — as an
iconographic representative of Star Trek memories. This is how people would

"remember" or "see" her. Adams, by wearing the *Trek* uniform, caused the imaginary entertainment environment of *Star Trek* to become part of the real world (a fantasy that solidified into a virtual image when the strips of *Star Trek* behavior were projected within the presence of a real-world event). In effect, Adams tried to subvert the real courtroom environment by introducing herself as an interface into the values associated with *Star Trek*.

A community of fans would now recognize one of their own outside that environment set aside for "play." The desires of science fiction fans activate strips of behavior contained in their favorite novels, art, television, and films. They perform these desires mainly at science fiction conventions as they circulate themselves in the presence of other fans and their favorite authors. The "performance" of these fictional characters and settings by fans activates a world of fiction through an interface (such as a uniform), which then activates entire imaginary environments represented by these interface objects. Through this very process science fiction fans build communities. Some may question whether the function of art (explored here as material artifacts and consumable mass market commodities) has a ritual, transformative function or merely offers a pleasurable aesthetic distraction. I believe it's a combination of both. However much one buys into capitalist consumption, as Adams did with *Star Trek*, certainly there really is no dysfunction in participating in the entertainment process. Wearing a *Trek* uniform in court is not necessarily dysfunctional. Killing yourself so you can be transported to a nonexistent UFO is. Ultimately, the desire to build communities around narrative worlds meets a mythic need.

Mythology of a Technological Age

Creating a community around which individuals' desires are circulated is not new. This desire has been around since primeval times. Nietzsche, in *Human, All Too Human*, says that "everything essential in human development occurred in primeval times" (1984:14). Is Nietzsche saying that present knowledge cannot determine (or be applied to) the past, but the past is essential to determine the present and the future? If this is so, according to Nietzsche, present knowledge cannot determine present humanity because the essentials of human development occurred in primeval times, when, as I understand his argument, story and myth (the earliest form of fantastic "literature") created sustainable worldviews in different cultures. Time or technology does not change these mythological occurrences. Fans (and even the UFO cults), those who circulate and are circulated through various fantasy and science fiction sites, are exploring the possibilities of alternative worldviews, searching for ways to live in and come to terms with an advancing technological age.

This would follow under Don Ihde's model of existential praxis, as outlined under the section "Technology and Human Self-Conception" in *Existential Technics* (1983). He explains how a "concrete pattern of actions ... always include[s] relations with things of a material sort" (15). The material (the stories that allow people to make sense of their world) is the interface into imaginary environments. Ihde explores mythology in relationship to the reflection of intentional phenomena — how the self expresses itself to the world and the world reflects this back to the self — in three different variations of human society: hunter/gatherer, agricultural, and technological.

A preindustrial, preagricultural nomadic hunter/gatherer society creates its own kinds of myth. It does this, Ihde says, by projecting an ideal "existential praxis into some non-ordinary time or place in the form of cultic behavior" that provides a foundation for society from which members of society can learn — "from it emerges a type of self-understanding in which the human becomes 'like' the 'world' which is projected" (1983:16). He adds that this same process of existential praxis occurs in agricultural and technological societies as well. Ihde believes that we are influenced by this "invariant" process and that is how we create knowledge — reflecting and internalizing "the very projected 'world' we find ourselves in" (18).

This projection of worlds we find ourselves in is more simply stated by Mary Baker Eddy (who stands out today as one of the more radical metaphysical philosophers of the late nineteenth and early twentieth centuries): "The physical universe expresses the conscious and unconscious thoughts of mortals" (Eddy 1906:484). For her the material laws of the universe — from Newtonian mechanics to sickness of the body — are but objective states of what she terms mortal mind. This relates to how Ihde sees the invariant self-interpretation as being invariant because, as Nietzsche said, the essential does not necessarily occur in our technological modern age, but it has already occurred in primeval times. This essentiality Eddy calls mortal mind. So in Ihde's words, "We end up modeling ourselves upon the very 'world' we project and interpret ourselves in terms of technology" (1983:22). If some people believe in the existence of UFOs, they may believe in a reality constructed from this false belief, even building a community of followers from such beliefs. The same goes for the *Star Trek* fans. Thus myth becomes reality. It becomes enacted, performed. Roland Barthes would call this the process of mythic consumption: "the reader lives the myth as a story at once true and unreal" (1972:128). The image becomes so "natural" that the consumer of myth no longer questions the assumption of its constructed and artificial meaning. This is how Captain Picard and not the judge of a United States district courthouse comes to represent law for Adams. And this is why a comet — an image already steeped in mythological astrology — could become closely allied to UFOs, a New Age phenomenon. For the Heaven's Gate cult the UFO image became so naturalized that there was no mistaking the power of the virtual Internet image.

The late astronomer Carl Sagan calls this mythical-consumption process "hypnogogic imagery." Sagan discovered parallels among the stories of contemporary alien abductions with those of an earlier European mythology composed of a pantheon of gods, demons, spirits, and fairies. All of the stories and sightings of these mythical beings evolve into new forms, "and when the old myths fade and we begin thinking that extraterrestrial beings are plausible, then that's where hypnogogic imagery tends" (1996:130–131). Hypnogogic imagery is an expression of the imagination — a physicalization of mortal mind. Eddy, the nineteenth-century metaphysician, wrote: "Mortal mind sees what it believes as certainly as it believes what it sees. It feels, hears, and sees its own thoughts" (1906:86). There certainly is a difference between science fiction used as a literary device and ufology that comes from a *belief* in something out *there*. The latter is based more on a faith that is neither science nor fiction — it is a faith in the supernatural, a perception of something that is not really there but seems so to a belief influenced by a mental environment that would think these imaginary visitations plausible. Sagan, in fact, was concerned by how the mind can be so easily influenced by belief in the imaginary: "And if the alien abduction accounts are mainly about brain physiology, hallucinations, distorted memories of childhood, and hoaxing, don't we have before us a matter of supreme importance — touching on our limitations, the ease with which we can be misled and manipulated, the fashioning of our beliefs...?" (188). The question "Do you believe in UFOs?" is similar to "Do you believe in demons?" One cannot equate that question with "Do you believe in science fiction?" Fictional stories are not a question of belief or faith, although classical mythology used stories as a way to understand the world. Ihde places science fiction within this tradition of mythology.

Science fiction conflates Ihde's three variations (hunter/gatherer, agricultural, and technological), presenting story and myth in a futuristic setting. It is a fantasy projection of our current technological society, which itself grew out of an earlier historical period. If earlier societies created their own myths and rituals to understand the world, then, according to Ihde, technological societies must create their own myths, and these myths will be presented in a way that today's society can understand, "embodying the imagination in a form appropriate to the respective 'world' reflected." If a snake dancer represented "a sacred and dramatized being" in the ritual of a hunter/gatherer society, then, Ihde contends, our contemporary society has its myths "embodied in various technological representations, the most notable candidates being film and television." So he believes that a "fascination of utopias, science fiction, UFOs, and such phenomena as *Star Wars*, *Battle[star] Galactica*, and the like illustrate" a contemporary mythology. He calls this kind of science fiction "a genre of projections placed in irreal future time" (1983:20). Straczynski, the creator of the multiple-award-winning science fiction television saga, *Babylon 5* (1993–1998), echoes in some ways Ihde's belief: "We listen for the voice that is ancient in us, and recast our core myths in more contemporary clothing, to better understand them and ourselves. Providing these myths is the responsibility of the storyteller.... The myth-maker points to the past but speaks in the voice of future history" (1995:9).

Science fiction fandom happens when these fictional projections into future time, however irreal, reflect back into our real present time as the hyperreal — simulations that, as Baudrillard says, are "characterized by a precession of the model ... their circulation, orbital like that of the bomb, constitutes the genuine magnetic field of the event" (1994:16). But it is exactly this attraction to the "magnetic field"— the circulation of film and television products — that film and television history gets performed. The purchase and display of film memorabilia (T-shirts, models, toys, role-playing games, and so forth) are how a"film gets articulated after people have seen it," Abdul-Karim Mustapha says (1996b). He adds that the film is the absolute reference and that these objects signify this reference, so, he believes, the objects of fantasy become the empirical history of the film as it gets performed in everyday life. By wearing memorabilia references (the interface) to a film or television show, fans' values become represented by means of a performance through which strips of behavior activate references to an entire imaginary entertainment environment. The environment's values become the fans' values. This is what Adams expressed in the Whitewater courtroom.

On the other hand, the Heaven's Gate cult crossed the line from enacted representation into what Schechner calls "dark play," exploding Baudrillard's orbital bomb. Fantasy becomes dangerous when a person's fantasy subjunctive transforms into an indicative reality (see Schechner 1993:36–39)— when they make the fantasy real or play at a fantasy when people around the fantasists are not aware that they have been placed within another's fantasy. The illusory Hale-Bopp UFO became the interface into Heaven's Gate's previously constructed imaginary environment, which was built from a UFO mythos. The photograph became the kernel that activated a ritual performance of death in the hopes that the ritual would take them to the craft. The belief of this flying object performed on their underlying and naturalized UFO mythos, opening a gateway — like the snake dancer's charm — to an alternative world. The snake dancer's audience knows that the performance is not deadly, however. Spring will come despite the nature-bound ritual performance. The Heaven's Gate technological ritual of death had to be performed because it was the only behavior that would get them to that UFO, since it did not exist. After several months of hope, they knew it was not coming. They had to go to it. The ritual performance transformed an unreality into an illusion of hope just within reach like a virtual image on the other side of a glass. Adams, however, knew that her costume represented a fiction. She (however seriously) played at tweaking the courtroom system.

Creating Community Through Mythology

Ihde's intentionality of a future projection into an irreal future becomes interactive in an actual present as commodities (like UFOs and *Star Trek*) circulate within a community. Fans and various cult groups embrace commodities and intentionally express the values of that irreal future that the commodities represent. Communities, like in early hunter/gatherer societies, get built around such circulation. Schechner would say that the performance of ritual in hunter/gatherer societies represented the theater of the day: "The first theaters were ceremonial centers," he says, and the entire process of hunting/gathering revolved around "a seasonal schedule" in which they would meet others and celebrate, "marking the celebration by some kind of writing on a space: an integration of geography, calendar, social interaction, and the proclivity of people to transform nature into culture" (1988:156). Today, in our technological age, we no longer move from place to place looking for food and marking ceremonial sites of performance. Or do we?

Science fiction fans move from one site of media consumption to another, and they meet others and share stories at an intersection of public space called the science fiction convention. Cult groups select a more private space, such as the one the Heaven's Gate followers created. Rituals of an earlier age have been translated into rituals of a technological age. An individual may have once identified with brother bear by wearing a mask in a ritual of an earlier period. But now individuals are more apt to wear a *Star Trek* uniform and through this performance circulate and identify with the values not of brother bear but of Captain Kirk. The science fiction convention becomes a central community for the sharing of sf rituals and values. However, these conventions do not transform nature into culture, for they themselves transform nature (in many cases, a hotel) into a self-contained virtual starship/time machine, an imaginary environment housing aliens, people, literature, movies, and so on. In contrast, the Heaven's Gate cultists performed a ritual in order to create a reality from an illusion, the UFO that existed only in their imaginations. The performance, however, made it real in the minds of those who watched and read about the aftereffects of their fantasy, their suicides.

Professor Reed would have us think that there is a similarity of intent between how UFO cults alter people's worldviews and how people buy into science fiction fandom. Because people build communities from the popular culture of science fiction, Reed would say that sf fans are cultic. I contend that this is not the case. Although I'm sure some science fiction fans have their romantic notions about UFOs, I have a hunch that most of these fans remain reasonably skeptical. Cult groups simply perform a different kind of function and intent than science fiction fandom. Science fiction fans certainly are not cultic or quasi-cultic. That belief is bred on stereotype and ignorance. SF fans would never revolve themselves around a cultic figure (with the exception, perhaps, of L. Ron Hubbard), and if they did, they would never jump into a suicide pact thinking they would accelerate their salvation from this world.

An sf convention is a site where people go to not only have fun and perform various roles but to have intelligent conversations among themselves and with their favorite authors. C. J. Cherryh, author of such award-winning novels as *Downbelow Station* (1981) and *Cyteen* (1988), spoke at a science fiction convention in Rye Brook, New York (Lunacon 1997). She knew more about the consequences of cloning than most other people because she has thought through these issues at the human level in her novels. *Cyteen* for example deals especially with issues of cloning. As our congressional leaders and fundamentalists debate the morality of cloning, Cherryh provided two comments that cut to the heart of the issue: 1) cloning is a way to preserve endangered species; 2) if a person is cloned, the clone should be made the legal heir to the person cloned. These thoughts were debated not in the halls of Washington but at a science fiction convention (that location where supposedly nuts and cultists worship at the feet of their favorite authors). Those 1,500 people would not commit suicide in the name of Cherryh. What happened to them instead? They got an education through exposure to literary ideas that debate contemporary scientific and social issues metaphorically.

Like myths, the works of literary sf circulating throughout science fiction conventions are meant to educate and entertain contemporary society about the world and our place in it. Most sf fans dream about exciting possible futures and want to improve their world, not escape from it. The UFO cults are looking for something to take their hand and lift them out of a world they apparently no longer care about.

UFOs are the product of "sci-fi," that pejorative term designating what author Harlan Ellison calls "cheapjack foolishness." Its like is found in the "tabloid mentality of UFO abductions, triangular-headed ETs, reinterpreted biblical apocrypha, and just plain bone stick stone gullibility" that the Heaven's Gate cultists got caught up in, he explains (Ellison 1997). Literary science fiction, like *Babylon 5* (1993–1998), for example, is an outcome of myth. Straczynski explains: "As a culture, we have come adrift and are searching for guideposts to the next five years, the next 10 years, the next millennium." Much of today's literature, he believes, fails to explore large mythic themes that create these guideposts. "The mainstream literary establishment has walked away from the mythmakers, the storyteller's obligation to point to the horizon and tell us where we are going," he says. And he believes that "science fiction is the only genre dealing with the issues of the future and our place in it" (Lancaster 1997b). Ellison and Straczynski are not cultists. They believe in the possibilities of a literary imagination, not fantasy escapism. So why would reporters and religious professors confuse the issue?

Highbrow and Lowbrow Culture

I believe that the root of the debate, or concern, in comparing ritualistic UFO cults with science fiction fandom lies within the invention of "highbrow" versus "lowbrow" culture — the perceived illusion between what Schechner calls efficacy and entertainment. I mentioned earlier how Benjamin says that there is no place for social function within pure art (1968:224). According to Lawrence

Levine's extensive historical research, the notion of how we must stand in silent awe when in the presence of respected art was born in the second half of the nineteenth century. Levine writes: "What was invented in the late nineteenth century were the rituals accompanying that appreciation [of high art]; what was invented was the illusion that the aesthetic products of high culture were originally created to be appreciated in precisely the manner late nineteenth-century Americans were taught to observe: with reverent, informed, disciplined seriousness" (1988:229). Cultural hegemony prevailed because nineteenth-century culture mavens perceived certain works of art as having the potential to give enlightenment. If only individuals would appreciate art in a reverent way, the argument goes, they too would become enlightened (and culturally homogenous).

These connoisseurs felt that their way (in viewing art) was the way the creators and appreciators of the original works of art experienced them — that the reverent way they experienced art "was the way Shakespeare, Beethoven, and Greek sculpture were meant to be experienced and in fact had been experienced always by those of culture and discernment" (Levine 1988:231). The historical fact remains, however, as Levine points out so well, that in the first half of the nineteenth century there really was no high art versus low art. I know that this is simplifying the argument. There were certainly those who appreciated art with different levels of awareness — but it is also true that the appreciation (albeit at different levels) was shared by all. There were no cultural categories separating Shakespeare from burlesque, for example. Shakespeare, opera, and other so-called high art was appreciated with as much enthusiasm and with the same popularity as today's rock concerts and sporting events. This was not to last.

Art appreciation shifted from entertainment to reverence (or efficacy), and so we have the phrase (directed at those who don't go to museums, theater, or classical music concerts), "Why don't you go out and get some culture?" And more importance, many are taught how to receive high culture — with the respected silence of worship. Thus, those who invented the belief in high culture ended up creating an exclusive way to appreciate art. They closed doors on many who did not want to be contained as passive observers of art. So popular culture substituted this need (which "high" art once supplied). A large segment of the population, in order to satisfy "aesthetic cravings," turned to "the blues, jazz or jazz-derived music, musical comedy, photography, comic strips, movies, radio, popular comedians" (Levine 1988:232). And so high art is meant to educate, enlighten, instill culture, whereas popular art is considered mere entertainment for the unenlightened masses. The real reason sf fans are looked down upon by much of the mainstream press and by a large segment of the population that has no interest in science fiction, is because sf is not considered art: it is either of the masses or of the fringe and therefore not of value. Perceived in this way, science fiction fans are easily labeled as fringe cultists. The dichotomy of high art versus low art is an invention and in a world growing increasingly postmodern is really of no use. Let's bury these invented nineteenth-century dichotomous concepts. Rather than placing value judgments on popular culture or art, I'm more interested in studying how performances are constructed — how they work and what they mean. The fact remains that art and popular culture have more in common with each other than the cultural snobs and critics have with art.

Many of today's cultural theorists realize the utter falsity and unimportance of cultural valuations. Schechner believes that all performances are a mixture of efficacy and entertainment. He lists the qualities of an efficacious performance: "results, link to an absent Other, symbolic time, performer possessed as in a trance, audience participates, audience believes, criticism discouraged, collective creativity." On the other side of the spectrum is entertainment, which includes such qualities as: "fun, only for those here, emphasis now, performer knows what s/he's doing, audience watches, audience appreciates, criticism flourishes, individual creativity" (1988:120). Different performances stress certain qualities over others — it is not a question of highbrow versus lowbrow. An efficacious performance is one that transforms. The Heaven's Gate cultists created an efficacious performance: they were looking for a permanent result, and their belief was linked to an absent Other. The whole group participated in a "trance"-like behavior that would symbolically send them away to another time/place. Essentially they created, then sacralized, an imaginary environment. Adams's courtroom experience, on the other hand, possessed more of the qualities of performed entertainment. Yet, despite the fact that sf conventions share many qualities of an efficacious performance, they do not transform these sites into a cultic environment. Nor are they any less important than, for example, a Shakespearean performance. There are only different efficacious/entertainment attributes shared and stressed in various ways throughout different styles and sites of performance.

Segments of our population are reacting against a culturally ingrained, individualistic approach to art spectatorship/appreciation — against the reverent sacralization invented in the latter half of the nineteenth century. As explicated by Levine: "With important exceptions — particularly in the areas of sports and religion — audiences in America had become less interactive, less of a public and more of a group of mute receptors. Art was becoming a one-way process: the artist communicating and the audience receiving" (1988:195). Today, at the cusp of the twenty-first century, people are looking for alternative forms of performance-entertainments that have less to do with reverent sacralization and more to do with collective participation. Science fiction conventions offer such participatory environments that react against the nineteenth-century desire that wormed its way into twentieth century notions of how audiences receive traditional theater, novels, movies, and TV.

Today's immersive participatory forms can be found in nontraditional postcinematic forms of performance-entertainments such as those described in this book, including fantasy role-playing games, interactive computer games, environmental theater (and murder-mystery dinners), Disney-like theme parks, Renaissance fairs, science fiction conventions, among many others. In between Whitewater and Heaven's Gate lie today's participatory and immersive interactive performances. Around these "fires" we experience the myths and rituals of a technological age.

10

The Pseudotragedy of
Star Wars and Reagan's
Pax Americana

"When Ben Kenobi says, 'May the Force be with you,' he's speaking of the power and energy of life, not of programmed political intentions."

Joseph Campbell (1991:178–179)

The Myth of Star Wars

The mythic elements of the *Star Wars* trilogy (1977–1983) have received much attention in the popular press, as well as among academics (most notably from myth scholar Joseph Campbell). As early as 1978 Andrew Gordon explained how Lucas's hero, Luke Skywalker, mirrors the hero-journey found in Campbell's classic, *The Hero with a Thousand Faces* (1972). *Star Wars*, although held together "by the standard pattern of adventures of a mythic hero," Gordon says, was "fashioned out of bits and pieces of twentieth-century American popular mythology — old movies, science fiction, television, and comic books" (1978: 315). Denis Wood, writing in the same journal as Gordon, argues that there is also a strong connection between *Star Wars* and the mythic works of J. R. R. Tolkien (*The Hobbit, The Lord of the Rings, The Silmarillion*) and T. H. White (*The Once and Future King, The Book of Merlyn*). Wood believes these connections include an "exotic mise-en-scène," lack of sex (a preadolescent view of the world), and the focus on "a parentless young man who, under the guidance of a wise but mysterious tutor ..., finds himself on a perilous venture he never sought, the outcome of which is crucial in a larger contest between opposing cosmic forces" (Wood 1978:327–329). These elements clearly resonate within the context of a classic monomyth, as explicated by Campbell. And the recent publication of *Star Wars: The Magic of Myth* (1997), a companion book to the Smithsonian exhibit in Washington, D.C., further valorizes the mythic structure of *Star Wars*. Daniel Mackay, however, believes that this "authority behind the *Star Wars* story is not a universal mythic faculty within the human consciousness or unconsciousness, but it is Joseph Campbell," because it is "*his* mythic themes, the ones he universalized and identified" that Lucas used as a "blueprint" for his movies, "thereby validating the 'universality' of the films" (1999).

Little, if any, however, has been said about the Aristotelian moments of tragedy — an important element of Campbell's monomyth — in the *Star Wars* trilogy. Campbell examines this connection: "The happy ending of the fairy tale, the myth, ... is to be read, not as a contradiction, but as a transcendence of the universal tragedy of man," Campbell writes (1972:28). He contends that both tragedy ("the shattering of the forms and of our attachment to the forms") and comedy ("the wild and careless, inexhaustible joy of life invincible") "together constitute the totality of the revelation that is life"— this transcendence occurs through catharsis (28). "It is the business of mythology proper, and of the fairy tale," he adds, "to reveal the specific dangers and techniques of the dark interior way from tragedy to comedy" (29). So it is really no surprise that George Lucas attempted to create such a tragic hero with Luke Skywalker, who faces tragedy in *The Empire Strikes Back* (1980), but unlike a typical classical hero such as King Oedipus, he recovers from his tragedy in *The Return of the Jedi* (1983). However, in the process Luke causes his father to face his sins, ultimately leading to his death and ultimate transcendence and re-transformation into Anakin Skywalker, who stands as a ghost-like image alongside the similarly depicted Ben Kenobi and Yoda at the end of the film.

Typical of the Campbell school of scholars is the argument that our age has lost its heroes. Lucas, they say, has brought heroes back into our culture: "In an era in which Americans have lost heroes in whom to believe, Lucas has created a myth for our times" (Gordon 1978:315); "When the first film in the *Star Wars* trilogy appeared in 1977, the ancient myths no longer seemed relevant for many people in this culture" (Henderson 1997:6). Campbell believes that "myth is the secret opening through which the inexhaustible energies of the cosmos pour into human cultural manifestation" (1972:3). Further, he contends, these tales are "spontaneous productions of the psyche, and each bears within it, undamaged, the germ power of its source" (4). The notion of Jung's concept of the collective unconscious rings throughout Campbell's work. And it is here that we supposedly identify with a mythology imbued with the "inexhaustible energies of the cosmos" in an attempt to bring healing to society's damaged psyche.

Pseudotragedy and Catharsis

Lacan argues against Jung's unified collective unconscious, stating that "the unconscious is the condition of linguistics" (1985:205). Myth is a linguistic structure coded with society's cultural tropes and not the "germ power" of a cosmic force. "Linguistics gets its force from the fact that the subject is marked from the beginning by division" (204)—created by the split self during the mirror-image stage. This split creates a desire for the imaginary (mythology) and manifests itself in the symbolic (through diverse and multiple texts and images). *Star Wars* offers its mythology at this level. Seen in this way, it is not a unifying myth, as some of the writers mentioned earlier suggest. Even Campbell acknowledges the fact that there are no unification myths today: "In the absence of an effective general mythology, each of us has his private, unrecognized, rudimentary, yet secretly potent pantheon of dream" (1972:4). From this premise Campbell takes the argument to a new level: "The latest incarnation of Oedipus, the continued romance of Beauty and the Beast, stand this afternoon on the corner of Forty-second Street and Fifth Avenue, waiting for the traffic light to change" (4).

I contend, however, that if mythology can only be found on the level of individuality, then it is not a true mythology, despite the fact that it does borrow elements from mythology, including elements of tragedy. The tragedies of ancient Greece, on the other hand, offered cathartic myths on a community-wide scale. Tropes within these myths resonated throughout a unified polis. (Athens may have been the best model of this; however, this unification was only for a certain class—the slaves certainly did not share the idealism of the Athenian.) Because *Star Wars* is not placed in an arguable unified polis, it fails to achieve a community-wide purgation, despite the fact that it attains moments of mythic tragedy. It is a pseudotragedy because it failed to deliver purgation within the nonunified polis of the United States in the 1970s and early 1980s. Today, instead of offering a reconciliation of a polis, the catharsis of films tends to create a desire on the part of some spectators to build microcommunities, where fans share the world and values of a film in an attempt to re-live the cathartic moment found in the contemporary mythologies (and their attendant tragic elements) of popular culture.

Catharsis, Aristotle says, is found in tragedy, which "is an imitation of an action that is serious, complete, and of a certain magnitude; ... through pity and fear effecting the proper purgation of these emotions" (1961:61). Tragedies offer catharsis for the spectator. Luke Skywalker certainly embodies the Aristotelian elements of tragic flaw at the end of *The Empire Strikes Back* (1980) when he confronts his nemesis, Darth Vader. At this moment, two-thirds into the trilogy, Vader reveals to Luke that he is his father, and we see Luke's transformation from the boy hero of *A New Hope* (1977) to a tragic hero who will redeem himself in *The Return of the Jedi* (1983). For me this represents a classic moment of Aristotelian tragedy—Luke's sudden realization of his own hubris forces him to look at life in a new way. I will argue later in more detail that however much this scene resonates with Greek tragedy, it fails to provide catharsis on an Aristotelian scale, for unlike the perceived unified community of ancient Athens, the population of the United States is disconnected from its polis. The original *Star Wars* films appeared in the political climate of the 1970s and 1980s, a time of extreme political disaffection that removed any possibility of a polis-like milieu. And this is why the *Star Wars* movies cannot provide purgation typical of the interconnectedness between ancient Greek plays and their own population, despite the fact that the megablockbuster status of *Star Wars* does indicate its close relationship to the public at large. Instead, contemporary films offer escape from political reality. Audiences do not reintegrate into the society at a social *and* political level.

If *Star Wars* represents such "B-movie culture" and World War II–era values of "unity, self-sacrifice for a higher calling, clarity of purpose against an evil enemy, implacable will toward ultimate victory," as film historian Robert Sklar contends in *Movie-Made America* (1994:342), then it does so in the wake of the United States's Vietnam debacle and as a precursor to Reagan's election and subsequent imperial policy of Pax Americana. When Oedipus, in Sophocles's *Oedipus Rex* (a consummate example of Aristotelian tragedy), realizes his unwitting patricide and Oedipal relationship to his mother, he blinds and exiles himself in order to offer penance to the community suffering from a curse caused by his sins. In such a tragedy the model spectator supposedly "will thrill with horror and melt to pity at what takes place," Aristotle says, adding: "This is the impression we should receive from hearing the story of *Oedipus*" (1961:78).

Pax Americana's Oedipal Curse

Post–World War II Pax Americana failed tragically during the undeclared Vietnam War — in the midst of which the United States bore a curse of Oedipal proportions, suffering economic recession, populous uprising, and fuel shortages. The United States found no purgation for the failure of its young men — hoping to ape the successful moral victory of World War II — sent off to a war without hope, many returning home with patricidal guilt and failure weighing them down in homeless, wounded poverty. However, no less than Oedipus, members of the United States realized somehow that *it* caused this curse. Thus we had popular protests against the Vietnam War. Like Oedipus's Thebes, the United States felt the bite of an unseen sin. Oliver Stone's *Platoon* (1986), perhaps, attempted to offer purgation for the veterans of that war — its popularity, box office success, and Academy Award for best picture would seem to indicate such a scenario. If, however (as some scholars contend), *Star Wars* presented mythic tropes found in the popular culture of comic books, old movies, and so forth from which it constructed its *fantasy*, then, *Platoon* presented what Thomas Prasch calls a "surface reality" of the war by reconstructing such realistic and tragic tropes as civilian murders, rapes, and village razing conducted by United States Marines during the war (1988:198–199). (I'm not discounting the fact that many people, including veterans, did receive some kind of purgation through Stone's film, however, it did not occur on a community-wide scale to the point where spectators were, en masse, reintegrated into the polis.)

In both cases these films, like original myths, reflect a cultural code common to many people. Roland Barthes, in a "Textual Analysis of a Tale of Poe," defines the cultural code as a "code of knowledge, or rather of human knowledge, public opinion, of culture transmitted through books, education ...; the referent of this code is knowledge, as a body of rules elaborated by society" (1985:94). He then goes on to describe the scientific, rhetorical, chronological, and sociohistorical codes that authors such as Poe use to convey their stories. According to Barthes the codes become commonplace — so "banal," "insignificant," and "widely used that we take them as natural features" of our society, yet without these codes the story "would very quickly become *unreadable*" (94). Stone and Lucas drew upon these cultural codes common to many people when constructing their movies, whether representing tropes of a jungle war or tropes from space fantasy. Dennis Muren, senior visual effects supervisor at Industrial Light and Magic, responding to a question during a press conference at the Smithsonian's Air and Space Museum on October 29, 1997, said that George Lucas and Steven Spielberg are successful filmmakers because they are "hardwired" to deliver audience expectations. They are accomplished because they know how to manipulate cultural codes.

George Lucas began his filmmaking career during the Vietnam War, releasing *THX 1138* in 1970 and *American Graffiti* in 1973. Mary Henderson, in *Star Wars: The Magic of Myth*, believes that the following events "contributed their own cultural flavor" to Lucas's next film, *Star Wars*, in 1977: the Watergate scandal, the Arab-Israeli Yom Kippur War (and Kissinger's "first nuclear alert since the Cuban missile crisis"), an OPEC oil price increase, economic decline, withdrawal from Vietnam, deployment of SS-20 missiles by the Soviets, as well as their support of "Communists incursions" in Angola, Mozambique, and Ethiopia. "For some viewers" of *Star Wars*, she concludes, "the trilogy, with its democratic allies fighting a totalitarian power, seemed reminiscent not just of World War II but of the ongoing Cold War" (1997:149). Ultimately, Henderson believes that the destructive power of the Death Star represented the destruction of a potential nuclear war so dominant in cold war scenarios.

For some, the priest's words to Oedipus, who queried him about his people's supplication for relief from the curse of Thebes, reflected the tragic crisis of the United States in the 1970s:

> Thebes is tossed on a murdering sea
> And can not lift her head from the death surge.
> A rust consumes the buds and fruits of the earth;
> The herds are sick; children die unborn,
> And labor is vain. The god of plague and pyre
> Raids like detestable lightning through the city,
> And all the house of Kadmos is laid waste,
> All emptied, and all darkened: Death alone
> Battens upon the misery of Thebes. (Sophocles 1996:46)

In a culture of gods and fate *Oedipus Rex* probably provided cathartic moments and purgation for a majority of an ancient Athenian audience. But today this play cannot reach people in the same way as in its original time. "Modern audiences, though, sometimes find the play baffling," one critic contends, because of the prophecy deciding Oedipus's fate (Worthen 1996:44). However, in the time of Sophocles tragic plays were tightly woven within the fabric of the (dominant) community, and because these cultural tropes were embedded in a collected consciousness, the social polis received periodic purgation through dramatic catharsis. United States culture provided no such pathos, despite how some scholars say that *Star Wars* is a myth for our times. It spoke to a large populace, but its mythic function, however coded, could not deliver a community-wide catharsis to a fractured society — unified only by a common link to popular culture media images that really did not offer any real or unmediated connection to the social and political fabric.

Theater, however, supposedly offered such a communal experience in ancient Greece. It provided catharsis to the majority population. As I mention in another essay, they

> exemplified a reflexive relationship between what anthropologist Victor Turner describes as two models of human inter-relatedness: 1) people segmented into the various political, legal, and economic positions of a structured, democratic society; and 2) people unified as equal individuals in the *comitatus* of the theater (1969:96). The Greeks presented an effective model for cathartic theater. The relationship between theater and society, performer and spectator linked closely together. For example, "the plots of all Greek plays were already well known to the audience," Turner writes (1982:103–104); consequently it can be seen how the playwrights provided a reflexive cathartic experience for the spectator by tapping into the ingrained cultural values of a unified Greek community. In addition, as a part of the main religious festivals, Greek theater included the "audience as active participant," Susan Bennett describes. The theater was "clearly inseparable from the social, economic, and political structures of Athens," she writes (1990:2–3). Furthermore, this kind of relationship existed because "unity existed prior to theatrical creation," Helen Chinoy states, adding: "The concord sprang from a cohesive society whose common thoughts and emotions found in an 'idea of a theater' a basic vision of human life" (1963:7). This cohesive status between theater and society changed over time. (Lancaster 1997a:75–76)

No longer would plays, or even their close ally, cinema, provide a community-wide cathartic experience for spectators. Spectators and the media of cinema, television, and theater are not connected to a shared "religious festival" that instills a unifying value system to our culture. Our media may unify the population into shared visions of popular culture, but these images do not reintegrate spectators into a unified "social, economic, and political" cohesive whole.

If the United States seemed "all emptied, and all darkened" in the 1970s, there was no Oedipus to step forward to take the blame and purge the nation of its sins. Even Nixon's resignation — surely a sign of a leader admitting his guilt — failed to provide cathartic responsibility, as historian Howard Zinn observes: "The word was out: get rid of Nixon, but keep the system.... Nixon's foreign policy remained. The government's connections to corporate interests remained" (1990:543). The United States, rather than blinding itself and stepping away from a failed imperialistic policy, would in a few years after Vietnam elect a president who during his eight-year reign oversaw the rise of a new corporate imperialism rampant in the materialism of a greedy corporate America and multinational corporations. (Donald Trump was one figure espousing his *Art of the Deal* so that all could potentially reap the same billion-dollar rewards as he.) It is ironic that Lucas and company would create their own multimillion-dollar art of the movie-making deal, indirectly helping to spawn the megablockbuster action movie genre. Sklar makes the connection: The "revival of B-movie culture — launched by *Star Wars* and expanded through Reagan's election — becomes a defining aspect of popular rhetoric in the 1980s, prevalent both in box-office hit movies and presidential politics" (1994:342).

It could be argued that *Star Wars* was one attempt to offer a purgation for a 1970s United States "tossed on a murdering sea and can not lift her head from the death surge." Despite the fact that "[n]ot even the cultural theory of mediation, which holds that works such as movies interpose themselves between society and the spectator's consciousness, seems entirely satisfactory" (Sklar 1994:329), some (namely Campbell) have explained that the popularity of *Star Wars* stems from the fact that it is rooted in a mythology resonating across time and cultures. It is my belief, however, that *Star Wars* is a pseudomyth pretending to offer solace to failed national policies and individual lives of the 1970s and 1980s. Because we do not live in a unicultural polis, as the ancient Greeks did, *Star Wars* cannot offer the same cathartic purgation of an *Oedipus Rex*. Yet, ironically, *Star Wars* reaches more people than Sophocles's play, and it certainly contains elements gleaned from ancient Greek tragedy.

Luke Skywalker's Peripeteia, Recognition, and Suffering

Aristotle lists plot as the most important facet of tragedy. It should, he says, "imitate actions which excite pity and fear, this being the distinctive mark of tragic imitation. ...pity is aroused by unmerited misfortune ... that of a man who is not eminently good and just, yet whose misfortune is brought about ... by some error or frailty. He must be one who is highly renowned and prosperous" (Aristotle 1961:75–76). In addition, "the most powerful elements of emotional interest in Tragedy" are peripeteia ("reversal of the situation") and recognition (63) — what I call the Oedipal moment of hubris: when the hero recognizes that his whole life or mission has been founded on false reasoning. "This recognition, combined with Reversal," Aristotle says, "will produce either pity or fear; and actions producing these effects are those which, by our definition, Tragedy represents" (73). So there are three elements of plot that hinge upon catharsis: peripeteia, recognition, and suffering. "The Scene of Suffering is a destructive or painful action, such as death on the stage, bodily agony, wounds and the like" (73). These three elements are projected through the character of Luke Skywalker.

In *The Empire Strikes Back* (1980) Luke begins the story as a hero of the rebellion, victor over the Death Star, reflecting the "inexhaustible joy of life invincible" and a person "highly renowned and prosperous." However, right at the beginning of the story he is attacked and wounded by an ice monster, the rebellion is forced to retreat from its base on Hoth by the forces of the Empire, and Luke's friend Han Solo is betrayed and captured near the end of the film. Luke, on a mission to avenge his father's death, attempts to track down and kill Darth Vader. What he doesn't realize is that Vader is looking for him in an attempt to either bring Luke to the emperor or convert him to his side. The first time we see Luke confronting Vader face-to-face is in the scene inside the tree cave on Yoda's planet, Dagobah. Luke, in a vision, cuts off Vader's head, revealing Luke's own face beneath the mask. This scene foreshadows the patricidal inclinations of Luke and hints at his "dark side" tendencies. Later he walks into Cloud City, floating high in the stratosphere of Bespin (reminiscent of Stratos in the 1969 *Star Trek* episode "The Cloud-Minders"). He is sure of his moral stance, trained by Ben Kenobi and Yoda in the ways of the Jedi, who were once the "guardians of peace and justice in the Old Republic. Before the dark times, before the Empire" (*Star Wars*). Having the moral authority of the Jedi behind him, Luke walks into the depths of Cloud City to the carbon-freezing chamber and into the reactor control room and shaft in the heart of the city. Three scenes — a beginning, middle, and end — depict Luke's encounter with Vader. This sequence encapsulates the tragic moments of Aristotelian reversal, recognition, and suffering for Luke.

The first scene is a prelude, when Luke walks into the carbon-freezing chamber. Shortly before this we saw Han Solo being encased in carbonite in this same room. Vader hopes to process Luke in the same way "for his journey to the Emperor" (*The Empire Strikes Back*). Luke walks warily into the empty room, steam hisses, and we see Vader silhouetted in a long shot, speaking: "The Force is with you, young Skywalker. But you are not a Jedi yet." Luke walks toward Vader, and in a telling moment of hubris Luke draws his lightsaber first. Earlier in the film, when Luke is training with Yoda, he asks him about the dark side of the Force:

LUKE: Is the dark side stronger?
YODA: No ... no ... no. Quicker, easier, more seductive.
LUKE: But how am I to know the good side from the bad?
YODA: You will know. When you are calm, at peace. Passive. A Jedi uses the Force for knowledge and defense, never for attack.

When Luke draws his lightsaber first, we realize that Luke is not playing on the defensive. Overconfident, he swings his blade at Vader, who easily parries the blow. The beginning of Luke's tragic flaw is depicted here, for he is drawing not on the Force of good, of passivity, of defense but on the easier and seductive path of the dark side. In *Star Wars: The Annotated Screenplays*, Bouzereau, referring to a story conference transcript dated November 28–December 2, 1977, mentions that the "challenge with the confrontation between Luke and Vader was to play it like a seduction, a temptation; the audience knows that Luke is not going to die, so the ultimate hook is the fear that Luke might turn to the dark side" (1997:210). It appears that Luke's tragic flaw lies in the fact that he may be seducible by the dark side of the Force. But this only hides the fact that Luke is expressing moral righteousness to exact revenge for his perceived father's death (as revealed to him by Ben Kenobi in *A New Hope*). His rashness and overconfidence (similar traits acted out by the United States's headlong rush into Vietnam) is what reveals the beginning of the tragedy that will lead to a major reversal and recognition for Luke. This prelude lasts only a few moments, but it sets up Luke's relationship to Vader. We then cut to the scene where Lando frees Leia, Chewie, and Threepio from the stormtroopers.

We then move back in continuation of Luke and Vader's lightsaber duel. Vader goes on the offensive and drives Luke into the carbon-freezing pit. Luke quickly leaps out of the trap, receiving the accolade from Vader, "Impressive ... most impressive." He insists to Luke, "Only your hatred can destroy me"—knowing that the more Luke uses his hatred, the easier it will be for Vader to turn him over to the dark side. Luke attacks Vader again, forcing him over the edge of a pit. Luke deactivates his lightsaber and finds an alternate route down into the depths. The second scene begins here. No dialogue occurs in this scene. Luke walks through a tunnel into the reactor control room, where Vader stands in the shadows, waiting for him. Luke again activates his saber, but this time Vader wants to show him the power of the dark side. Vader uses the energy of the Force to tear pipes, cables, and other technological paraphernalia from off the wall. Luke turns to parry the flying objects with his saber. One large object smashes open a huge window overlooking the gargantuan reactor shaft. Too many objects impact him, and he is knocked off his feet and subsequently sucked out the window. At this moment Luke has faced a tragic reversal, the first part of the cathartic sequence. No longer is he the overconfident Jedi warrior coming to exact righteous justice on Vader. Luke's hubris has led him to his nemesis. He is now fighting for his life. The movie then cuts to Lando, Leia, and company who fail in their attempt to rescue Han from the bounty hunter, Boba Fett.

The final confrontation with Vader, David Wyatt argues, collapses "the Satanic Temptation with the Recognition of the Father" (1982:605). The scene begins when Luke, after being sucked out the window in the previous scene, catches hold of a girder extending out into the cavernous reactor shaft. He climbs up into another control room area that overlooks a gantry platform overhanging the pit. In the control room Vader mounts a ferocious attack, driving Luke out onto the gantry precipice, where Vader cuts off Luke's hand. John Rieder calls Vader the "'death father,' who symbolically castrates his son (by cutting off his right hand)" (1982:34). Wounded and in fear, Luke sidles his way out onto the end of the gantry. Below him the abyss drops thousands of feet. Vader attempts to persuade Luke to join him, revealing Vader's desire to replace the emperor:

> VADER: There is no escape. Don't make me destroy you, Luke. You do not yet realize your importance. You have only begun to discover your power. Join me and I will complete your training. With our combined strength, we can end this destructive conflict and bring order to the galaxy.
> LUKE: I'll never join you!
> VADER: If you only knew the power of the dark side.

Luke has reached the moment of suffering, but this suffering is minuscule compared to the suffering brought about by his moment of tragic recognition. Vader gives Luke the verbal coup de grace that seals the failure of his entire hero's mission up to this point:

> VADER: Obi-Wan never told you what happened to your father.
> LUKE: He told me enough! He told me you killed him.
> VADER: No. *I* am your father.
> LUKE: No. No. That's not true! That's impossible!
> VADER: Search your feelings. You know it to be true.
> LUKE: No! No!

The realization rends words of denial from Luke: he was on a quest to kill the slayer of his father, but through a tragic recognition he perceives his patricidal error. The recognition of his hubris racks Luke with horror. He feels betrayed by Ben Kenobi, whose lie to him about Vader's real identity could have potentially led Luke, like Oedipus, to unwittingly kill his own father.

Vader has other plans for Luke and tries to entice him to become a crown prince of the Empire: "Luke. You can destroy the Emperor. He has foreseen this. It is your destiny. Join me, and together we can rule the galaxy as father and son. Come with me. It is the only way." Rather than allying himself to the dark side, and wanting to escape his patricidal desire, Luke leaps to what he believes to be his own death. Even though he does not in fact die (he falls down a side shaft that sucks him down to the bottom of the city, where he hangs onto a weather vane as Lando, Leia, and Chewie rescue him in the *Millennium Falcon*), his entire outlook on life has changed. He has transformed from the idealistic righteous boy-hero of *A New Hope*, to a humble man, taking on the qualities and confidence of a Jedi Knight, which we see enacted in the third part of the trilogy, *The Return of the Jedi* (1983). In this movie Luke redeems his father from the dark side and destroys the emperor. The rebellion is victorious. In a ghost-

like image we see Vader in his original form of Anakin Skywalker, before his fall
to the dark side. Lucas's *Star Wars* prequel trilogy, beginning with *The Phantom
Menace* (1999), will depict the rise and fall of Luke's father.

Reagan's Pax Americana and the Manipulation of Cultural Codes

The Empire Strikes Back, although fulfilling moments of Aristotelian tragedy,
lacked a polis wherein the cathartic experience could be fully realized. The United
States, pulling out of its own 1970s peripeteia, recognition, and suffering, failed
to create a political consensus, a polis wherein a mythic story and its elements
of tragic catharsis could resonate not just within the audience escaping from the
pressures of a failing world outside the darkened room of a movie house but
throughout the entire social fabric. It was impossible for catharsis to effect a
polis-wide purgation then, as it is today, because of a fractured political and cultural climate. Rieder argues that "a political interpretation of [Skywalker's] rebellion leads us to the paradoxical conclusion that the films also appeal to a 'youth
movement' reaction against military-industrial imperialism" (1982:34). If *Star
Wars* sent a message that military-industrial imperialism could be overcome, it
never happened because, as Rieder contends, the ideology of the films is consumption: "What is being marketed is the *fantasy* of rebellion" (34). Brazilian
theater director Augusto Boal argues in fact that the entire model of Greek
tragedy is a formula for repressive passivity, allowing the dominant social order
to maintain its unquestioned policies (Boal 1979). *Star Wars*, modeled on the
Aristotelian drama, shares the repressive passivity of this form. Lacking a polis-
wide reconciliation through purgation, it becomes a fantasy of tragedy.

Two things happen to displace the classical model of tragic catharsis in contemporary society. First, instead of a purgation that offers reconciliation of society to its polis, we see an arrested form of reintegration — an escape from any
possible reconciliation. Individuals who have been touched by the cathartic elements of tragedy in a film may become purged from the pain of daily social structure of the polis, but instead of reintegrating themselves into society after being
exposed to this catharsis, they build a fan community in an attempt to relive this
moment of purgation. Marshall Blonsky, commenting on the "crisis" of Aristotelian catharsis, writes: "In the old world you felt cleansed upon leaving a
church or theater. In the new and in its theater of advertising, you feel aroused:
American advertising has transformed catharsis into desire" (1992:370). Fans
build communities around the commodification of film. This is where advertising — the desire for objects and the art of marketing — embodies itself in the fan.
Such fans, Henry Jenkins says, enter a "realm of the fiction as if it were a tangi-
ble place they can inhabit and explore" (1992:18) and where they are "active producers and manipulators of meanings" (23). So fans see films dozens of times,
perform in role-playing games, dress up in costumes, play computer games, read

novels based on the films, and so forth — all in an attempt to capture the original cathartic moment felt during the first viewing of the film. Mackay calls this process of playing in what he calls an Imaginary Entertainment Environment (such as *Star Wars*) "a recuperation of popular culture," through which role-players "create a series of performances that put a real life — the everyday ordinary life of the player — behind the fantastic mask and enchanting forms of popular culture" (1997:60). This recuperation is a desire for immersion into fantasy and, in fact, reflects a post-cinematic form wherein new kinds of participatory performances, such as those found in role-playing games, revolve around the commodification of a fictional fantasy universe. "The esthetic experience today, dominated by advertising," Blonsky argues, "leads you to want to possess and to do" — this is what "has pushed catharsis into a corner" (1992: 370). It is no longer enough to just watch a movie. Fans want to play with images from it.

The second thing that displaces the classical model of catharsis is the appropriation of a cultural product, such as *Star Wars*, by politicians, who place it into their own political ideology. Ronald Reagan's Strategic Defense Initiative — an orbital facility that was to be used to intercept potential ICBM nuclear attacks by the "evil empire" — was quickly dubbed "Star Wars." As Sklar points out, Reagan, during the B-movie period (from which *Star Wars* received some influence), played a Secret Service agent in a series "that culminated with the unveiling of a mystery ray gun capable of shooting spy planes from the sky." Some claim that these films "are progenitors of Reagan's Strategic Defense Initiative: the missing link, perhaps, between *Star Wars* and 'Star Wars'" (1994:342). This 1980s analogy is still being made today. The United States Army at the end of October 1997 test-fired a laser at one of their own older military satellites orbiting 260 miles above Earth. This program is run by Tom Meyer, the former head of laser research for "President Reagan's Strategic Defense Initiative (SDI), known as 'Star Wars'" (Landay 1997:4). A photo caption of an artist's rendering of a satellite laser platform states: "Mr. Reagan's Dream Come True?" The journalist, apparently buying into the $28-billion-a-year program, goes on to write, "Officials claim the test is defensive — not aimed at creating a satellite killer that would shatter the neutrality of space and could trigger a new global arms race" (1). However, if the heat from the laser is powerful enough to "detonate a missile's fuel or weaken its body until it shattered under high-speed stress" (4), what would prevent the military from using it against enemy planes, ships, or even tanks of oil reserves? The report talks about the potential for other countries to develop laser technology that could be used against "American satellites." No mention is made, however, of the other "quicker, easier, more seductive" darker side offensive capabilities of this technology. This is the ideology of a Death Star mentality found in the Empire of the *Star Wars* movies.

Janice Rushing, analyzing Reagan's 1983 SDI speech, argues that he used the rhetoric of "America's identity-defining myths" of the frontier to convey the legitimacy of "Star Wars" (1986:417). The Old West frontier myth represents an individualistic hero living outside the community. Even in the space age, when the "frontier scene has now shifted from finite land to infinite space," the hero is still modeled on the Old West form. Ever since the release of the original *Star Wars* film, writers have connected it with the Western (Gordon 1978 and Henderson 1997 being two such examples). However, the self-sufficient hero of the mythic Old West is "woefully ill-equipped" to transcend a "technological counter-agent, and the attempt to conquer technology with technology results in the diminution of the hero" (Rushing 1986:417). It is in the third, final stage that the hero reaches the "transcendent phase of the New Frontier," Rushing says, and the "reintegrated hero becomes consubstantial with the infinite scene s/he occupies and dissolves the dialectic between hero and enemy" (417). It is in science fiction that we see this myth enacted. Luke became a hero by overcoming the might of the Empire through the Force, not through technology. Rushing believes that Reagan was able to "grasp the widespread yearning for this wholistic phase, and to convert these hopes and dreams to his own political advantage" (418). He did this by eliding the technological nature of SDI: "Reagan subordinates technical reasoning to the purpose of maintaining the peace," Rushing contends (418). He, instead, seems to evoke the myth of Western Luke Skywalker–like heroes overcoming technologically developed evil empires through the determination of rugged individualism as found in *Star Wars*.

Lucas even said once that he wanted to create a fantasy that had since been lost: "Once the atomic bomb came ... they forgot the fairy tales and the dragons and Tolkien and all the *real* heroes" (Gordon 1978:314). Reagan draws on the same desire for what Gordon calls a "prelapsarian era." *Star Wars*, he contends, reflects a "yearning ... for innocence of the time before the bomb" (315). Reagan yearns for *Star Wars* by ostensibly creating his own "Star Wars." However, to use "Star Wars" as an ostentation to evoke the message of the *Star Wars* films is to misunderstand what Lucas was trying to convey — but it certainly shows the disunity, the disconnection of a culture from its polis.

Every time the press or politicians valorize Reagan's "Star Wars" dream they are speaking about the technological might of the Empire that crushed the democracy of the Old Republic. Mackay calls the rational, empirical scientific method of living — represented by the bureaucracy of the stormtroopers — the mythology of contemporary society. *Star Wars* speaks against this mythology, and, so he argues, Lucas's trilogy is actually an "anti-myth": "The *Star Wars* message is, in fact, an anti-mythological message, precisely because it is assembled from the remnants of the old mythologies — mythologies that no longer carry weight in the way we live our lives today" (Mackay 1999). Reagan's "Star Wars" is a myth. Lucas's *Star Wars* is an antimyth. In *A New Hope* the Force could overcome the domination of technology as a utopian tool. The first wave of Y-Wing fighters (as well as the second wave of X-Wings) flying down the Death Star trench failed to destroy it because the pilots were using their computers. However, Luke Skywalker (urged on by the mystic voice of the dead Ben Kenobi, "Use the Force, Luke" and "Trust your feelings"), turned off his targeting computer and used the Force to guide the proton torpedoes to the Death Star's destruction. Joseph Campbell, responding to Bill Moyers, who asked about the theme of this scene, states, "It asks, Are you going to be a person of heart and humanity — because that's where the life is, from the heart — or are you going to do whatever seems to be required of you by what might be called 'intentional power'? When Ben Kenobi says, 'May the Force be with you,' he's speaking of the power and energy of life, not of programmed political intentions" (Campbell 1991:178–179).

A discontiguous United States polis, at times seduced by the programmed intentions of the government, allows an acceptance of political laissez-faire and assures the continued existence, in Campbell's words, of a "world full of people who have stopped listening to themselves or have listened only to their neighbors to learn what they ought to do, how they ought to behave, and what the values are that they should be striving for" (1991:181). *Star Wars*, containing mythic (or antimythic) themes and Aristotelian moments of tragedy, will continue to offer an entertaining message of hope for some people, and serve as a source for many fan communities, but it will have to be placed within an impossible unified polis to instigate community-wide catharsis. Instead, we get a redemption from the Vietnam War through the resounding success of the Gulf War — and the myth of a "New World Order" attempts to shield us under the virtual umbrella and technological might of Pax Americana.

Bibliography

Adcock, Craig. 1992. "Marcel Duchamp's Gap Music: Operations in the Space Between Art and Noise." In *Wireless Imagination: Sound, Radio, and the Avant-Garde,* edited by Douglas Kahn and Gregory Whitehead. Cambridge and London: Massachusetts Institute of Technology Press.

America Online. 1995. Interview transcript of J. Michael Straczynski and Bruce Boxleitner. 25 October.

Ames, Michael M. 1986. *Museums, the Public and Anthropology: A Study in the Anthropology of Anthropology.* Vancouver: University of British Columbia Press.

Anderson, Jay. 1984. *Time Machines: The World of Living History.* Nashville: American Association for State and Local History.

Aristotle. 1961. *Poetics.* Translated by S. H. Butcher. New York: Hill and Wang.

Aronson, Arnold. 1981. *The History and Theory of Environmental Scenography.* Ann Arbor: UMI Research Press.

Artaud, Antonin. 1958 [1938]. "No More Masterpieces." In *The Theater and Its Double.* New York: Grove Press. 74**83.

Associated Press. 1996. "Star Trek juror is bounced from the Whitewater case." *Fort Worth Star-Telegram.* Thursday, March 14.

Aukstakalnis, Steve, and David Blatner. 1992. *Silicon Mirage: The Art and Science of Virtual Reality.* Edited by Stephen F. Roth. Berkeley: Peachpit Press.

Austin, J.L. 1975 [1957]. *How to Do Things with Words.* Cambridge: Harvard University Press.

Bailey, James. 1996. *After Thought: The Computer Challenge to Human Intelligence.* HarperCollins.

Barker, Juliet, R.V. 1986. *The Tournament in England: 1100–1400.* Suffolk, England: St. Edmundsbury Press.

Barrett, Edward. 1995. "Hiding the Head of Medusa: Objects and Desire in a Virtual Environment." In *Contextual Media: Multimedia and Interpretation,* edited by Edward Barrett and Marie Redmond. Cambridge: MIT Press.

Barthes, Roland. 1985. "Textual Analysis of a Tale of Poe." In *On Signs,* edited by Marshall Blonsky. Baltimore: Johns Hopkins University Press. 84–97.

_____. Barthes, Roland. 1972 [1957]. *Mythologies.* Translated by Annette Lavers. New York: Hill and Wang.

Bates, Joseph. 1994. "The Role of Emotion in Believable Agents." CMU-CS-94-136. Pittsburgh: Computer Science Documentation, Carnegie Mellon University. April.

_____. 1992. "The Nature of Characters in Interactive Worlds and the Oz Project." CMU-CS-92–200. Pittsburgh: Computer Science Documentation, Carnegie Mellon University. October.

Baty, S. Paige. 1995. *American Monroe: The Making of a Body Politic*. Berkeley: University of California Press.

Baudrillard, Jean. 1994. *Simulacra and Simulation*. Ann Arbor: University of Michigan Press.

Beacham, Richard. 1987. *Adolphe Appia: Theatre Artist*. Cambridge and New York: University of Cambridge Press.

Belsie, Laurent. 1994. "Our Correspondent Meets the Vice President in Cyberspace." *Christian Science Monitor*, 19 January, 7.

Benedikt, Michael. 1991a. "Cyberspace: Some Proposals." In *Cyberspace: First Steps*, edited by Michael Benedikt. Cambridge: MIT Press.

_____. 1991b. "Introduction." In *Cyberspace: First Steps*, edited by Michael Benedikt. Cambridge: MIT Press.

Benjamin, Walter. 1968. "The Work of Art in the Age of Mechanical Reproduction." In *Illuminations*, edited by Hannah Arendt. New York: Schocken Books.

Bennett, Susan. 1990. *Theater Audiences*. London: Routledge.

Benton, Louisa. 1990. A Marriage Made Off Broadway Takes the Cake." *New York Times*, 15 July, H5+.

Bernheimer, Richard. 1956. "Theatrum Mundi." *Art Bulletin*, December, 225–247.

Betancourt, Stephanie. 1995. Interview with author. New York, 11 December.

Blau, Herbert. 1995. *To All Appearances: Ideology and Performance*. New York: Routledge.

Blonsky, Marshall. 1992. *American Mythologies*. New York: Oxford University Press.

Boal, Augusto. 1979. *Theater of the Oppressed*. Translated by Charles A. and Maria-Odica McBride. New York Theater Communications Group.

Bouzereau, Laurent. 1997. *Star Wars: The Annotated Screenplays*. New York: Ballantine.

Brecht, Bertolt. 1992 [1962]. *Brecht on Theater: The Development of an Aesthetic*. Edited and translated by John Willett. New York: Hill and Wang.

Bricken, Meredith. 1991. "Virtual Worlds: No Interface to Design." In *Cyberspace: First Steps*, edited by Michael Benedikt. Cambridge and London: MIT Press.

Brockman, John. 1996 [1995]. *The Third Culture*. New York: Touchstone.

Brown, Joe. 1995. "The 'Gathering' Storm." *Washington Post*, 26 May, W13.

Brown, Ronald D. 1995. "Opening Remarks: Bioastronomy and Pseudo-Science." In *Progress in the Search for Extraterrestrial Life*, edited by G. Seth Shostak. ASP Conference Series, vol. 74. San Francisco: Astronomical Society of the Pacific.

Bruckner, Sandra. 1996. "DC Gathering." *Zocalo* #50. 26 February.

Burgin, Victor. 1995. "The City in Pieces." In *Prosthetic Territories: Politics and Hypertechnologies*, edited by Gabriel Brahm Jr. and Mark Driscoll. Boulder: Westview Press.

Caillois, Roger. 1979. *Man, Play, and Games*. New York: Shocken Books.

Campbell, Joseph 1972 [1968, 1949]. *The Hero with a Thousand Faces*. Princeton: Princeton University Press.

_____ (with Bill Moyers). 1991 [1988]. *The Power of Myth*. New York: Anchor Books.

Capra, Fritjof. 1996. *The Web of Life: A New Scientific Understanding of Living Systems*. New York: Doubleday.

Carroll, Jon. 1994. "Guerrillas in the Myst." *Wired*, August, 69–73.

Cartwright, Glenn F. 1994. "Virtual or Real? The Mind in Cyberspace." *Futurist* March–April, 22–26.

Castle, Terry. 1986. *Masquerade and Civilization*. Stanford: Stanford University Press.

Caughey, John L. 1984. *Imaginary Social Worlds: A Cultural Approach*. Lincoln: University of Nebraska Press.

Cherryh, C. J. 1986. *Visible Light*. New York: DAW Books.

Chinoy, Helen. 1963. "The Emergence of the Director." In *Directors On Directing*, edited by Toby Cole and Helen Chinoy. Indianapolis: Bobbs-Merrill.

The Christian Science Monitor. 1996. "The News in Brief." 11 September, 2.

CpowellRun. 1995. "Cancellation Notice." *Star Trek* Forum, America Online, 3 November.

Critical Art Ensemble. 1994. *The Electronic Disturbance.* New York: Autonomedia.

Dasgupta, Gautam. 1985. "From Science to Theatre: Dramas of Speculative Thought." *PAJ* #9.2/3 (26/27) 237–246.

Davenport, Glorianna, and Larry Friedlander. 1995. "Interactive Transformational Environments: Wheel of Life." In *Contextual Media*, edited by Edward Barrett and Marie Redmond. Cambridge: MIT Press. 1–25

Davis, Ben. 1995. "Wheel of Culture." In *Contextual Media*, edited by Edward Barrett and Marie Redmond. Cambridge: MIT Press. 247–257.

Davis, Tracy. 1995. "Performing the Real Thing in the Postmodern Museum." *Drama Review* 39.3 (Fall):15–40.

Dear, William. 1984. *The Dungeon Master.* Boston: Houghton-Mifflin.

de Certeau, Michel. 1984. *The Practice of Everyday Life.* Berkeley: University of California Press.

DeWitt, Karen. 1979. "Fantasy Game Finds Unimagined Success." *New York Times*, 3 October, 3.5.

Dieckmann, Hans. 1986. *Twice-Told Tales: The Psychological Use of Fairy Tales.* Translated by Boris Matthews. Wilmette, IL: Chiron Publications.

Disney. 1996. Plaque on wall at Walt Disney Imagineering Studios, Burbank, California.

Doyle, Laurence. n.d. Lecture given at The Principia, St. Louis.

Duncan, Carol, and Alan Wallach. 1980. "The Universal Survey Museum." *Art History* 3.4 (December): 448–468.

Dyson, Frances. 1992. "The Ear That Would Hear Sounds in Themselves: John Cage 1935–1965." In *Wireless Imagination: Sound, Radio, and the Avant-Garde*, edited by Douglas Kahn and Gregory Whitehead. Cambridge: MIT Press.

Eddy, Mary Baker. 1906 [1875]. *Science and Health with Key to the Scriptures.* Boston: The First Church of Christ, Scientist.

Ellison, Harlan. 1997. "Harlan Ellison on Heaven's Gate." *http://harlanellison.com/-text/ellicult.htm*, 4 April. (A "watered-down" version of this essay appeared in *Newsweek* 5 April 1997.)

Eno, Brian. 1983. *Apollo.* Audio recording. EG Music.

_____. 1985. *Thursday Afternoon.* Audio Recording. EG Music.

Fannon, Sean Patrick. 1996. *The Fantasy Role-Playing Gamer's Bible.* Rocklin, CA: Prima Publishing.

Figueroa-Sarriera, Heidi J. 1995. "Children of the Mind with Disposable Bodies." In *The Cyborg Handbook*, edited by Chris Hables Gray. New York: Routledge 127–135.

Fine, Gary Alan. 1983. *Shared Fantasy: Role-Playing Games as Social Worlds.* Chicago: University of Chicago Press.

Frakes, Jonathan (Director). 1996. *Star Trek: Klingon* (CD-ROM). New York: Simon & Schuster Interactive.

Fraquet, Cecile. 1995. Interview with author. New York, October.

Frase, Tuesday, Chris McCubbin, and Melissa Mead. 1995. *Origin's Official Guide to Wing Commander III.* Indianapolis: Brady Publishing.

Fulford, Robert. 1968. *This Was Expo.* Toronto: McClelland and Stewart.

Geer, Richard Owen. 1996. "Out of Control in Colquitt: Swamp Grave Makes Stone Soup." *TDR: the journal of performance studies* T150 (Summer):103–130.

Gerzoff, Sheila. 1996. "The Second Decade: Hearts of Space Glides into the New Ambient Frontier — An Interview with Stephen Hill." *www.hos.com/radio.html.* San Francisco: Heart of Space.

Goffman, Eriving. 1959. *The Presentation of Self in Everyday Life.* New York: Doubleday.

Gordon, Andrew. 1978. "*Star Wars*: A Myth for Our Time." *Literature Film Quarterly* 6.4 (Fall):314–326.

Greenblatt, Stephen. 1991. "Resonance and Wonder." In *Exhibiting Cultures: The Poetics and Politics of Museum Display*, edited by Ivan Karp and Steven D. Lavine. Washington: Smithsonian Institution Press.

Hall, Dennis. 1994. "New Age Music: A Voice of Liminality in Postmodern Popular Culture." *Popular Music and Society* 18.2 (Summer):13–21.

Hall, Susan Grove. 1994. "New Age Music: An Analysis of an Ecstasy." *Popular Music and Society* 18.2 (Summer):23–33.

Hamilton, Candy. 1995. "Where a Tomahawk Chop Feels Like a Slur." *Christian Science Monitor*, 25 October 3.

Haraway, Donna J. 1991. *Simians, Cyborgs, and Women*. New York: Routledge.

Hauser, Susan G. 1994. "Northwestern Oz: The Magus Behind a Teenage Obsession." *Wall Street Journal*, 27 December, A14.

Hawking, Stephen W. 1988. *A Brief History of Time*. New York: Bantam.

Heidegger, Martin. 1993. "The Question Concerning Technology." (1954). In *Martin Heidegger: Basic Writings*, edited by David Farrell Krell. Translation by William Lovitt with slight alterations by Krell. San Francisco: HarperCollins.

Heim, Michael. 1993. *The Metaphysics of Virtual Reality*. New York: Oxford Univ. Press.

Henderson, Mary. 1997. *Star Wars: The Magic of Myth*. New York: Bantam.

Hill, Stephen. 1988. "New Age Made Simple." San Francisco: Hearts of Space. *http://www. hos.com*.

Holly, Rob, Joe Nazzaro, Mo Ryan, Steve Spaulding. 1995. "The Master's Plan." In *The Official Babylon 5 Collector's Magazine*, edited by Mike Stokes. Lombard, IL: Sendai Licensing. 6–13.

HorizInc. 1995a. "CRUISE TREK '96." *Star Trek* Forum, America Online, 12 July.

_____. 1995b. STAR TREK TOURS." *Star Trek* Forum, America Online, 10 October.

Houlihan, Patrick T. 1991. "The Poetic Image and Native American Art." In *Exhibiting Cultures: The Poetics and Politics of Museum Display*, edited by Ivan Karp and Steven D. Lavine. Washington: Smithsonian Institution Press.

Huizinga, Johan. 1995 [1950]. *Homo Ludens: The Study of the Play-Element in Culture*. Boston: Beacon.

Ihde, Don. 1983. *Existential Technics*. Albany: State University of New York.

International Fantasy Gaming Society. 1989. *IFGS Fantasy Rules*. Boulder: International Fantasy Gaming Society.

Ivans, Molly. 1980. "Utah Parents Exorcize 'Devilish' Game." *New York Times*, 3 May, 8.

Jameson, Fredric. 1991. *Postmodernism, or, The Cultural Logic of Late Capitalism*. Durham: Duke University Press.

Jenkins, Henry. 1992. *Textual Poachers: Television Fans and Participatory Culture*. New York: Routledge.

_____. 1994. "*Star Trek* Rerun, Reread, Rewritten: Fan Writing as Textual Poaching." In *Television: The Critical View*. 5th ed. Horace Newcomb. New York: Oxford University Press.

Jindra, Michael. 1994. "*Star Trek* Fandom as a Religious Phenomenon." *Sociology of Religion* 55.1:27–51.

Kaku, Michio. 1994. *Hyperspace: A Scientific Odyssey Through Parallel Universes, Time Warps, and the 10th Dimension*. New York: Doubleday.

Kellman, Jerold L. 1983. "Games to Magazines to Children's Books is the Multimillion-Dollar Wisconsin Saga of TSR." *Publishers Weekly*, 8 July, 34–35.

Kelly, Kevin and Paula Parisi. 1997. "Beyond Star Wars." *Wired* 5.02 (February). Archived at: *www.wired.com/wired/archive/5.02*.

Kelso, Margaret Thomas, Peter Weyhrauch, and Joseph Bates. 1992. "Dramatic Presence." CMU-CS-92-195. Pittsburgh: Computer Science Documentation, Carnegie Mellon University.

Kirby, Michael. 1987. *A Formalist Theatre*. Philadelphia: University of Philadelphia Press.

Kirshenblatt-Gimblett, Barbara. 1991. Objects of Ethnography." In *Exhibiting Cultures: The Poetics and Politics of Museum Display*, edited by Ivan Karp and Steven D. Lavine. Washington: Smithsonian Institution Press.

_____. 1993. "Foreword" to *Performing the Pilgrims*, by Stephen Eddy Snow. Jackson: University Press of Mississippi.

Knanna. 1995. "Where are they?!" *Star Trek* Forum, America Online, 4 July.

Kuhn, Thomas S. 1996 [1962]. *The Structure of Scientific Revolutions*. Chicago: University of Chicago Press.

Kurkura. 1995. "Where are they?!" *Star Trek* Forum, America Online, 4 July.

Lacan, Jacques. 1985. "Sign, Symbol, Imaginary." In *On Signs*, edited by Marshall Blonsky. Baltimore: Johns Hopkins University Press. 203–209.

Lancaster, Kurt. 1994. "Do Role-Playing Games Promote Crime, Satanism, and Suicide Among Players as Critics Claim?" *Journal of Popular Culture* 28.2:67–79.

_____. 1997a. "When Spectators Become Performers: Contemporary Performance-Entertainments Meet the Needs of an 'Unsettled' Audience." *Journal of Popular Culture* 30.4:75–88.

_____. 1997b. "Epic Story of Babylon 5 Takes on the 'Big Questions.'" *Christian Science Monitor,* 5 June:13.

Landay, Jonathan S. 1997. "Dawn of Laser Weapons Draws Near." *Christian Science Monitor*, 20 October, 1, 4.

Laurel, Brenda. 1993 [1991]. *Computers as Theater*. 2d edition. New York: Addison-Wesley.

Le Guin, Ursula K. 1989. "Why Are Americans Afraid of Dragons?" In *The Language of the Night: Essays on Fantasy and Science Fiction*. Edited by Susan Wood and Ursula K. Le Guin. New York: HarperCollins.

Levine, Lawrence W. 1988. *Highbrow Lowbrow: The Emergence of Cultural Hierarchy in America*. Cambridge: Harvard University Press.

Leydon, Joe. 1996. "Terminator 2 3-D (3-D theme park attraction)." *Variety*, 6–12 May, 82.

Li-Ron, Yael. 1997. "3-D or Not 3-D? Chat is the Question." *Web Magazine*, January, 55–56.

Logan, Michael. 1998. "Starship Vegas." *TV Guide*, 3 January, 30–32.

Lombardi, Kate Stone. 1995. "Fantasy Game Tangles With Reality." *New York Times*, 7 May, WC1, 9.

MacCannell, Dean. 1989 [1976]. *The Tourist: A New Theory of the Leisure Class*, 2d ed. New York: Schocken Books.

Mackay, Daniel. 1997a [revised 5 Feb. 1998] "The Dolorous Role: Toward an Aesthetics of the Role-Playing Game." Master's thesis, New York University.

_____. 1999. "*Star Wars*: The Magic of the Anti-Myth." *Foundation* 76 (Summer) 8–9.

Magid, Ron. 1996. "Eminent Domain." *Cinescape* 2.6 (March): 24–34.

Magnus. 1995. "Where are they?!" *Star Trek* Forum, America Online, 13 August.

Mahsja. 1995. "Where are they?!" *Star Trek* Forum, America Online, 4 July.

Marquand, Robert, and Daniel B. Wood. 1997. "Rise in Cults as Millennium Approaches." *Christian Science Monitor*, 28 March, 1, 18.

Marsh, Lexie. 1995. Interview with author. New York, October.

McDowell, Edwin. 1995. "A Next Generation Casino With a *Star Trek* Theme." *New York Times*, 24 January, D4.

McNamara, Brooks. "Defining Popular Entertainment." Unpublished essay.

Milkowski, Bill. 1983. "Eno: Excursions in the Electronic Environment." *Down Beat* 50.6 (June):14+.

Miller, Carman. 1992. "*Online* interviews Dr. Thomas A. Furness III, Virtual Reality Pioneer." *Online*, November, 14–27.

Mitter, Shomit. 1992. *Systems of Rehearsal: Stanislavsky, Brecht, Grotowski, and Brook*. London: Routledge.

Morningstar, Chip, and F. Randall Farmer. 1991. "The Lessons of Lucasfilm's Habitat." In *Cyberspace: First Steps*, edited by Michael Benedikt. Cambridge: MIT Press.

Mow. 1995. Interview with author. New York, October.

Mulvey, Laura. 1988. "Visual Pleasure and Narrative Cinema." In *Feminism and Film Theory*, edited by Constance Penley. New York: Routledge. 57–68.

Mustapha, Abdul-Karim. 1996a. "Absolute Dictator/Absolute Spectator." *TDR: the journal of performance studies* T150 (Summer):7–10.

_____. 1996b. Interview with author. New York.

National Museum of the American Indian. n.d. "This Path We Travel: Celebrations of Contemporary Native American Creativity." Museum brochure.

New York Times. 1980. "Dungeons and Dollars." 2 November, 19.

New York Times. 1992. "The New Season/Arts & Artifacts, His Mission? An Indian Museum Like None Other," 13 September: 2, 53.

_____. 1995. "Schools on reservations crumbling for lack of repair money," 3 September, 17.

Nietzsche, Friedrich. 1984. *Human, All Too Human: A Book for Free Spirits*. Translated by Marion Faber. Lincoln: University of Nebraska Press.

Norbeck, Edward. 1971. "Man at Play." *Play, A Natural History Magazine Special Supplement*, December, 48–53.

Norman, Donald. 1990 [1988]. *The Design of Everyday Things*. New York: Doubleday.

_____. 1993. *Things That Make Us Smart*. New York: Addison-Wesley.

Ottawa Citizen. 1995. "Brutal tales of Indian school finally get told," 26 August, A5.

Parisi, Paula. 1995. "The New Hollywood: Silicon Stars." *Wired*, December, 142+.

Payne, Roger. 1995. *Deep Voices* (audio recording). Litchfield, CT: Earth Music Productions.

Peterson, Ivars. 1992. "Wizard of Oz: Bringing Drama to Virtual Reality." *Science News*, 19 December, 440.

Plato. 1945. *The Republic of Plato*. Translated by Francis MacDonald Cornford. New York: Oxford University Press.

Pomian, Krzysztof. 1990 [1987]. *Collectors and Curiosities: Paris and Venice, 1500–1800*. Translated by Elizabeth Wiles-Portier. Cambridge: Polity Press.

Porush, David. 1993. "Cyberspace: Portal to Transcendence?" *OMNI*, April, 4.

Prasch, Thomas. 1988. "*Platoon* and the Mythology of Realism." In *Search and Clear*, edited by William J. Searle. Bowling Green: Bowling Green State University Press. 195–215.

Project on Disney. 1995. *Inside the Mouse: Work and Play at Disney World*. Durham: Duke University Press.

Randle, Kevin D., and Donald R. Schmitt. 1994. *The Truth about the UFO Crash at Roswell*. New York: Avon Books.

Rheingold, Howard. 1991. *Virtual Reality*. New York: Summit Books.

Richards, Ron. 1992. *A Director's Method for Film and Television*. Boston: Focal Press.

Ricky1701D. 1995. "DEAD!" *Star Trek* Forum, America Online, 28 July.

Rieder, John. 1982. "Embracing the Alien: Science Fiction in Mass Culture." *Science Fiction Studies* 9.1: 26–37.

Roach, Greg. 1993. *Quantum Gate* (CD-ROM). Fremont: Media Vision; Hyperbole Studios.

Roach, Joseph. 1996. *Cities of the Dead*. New York: Columbia University Press.

Roberts, Chris. 1996. *Wing Commander IV: The Price of Freedom* (CD-ROM). Origin Systems.

Roberts, Mary Nooter, and Susan Vogel. 1994. *Exhibition-ism: Museums and African Art*. New York: Museum for African Art.

Rushing, Janice Hocker. 1986. "Ronald Reagan's 'Star Wars' Address: Mythic Containment of Technical Reasoning." *Quarterly Journal of Speech* 72.4:415–433.

Sagan, Carl. 1980. *Cosmos*. New York: Random House.

_____. 1996. *Demon Haunted World: Science as a Candle in the Dark*. New York: Random House.

Santino, Jack. 1983. "Halloween in America." *Western Folklore*, June, 1–20.

Schechner, Richard, and Mady Schuman. 1976. *Ritual, Play, and Performance*. New York: Seabury Press.

Schechner, Richard. 1985. *Between Theater & Anthropology*. Philadelphia: University of Pennsylvania Press.

_____. 1988. *Performance Theory*. New York: Routledge.

_____. 1990. "Performance Studies: The Broad-Spectrum Approach." *Phi Kappa Phi Journal* (Summer):15–16.

_____. 1992. "Theatre Departments, Rejoin and Reform the Humanities in a Big Way." *New England Theatre Journal* 3.1:1–13.

_____. 1993. *The Future of Ritual*. New York: Routledge.

_____. 1994 [1973]. *Environmental Theater*. New York: Applause Books.

Schivelbusch, Wolfgang. 1986 [1977]. *The Railway Journey: The Industrialization of Time and Space in the 19th Century*. Berkeley: University of California Press.

SF Unicorn. 1995. "USS *Atreides* on the way." Star Trek Forum, American Online, 21 October.

Shaw, Brenda. 1993. "Plugging into the Net." *Oregonian*, 6 December, D1, D6.

Sklar, Robert. 1994 [1975]. *Movie-Made America: A Cultural History of American Movies*. New York: Vintage Books.

Skywalk925. 1995. "Where are they?!" *Star Trek* Forum, American Online, 27 August.

Slizewski, Tom. 1997. "Garfield Granted CCG Patent." *Inquest* 32 (December):12.

Sloterdijk, Peter. 1987. *Critique of Cynical Reason*. Translated by Benjamin Sher. Elmwood Park, Ill: Dalkey Archive.

Smith, Leo. 1995. "Magic in the Air." *Los Angeles Times*, 30 May, B10, 11.

Smolin, Rick. 1995. *Passage to Vietnam* (CD-ROM). Sausalito: Against All Odds/Interval Research.

Sophocles. 1996 [1993]. *Oedipus Rex*. Translated by Dudley Fitts and Robert Fitzgerald. In *The Harcourt Brace Anthology of Drama*, edited by W. B. Worthen. New York: Harcourt Brace College Publishers.

Stanislavsky, Konstantin. 1948a. *An Actor Prepares*. Translated by Mary Elizabeth Hapgood. New York: Theater Arts Books/Methuen.

_____. 1948b. *Building A Character*. Translated by Mary Elizabeth Hapgood. New York: Theater Arts Books/Methuen.

Stearns, Michael. 1985. *Planetary Unfolding* audio recording). Sonic Atmospheres.

_____. 1988. *Encounter: A Journey in the Key of Space* (audio recording) San Francisco: Hearts of Space.

_____. Accessed 1996. <http://www.nets.com/stearns/>.

Stokes, Mike. 1995. *The Official Babylon 5 Collector's Magazine*. Edited by Mike Stokes. Lombard: Sendai Licensing.

Stone, Allucquere Rosanne. 1991. "Will the Real Body Please Stand Up?: Boundary Stories about Virtual Cultures." In *Cyberspace: First Steps*, edited by Michael Benedikt. Cambridge: MIT Press. 81–118.

Straczynski, J. Michael. 1994. *Babylon 5* (from season one opening credits). Warner Bros.

_____. 1995. *The War of Desire and Technology at the Close of the Mechanical Age*. Cambridge: MIT Press.

Straczynski, J. Michael. 1995. "Approaching Babylon." *Foundation: The Review of Science Fiction* 64:5–19.

Thomas, F., and O. Johnston. 1981. *Disney Animation: The Illusion of Life.* New York: Abbeville Press.

Toffler, Alvin. 1970. *Future Shock.* New York: Random House.

Toles-Patkin, Terri. 1986. "Rational Coordination in the Dungeon." *Journal of Popular Culture* (Summer):1–14.

Tolkien, J. R. R. 1981. *The Lord of the Rings.* Prepared for BBC Radio by Brian Sibley. New York: Bantam Doubleday Dell Audio Publishing.

_____. *The Lord of the Rings.* 1993 [1954, 1965]. Boston: Houghton Mifflin.

Toth, Margo I., editor. 1989. *Game Designer's Manual.* Boulder: International Fantasy Gaming Society.

Trumbull, Mark. 1994. "The Viewer Is in the Driver's Seat in This Movie for the 21st Century." *Christian Science Monitor,* 21 July, 1+.

Turkle, Sherry. 1995. *Life on the Screen: Identity in the Age of the Internet.* New York: Simon & Schuster.

Turner, Victor. 1969. *The Ritual Process.* Chicago: Aldine Publishing Company.

_____. 1982. *From Ritual to Theater: The Human Seriousness of Play.* New York: Performing Arts Journal Publications.

UFO Joe. 1993. "UFO Sightings by Astronauts," 17 February.

Ulmer, Gregory L. 1994. *Heuretics: The Logic of Invention.* Baltimore: John Hopkins University Press.

Vrgoc, Dubravka. 1996. "Deadly Criticism." *TDR: the journal of performance studies* (Summer):10–12.

Weiner, Rex. 1995. "CD Shoots Now Major League." *Variety,* 21–27 August, 24.

Weiss, Allen. 1994. *Perverse Desire and the Ambiguous Icon.* Albany: State University of New York Press.

_____. 1995. *Phantasmic Radio.* Durham: Duke University Press.

Wheat, Jack. 1994. "MTV: a totally new form of literacy?" *Oregonian,* 18 September, E12.

Wizards of the Coast. 1994. *Magic: The Gathering: A Fantasy Trading Card Game.* Renton, WA: Wizards of the Coast.

Wolmark, Jenny. 1994. *Aliens and Others: Science Fiction, Feminism, and Postmodernism.* Iowa City: University of Iowa Press.

Wood, Denis. 1978. "Growing Up Among the Stars." *Literature Film Quarterly* 6.4 (fall):327–341.

Woolley, Benjamin. 1992. *Virtual Worlds.* New York: Penguin Books.

Worthen, W. B. 1996 [1993]. *The Harcourt Brace Anthology of Drama.* New York: Harcourt Brace College Publishers.

WwestStyle. 1995. "Where are they?!" *Star Trek* Forum, America Online, 14 August.

Wyatt, David. 1982. "*Star Wars* and the Productions of Time." *Virginia Quarterly Review* 58.4 (Autumn):600–615.

Zane, J. Peder. 1994. "Trumps, Shmumps: I'll Play My Unicorn." *New York Times,* 14 August, 4.2.

Zinn, Howard. 1990 [1980]. *A People's History of the United States.* New York: Harper Perennial.

Zrzavy, Helfried C. 1990. "Issues of Incoherence and Cohesion in New Age Music." *Journal of Popular Culture* 24.2 (Fall):33–53.

Index